**Intention-Based Diagnosis
of Novice Programming Errors**

To Kimberley,
whose efforts and sacrifices made this work possible

W Lewis Johnson
Information Sciences Institute
University of Southern California

Intention-Based Diagnosis of Novice Programming Errors

Pitman, London

Morgan Kaufmann Publishers, Inc., Los Altos, California

PITMAN PUBLISHING LIMITED
128 Long Acre, London WC2E 9AN

A Longman Group Company

© W Lewis Johnson 1986
First published 1986

Available in the Western Hemisphere from
MORGAN KAUFMANN PUBLISHERS, INC.,
95 First Street, Los Altos, California 94022

ISSN 0268-7526

British Library Cataloguing in Publication Data

Johnson, W. Lewis
  Intention-based diagnosis of novice programming errors.
  1. Debugging in computer science
  2. Computer programs—Testing
  I. Title
  005'.14   QA76.6

  ISBN 0-273-08768-1

Library of Congress Cataloging in Publication Data

Johnson, W. Lewis.
  Intention-based diagnosis of novice programming errors.

  (Research notes in artificial intelligence, ISSN
0268-7526)
  Bibliography: p.
  Includes index.
  1. Debugging in computer science. 2. PROUST (Computer
program) 3. PASCAL (Computer program language)
I. Title. II. Series.
QA76.6.J653 1986   005.1'4   86-8765
ISBN 0-934613-19-2 (Morgan-Kaufmann)

Reproduced and printed by photolithography
in Great Britain by Biddles Ltd, Guildford

Preface

The work described in this book is an attempt to answer the following question: how good a job can machines do in debugging programs? Various systems exist which are capable of recognizing certain kinds of program bugs, such as syntactic errors; error-correcting compilers are good examples of such systems. These systems typically have the weakness of being unable to recognize broad categories of bugs. For example, an error-correcting compiler cannot tell whether or not a program generates the right output for a given set of inputs. Furthermore, debugging systems tend to be quite poor at determining where the bugs are in a given program. All Pascal compilers can detect when **end** statements are missing from a program, for example; none can do a very good job of figuring out where the missing **end** statements ought to go. When people debug programs, on the other hand, they are not limited to certain classes of bugs; furthermore, they usually can figure out what needs to be done to fix the bugs. People have trouble debugging not because they are unable to detect some kinds of bugs, but because they overlook bugs. It therefore is reasonable to ask whether a system can be built that can detect as broad a range of bugs as people can, but is not prone to overlook bugs.

A powerful debugging system, such as the one proposed above, is necessary in order to build an intelligent tutor to teach programming. Programming is a skill, one which is learned by doing. A tutoring system for programming needs to be able to supervise and observe students as they write programs, to give them help and suggestions when they make mistakes. A tutor therefore requires as a component a debugging system which can diagnose mistakes in the students' programs. If the debugging component is only able to recognize and diagnose a narrow range of bugs, the tutor will not be able to give the students the help they need.

What distinguishes human debuggers from most debugging systems is that people develop an understanding of what the buggy program is supposed to do, and debugging systems do not. People try to determine the intended behavior of the code, and relate it to the code's actual behavior. They try when possible to figure out how the original programmer intended the program to work, and fix the buggy code to make it agree with the programmer's intentions. It thus appears that the key to building a high-quality debugging system is to make the system try to understand the intentions underlying programs.

This book describes a program called PROUST which analyzes programs in an intention-based fashion. PROUST is designed to diagnose errors in novice programs; it generates diagnoses that could be used by an intelligent tutoring system. Empirical tests of PROUST have shown that it successfully diagnoses a large proportion of the bugs that novice programmers make when writing programs. It often rivals the best human debuggers in the accuracy and breadth of its bug diagnoses.

Various people have helped me to carry out and present the research described here. First, I would first like to express my thanks to my advisor, Professor Elliot Soloway of Yale University. My debt to him is manifold. Much of the work described here is a direct outgrowth of his own work. Professor Soloway has maintained a stimulating working environment and research group. He gave me many opportunities to present my work to the community at large, and taught me how to present it. But most important, he offered me a chance to do research in AI; without that opportunity, it is doubtful that I would be involved in research today.

William Swartout, Derek Sleeman, Drew McDermott, and Alan Perlis all read earlier drafts of this book, and made helpful comments. Drew offered critical insights at various points during the development of the work. Bill took great pains to work through the manuscript and identify places that needed reworking; his efforts are much appreciated.

Various people in the Cognition and Programming Project at Yale gave me inspiration and support over the years. Steve Draper worked with me to impose some order on the confusing domain of novice programming bugs. David Littman, Beth Adelson, Stanley Letovsky, and Jim Spohrer all helped to clarify some of my ideas. Jim provided useful feedback on an earlier draft of this thesis. In addition, people in CAPP helped build components of PROUST. David Littman built the mechanism for grouping bugs for presentation to students. Ben Cutler wrote the test-data generator. Paul Barth wrote the Pascal parser that PROUST uses.

Finally, I wish to thank my parents for their guidance and support. They knew all along that I should get involved in computers.

This work was co-sponsored by the Personnel and Training Research Groups, Psychological Sciences Division, Office of Naval Research and the Army Research Institute for the Behavioral and Social Sciences, under Contract No. N00014-82-K-0714, Contract Authority Identification Number, No. 154-492.

Contents

List of Figures

1 Introduction

1.1 Intention-based diagnosis

This book describes a process for identifying faults in designed artifacts; this process is called *intention-based diagnosis*. In intention-based diagnosis, faults are found in artifacts through a process of understanding the intended structure and function of the artifact, and determining whether or not those intentions were successfully realized. Intention-based diagnosis can identify a wider range of errors than other methods of error diagnosis, because it allows the diagnostician to detect deep faults resulting from design errors. Furthermore, it makes possible a richer account of why the artifact has faults, because the diagnostician is able to distinguish errors in intentions from errors in the realization of those intentions. Intention-based diagnosis has been implemented in a computer program called PROUST. PROUST analyzes programs written by novice programmers, diagnoses each program's non-syntactic bugs, and explains the bugs and their causes to the programmers. PROUST diagnoses bugs by inferring what the program was intended to do and how it was intended to work, and identifying errors in these intentions or in their realization.

Error diagnosis in general involves recognizing that some aspect of an artifact is not what it should be. Such recognition need not require any understanding of the intended function and structure of the artifact. For example, if when troubleshooting an electronic circuit one notices that a wire is loose, one doesn't have to know what the circuit does to recognize that the loose wire needs to be fixed. Compilers can detect whether or not a computer program is syntactically well-formed without any knowledge about the purpose of the program. In these cases errors are diagnosed using general knowledge about how distinguish a well-formed artifact from an ill-formed one.

However, in many domains, including electronics and computer programming, well-formedness criteria are inadequate for identifying all faults. Circuits can fail without exhibiting any obvious manifestations of failure such as loose wires or blown fuses. Computer programs can be syntactically correct, yet fail to compute the right results on a given set of input data. Furthermore, even if one can detect that an artifact has a fault, it may be difficult to localize the fault. For example, it is easy to detect whether or not a computer program is syntactically correct; it is much harder to determine precisely where the syntax errors are, and how best to correct them. Intention-based error diagnosis is best suited for those domains where fault detection and localization require more than general well-formedness criteria.

1.1.1 Domain of application: novice programming

The domain of novice programming has precisely the characteristics which make intention-based diagnosis necessary. Novice programs have the following characteristics:

- *Complexity*: programs are built out of many components, with complex interactions. Programs written by rank novices tend to be fairly simple; however, as students progress through a programming course they quickly reach the point where complex solutions are required. Bugs in such programs are difficult to localize to a particular line of code, because of the number of possibly buggy statements to choose from, and because of the interactions between statements as programs are executed.

- *Variability*: programs can be implemented in a variety of ways, and exhibit numerous errors. Furthermore, students in a given introductory programming class have a wide disparity in aptitude and command of the material. Thus some students write fairly good programs, whereas others only have the vaguest idea of how to write a program. It is therefore difficult for a bug diagnosis system to know what bugs to look for, and to distinguish buggy code from unusual but correct code.

- *Deep faults*: many bugs stem from design errors, mistaken intentions, and misconceptions. Novice programmers often have misconceptions about programming language syntax and semantics, resulting in large numbers of seemingly bizarre bugs. They also lack the expert's knowledge about how to analyze program specifications and design and implement algorithms. A single misconception can result in a number of buggy lines of code. A misinterpretation of the program requirements can result in a program which appears well-formed, but is buggy because the intended function of the program is incorrect.

The following statistics illustrate these points. We modified the Pascal compiler that students used in an introductory programming course so that whenever they attempted to compile a program a copy of their program was saved on tape.[1] We then analyzed these programs for bugs, to investigate the kinds of errors that novices make. To take a representative example, we analyzed the first syntactically correct versions that 206 different students produced for a single programming problem. This problem, called the Rainfall Problem, is shown in Figure 1-1. We chose the first syntactically correct versions in order to see the non-syntactic bugs in the students' original programs, before the students started debugging them.

Noah needs to keep track of rainfall in the New Haven area in order to determine when to launch his ark. Write a Pascal program that will help him do this. The program should prompt the user to input numbers from the terminal; each input stands for the amount of rainfall in New Haven for a day. Note: since rainfall cannot be negative, the program should reject negative input. Your program should compute the following statistics from this data:

1. the average rainfall per day;

2. the number of rainy days.

3. the number of valid inputs (excluding any invalid data that might have been read in);

4. the maximum amount of rain that fell on any one day.

The program should read data until the user types 99999; this is a sentinel value signaling the end of input. Do not include the 99999 in the calculations. Assume that if the input value is non-negative, and not equal to 99999, then it is valid input data.

Figure 1-1: The Rainfall Problem

The number of source lines in these programs gives a sense of the degree of complexity of the programs. The mean number of non-comment source lines was 44 in this sample. However, there was a wide range in the number of source lines per program. The minimum number was 16 lines; the maximum was 71.

The mean number of bugs per program was 3.81. Thus a system which diagnoses

---

[1]Jeff Bonar first set up this data collection system on a CYBER; B.J. Herbison and I subsequently set up a similar data collection system to run on VAX 750s.

bugs in these programs must be able to cope with multiple bugs as a matter of course. We find the range of frequency of bugs to be quite high; the standard deviation of the number of bugs is 2.45. The minimum number of bugs per program was 0; 26 programs were bug-free. The maximum number, on the other hand, was 11 bugs. The program which had the 11 bugs had only 37 non-comment source lines!

The bugs in these programs were caused by a wide range of errors and confusions. Some of them appeared to be accidental slips and omissions; others seemed to stem from misconceptions about Pascal syntax. Still others appeared to reflect errors in programming pragmatics, i.e., misconceptions about how programs are expected to interact with their environment. For example, many programs failed to deal properly with faulty input data.

These properties of novice programs make automatic bug diagnosis difficult. As a result, bug diagnosis systems have been severely limited in how they can diagnose program bugs. Techniques exist which do a fairly good job of identifying syntactic errors [6, 35] and of correcting them [39, 19]. Semantic and logical errors, on the other hand, are not so easily diagnosed. Most semantic and logical error detectors focus on narrow ranges of bugs, such as uninitialized variables [29] or spelling errors [67]. Yet although success in building automatic bug diagnosis systems has been limited, the benefits to be gained from such a system are great, particularly for novices. In order to learn how to use new programming constructs, novices need to make use of them in writing programs; the resulting programs, however, may have bugs which are unrelated to the constructs being practiced. Furthermore, novices frequently have misconceptions about programming language syntax and semantics, which lead to confusions when their programs behave differently from what they expect. We therefore decided to build a bug diagnosis system for novice programs, in spite of the potential difficulties. We believed that the intention-based approach would surmount these difficulties.

4

1.2. The PROUST program diagnosis system

PROUST is an on-line aid for novice programmers. It is designed to operate in an ordinary interactive environment. The students edit and compile their programs; whenever a program passes through the compiler without errors, it is automatically passed over to PROUST before it is executed. PROUST then analyzes the program for non-syntactic bugs.

For each programming problem that the students are assigned, a problem description is prepared, using a special problem description language. Currently these problem descriptions cannot be developed by the course instructor, but must instead be prepared by someone who is familiar with PROUST's knowledge base. The problem descriptions are collected into a library. When the student submits a program for analysis, PROUST retrieves the corresponding problem description from the library. Using the problem description as a guide, PROUST determines what exactly the student's program is intended to do, and how it was intended to do it, identifying bugs in the process.

For each bug in the program, PROUST determines where possible what the probable cause is, and uses this information in describing the bug to the student. If the bug was due to a misconception, then PROUST describes the misconception in English. An example of such a misconception is the following:

> The loop at line 39 doesn't do anything; it will loop forever. The statement in question is:

```
REPEAT ... UNTIL RAINFALL = SENTINEL
```

> In particular, it will not make the program loop back to the beginning, if that is what you had in mind.

If the bug results from a failure to check for boundary conditions, PROUST can generate an example of input data which exercises the program in a manner which the student may have overlooked. Here is an example of such data generation:

> You're missing a sentinel guard. When your program reads the sentinel, it processes it as if it were data. See what happens when you enter this data in your program:

```
-1 99999
```

> Here's the correct output:

```
There were O valid rainfalls entered.
```

PROUST's output must be such that the student can understand and make use of it. However, PROUST is not a programming tutor, and lacks sophisticated pedagogical expertise. There are bound to be cases where PROUST can identify the students' problems, but cannot explain them adequately to the students. We plan ultimately to build a programming tutor based upon PROUST, which will use information about each student's errors to guide the presentation of course material.[2] That is beyond the scope of the research described here. At present PROUST is designed to perform a detailed analysis of the students' bugs, such as a tutor would require, and then present this analysis to the students in some reasonably clear fashion.

Because PROUST is intended for a classroom setting, it must give reliable diagnoses. Many AI systems designed for actual use operate as "assistants"; i.e., the systems provide suggestions which may or may not be appropriate, and the users have the option of accepting the systems' advice or ignoring it. Such an assistant role is not appropriate for an instructional setting. If students doubt the correctness of PROUST's comments, they will ignore them when the comments disagree with their expectations. Furthermore, if PROUST's analysis is frequently incorrect the tutor which we plan to build will provide inappropriate instruction.

PROUST is designed to analyze programs which are written by students in the middle of an introductory programming course. That is, it can analyze programs with nested loops and conditional branches, but it cannot as yet analyze recursive programs. PROUST currently runs on two programming assignments, both of which are assigned toward the middle of an introductory programming course. These problems are moderately complex, requiring solutions of around a page in length. On these problems, PROUST has already attained a level of accuracy where it can be used effectively as an instructional tool. It successfully identifies 95% of the novices' bugs, provided that it understands the student's intentions. PROUST checks over its analysis before presenting it to the student, looking for inconsistencies which might indicate a failure to understand the programmer's intentions. If PROUST concludes that its analysis may be faulty, it restricts output to the student, rather than risk saying incorrect things. This happens in about 20% of the programs.

---

[2] David Littman is currently designing the PROUST tutor, called BERTIE.

1.3 An example of intention-based analysis

In order to give the reader a sense of what is involved in finding bugs in novice programs, an intention-based bug diagnosis for an example novice program will now be presented. The analysis will illustrate how knowledge of the programmer's intentions is key to the process of diagnosing bugs. The analysis will then be compared against what a non-intention-based analysis would provide. PROUST's analysis of the example program will then be shown.

1.3.1 The example and its analysis

The program that we will analyze is a solution to the Rainfall Problem, the problem that was shown in Figure 1-1. The Rainfall Problem requires that the student write a program which reads a series of numbers, each of which represents the amount of rain that fell on a particular day. The end of input is signaled when the user types a special sentinel value, 99999. The program is then supposed to compute the average and the maximum of the input values, and count the total number of rainfall inputs and the number of positive inputs.

The example program appears in Figure 1-2. This program was written by a novice programmer, and was among the set of novice programs that were collected using the altered Pascal compiler mentioned earlier.[3] This program has a number of different bugs; however, there is one bug that is of particular interest. The `while` loop that that starts at line 19 and ends at line 27 is an infinite loop. The loop tests the variable `Rain` against the sentinel value, 99999, but the body of the loop never modifies `Rain`. Therefore if the body of the `while` loop is entered, it will never be exited.

Further inspection of the program reveals other peculiarities. Most solutions to the Rainfall Problem have a single loop for reading the input data, processing it, and checking for the sentinel value. This program, however, has two loops which test the data against 99999. One is a `repeat` loop, starting at line 8 and ending at line 28. The other is the infinite `while` loop. The `while` loop is contained within the

---

[3]The indentation and use of upper and lower case in all novice code examples in this book have been cleaned up and made uniform, so that the reader can better understand the code.

```
 1 program Rainfall ( input, output );
 2
 3 var
 4   Rain, Days, Totalrain, Raindays, Highrain, Averain: real;
 5
 6 begin
 7   Rain := 0; .
 8   repeat
 9     writeln ('Enter rainfall');
10     readln;
11     read (Rain);
12     while Rain < 0 do
13       begin
14         writeln ( Rain:0:2,'is not possible, try again');
15         readln;
16         read ( Rain )
17       end;
18
19     while Rain <> 99999 do
20       begin
21         Days := Days + 1;
22         Totalrain :=  Totalrain + Rain;
23         if Rain > 0 then
24           Raindays := Raindays + 1;
25         if Highrain < Rain then
26           Highrain := Rain
27       end;
28   until Rain = 99999;
29
30   Averain := Totalrain / Days;
31
32   writeln;
33   writeln ( Days,'valid rainfalls were entered');
34   writeln;
35   writeln ('The average rainfall was',Averain,'inches');
36   writeln;
37   writeln ('The the highest rainfall was',Highrain);
38   writeln;
39   writeln ('There were',Raindays,'in this period');
40 end.
```

Figure 1-2: A buggy solution to the Rainfall Problem

`repeat` loop. Thus the infinite loop is not the only peculiar control structure of this program; the overall organization of the loops in this program is suspicious. Perhaps the error in this program is more profound than first appears.

Well-known non-intention-based analysis techniques such as data-flow analysis [29] are capable of detecting the infinite loop in the program in Figure 1-2. Data-flow analysis cannot detect that the overall control structure of a program is an unusual solution for a particular problem, however. If an infinite loop is a manifestation of a more significant programming error, then simply pointing out the infinite loop may distract the student away from correcting the true error. In particular, if a loop does not belong in the program at all, then the question of whether or not the loop is infinite is moot. Our empirical studies of how students debug programs indicate that novice programmers tend to correct the surface manifestations of bugs rather than the bugs themselves; thus proper descriptions of bugs are crucial.

We believe that the proper analysis of the bug in this program is as follows. The student did not intend the `while` statement at line 19 to loop at all. Instead, the effect of an `if` statement was intended. Since the input statements are at the top of the `repeat` loop, and the loop exit test is at the bottom of the `repeat` loop, there has to be a way for control to skip from the input statements to the end of the loop when 99999 is read. Otherwise the 99999 would be processed as if it were a rainfall amount. An `if` statement would serve this purpose, but the student has written a `while` statement instead. Empirical analyses of novice programming errors [42] have shown that novice programmers commonly confuse the meanings of `if` and `while`, particularly when they are embedded within other loops. If this bug were to be described to the novice programmer, the description should focus on the probable misconception about the meanings of `if` and `while`, rather than just on the fact that the `while` statement is an infinite loop.

Two kinds of knowledge about the programmer's intentions are required in order to come up with the above diagnosis:

- knowledge about the intended function of the program, and

- knowledge about how the programmer intended this function to be achieved.

9

Knowledge of intended function was required to determine what the input/output behavior of the program should be. Knowledge of how the function was to be achieved was needed in order to figure out what the `while` statement was really intended to do.

The key difference between the above analysis and the analysis that a data-flow analyzer would produce is the following. A data-flow analyzer analyzes the behavior of the program itself, independent of the intentions underlying it. In the above analysis, the focus was on understanding the intentions underlying the program, and then on referring to those intentions in diagnosing bugs. Thus the bug analysis presented above is an *intention-based* analysis; a data-flow analyzer, in contrast, performs non-intention-based analysis.

Note furthermore that analyzing the intentions underlying a program inevitably implies understanding something of the cognitive process which the programmer went through in forming and acting on those intentions. That is, we must follow the reasoning of the programmer to see what the buggy `while` statement was supposed to do, and why it is buggy. Thus intention-based error diagnosis can be defined as follows:

> A system for diagnosing errors in artifacts is *intention-based* if it finds errors based on an interpretation of the cognitive process which generated the artifact, rather than on an interpretation of the structure or behavior of the artifact itself.

1.3.2. PROUST's analysis of the example program

Figure 1-3 shows PROUST's output when analyzing the program in Figure 1-2. PROUST finds all of the bugs in the program, including the `while`-for-`if` bug. Bugs that appear to have a common cause are grouped together, and the misconceptions that may cause them are alluded to. Thus PROUST observes that none of the variables that should be initialized in the program are initialized, and therefore hypothesizes that the student has a misconception about variable initializations. PROUST bases its description of the bugs on its misconception hypothesis:

> Programs should not fetch values from uninitialized variables! If you don't initialize these variables to the values that you want, you will have no way of knowing what variables they will be initialized to.

NOW BEGINNING BUG REPORT:

>> Now Reporting CRITICAL Bugs in the SETUP part of your program:

You left out the initializations for the variables HIGHRAIN,
DRYDAYS, RAINDAYS, and TOTALRAIN. Programs should not fetch
values from uninitialized variables! If you don't initialize
these variables to the values that you want, you will have no
way of knowing what values they will be initialized to.

(TO CONTINUE, PLEASE PRESS CARRIAGE RETURN)

 >>> Now Reporting MINOR Bugs in the SETUP part:

The initialization at line 7 appears to be unnecessary.
The statement in question is:
        RAIN := 0

(TO CONTINUE, PLEASE PRESS CARRIAGE RETURN)

 >>> Now Reporting CRITICAL Bugs in the CONTROL part:

You used a WHILE statement at line 19 where you should have used
an IF. WHILE and IF are NOT equivalent in this context; using
WHILE in place of IF can result in infinite loops.
The statement in question is:
        WHILE RAIN <> 99999 DO ...

(TO CONTINUE, PLEASE PRESS CARRIAGE RETURN)

 >>> Now Reporting CRITICAL Bugs in the OUTPUT part:

The maximum and the average are undefined if there is no valid
input. But lines 34 and 33 output them anyway. You should
always check whether your code will work when there is no input!
This is a common cause of bugs.

You need a test to check that at least one valid data point has
been input before line 30 is executed. The average will bomb
when there is no input.

BUG REPORT NOW COMPLETE.

Figure 1-3: PROUST's output for the program in Figure 1-2

When PROUST describes the `while-for-if` bug, it notes that the loop is an infinite loop. It mentions this so that the student can better understand why the program malfunctions. However, PROUST does not *diagnose* the bug by looking for infinite loops, as in data-flow analysis. Rather, it tries to understand the intentions underlying the program, and in the process discovers that a `while` statement was used where an `if` statement should have been used. This understanding of intentions allows PROUST to discriminate between the `while-for-if` diagnosis and alternative diagnoses, such as the diagnosis that the student accidentally omitted a `read` statement from the `while` loop.

1.4 PROUST's approach

I will now describe the key features of PROUST's intention-based approach to program debugging. This will lay out some of the themes which will be explored in further detail in subsequent chapters.

1.4.1 The process: analysis by synthesis

PROUST gets an initial understanding of the student's intentions from the problem description provided by the instructor. These problem descriptions alone are insufficient for understanding the student's intentions, however. If the program is non-trivial, each programmer may produce a program which works in a different way. Furthermore, unless the problem is very simple and easy to state, the problem statement may not be a complete specification of the program. The programmer is likely to add details to the problem requirements, such as deciding how to deal with boundary conditions. In order for intention-based diagnosis to be effective, the diagnostic system must be able to take the problem description and a given solution, and figure out what exactly the solution is supposed to do and how it is supposed to work.

The approach that is taken in PROUST is to perform analysis by synthesis. The system attempts at each stage of the analysis to predict what the student was likely to be trying to do. This involves synthesizing possible realizations of the problem requirements, and suggesting possible elaborations of the requirements. The system then looks at the program and analyzes it in terms of the predicted realizations. In this way PROUST's analysis is guided at all times by what the student's intentions are likely to be, rather than by the behavior that the buggy code happens to exhibit.

The basic structure of diagnosis in PROUST is as follows. The system starts with a description of the problem. It selects some goal in the problem description to serve as a basis for analysis. Knowledge about program synthesis is used to construct alternative models of how the student intends to implement that goal. These models are then matched against the program. If one of them fits the code, then PROUST adds it to the interpretation that is being built for the program as a whole, and starts work on another goal in the problem description. If none of the predicted implementations matches the program, then PROUST must use knowledge about common bugs to try to explain why the implementations fail to match. The choice of implementation model depends upon how easy it is to explain the mismatches in terms of bugs.

A top-down approach is crucial in analyzing buggy novice programs because bugs can obscure the intended function of code. The program example in Figure 1-2 illustrates this. We were able to analyze the `while`-for-`if` bug in this program because we predicted that there would be a test inside of the loop for 99999, so that control flow can break out of the loop. When we found the `while` statement where the `if` statement was expected, we concluded that the programmer intended the `if` statement to function as a `while` statement. If we took a bottom-up approach, we would have to inspect every `while` statement in the program and consider whether or not it really was meant to be an `if` statement. The program has two `while` loops, so we would have to consider the possibility of a `while`-for-`if` bug in both `while` loops. We would have to consider all other possible interpretations of the `while` loops as well, such as the possibility that a `read` statement is missing from the infinite `while` loop. Without any expectations concerning what the code is supposed to do, there is an explosion of possible interpretations, and no way of deciding among the alternatives. If we try to reduce the number of interpretations by assuming that the code matches the student's intentions, we risk misinterpreting the code.

Another advantage of the analysis-by-synthesis approach is that it provides a natural means of differentiating possible interpretations of the code. There are frequently many possible ways of matching a goal against a program, depending upon what bugs are assumed to be present. The best way of choosing an interpretation is to compare the different matches in order to see which fits best, e.g., assumes the fewest misconceptions. Generation of alternatives comes naturally out of the analysis-by-synthesis approach: instead synthesizing just one realization of a goal, PROUST synthesizes many different realizations. A kind of differential diagnosis technique is used to decide among the possible goal realizations.

Top-down analysis imposes a limitation, however: it only works if the system's predictions are adequate for understanding the program. Novice programmers sometimes invent novel implementations, and frequently exhibit novel strains of bugs. It is virtually impossible to construct a knowledge base of programming knowledge and of bugs which covers all of the unusual cases. PROUST therefore performs analysis-by-synthesis only as far as it can. Since PROUST is attempting to analyze the entire program, it should be able to derive a consistent interpretation which establishes the role of every part of the program. If this cannot be done, either because the analysis has inconsistencies or because parts of the program are unexplained, then PROUST's analysis is probably wrong. PROUST edits out the dubious parts of the bug analysis in these cases, and thereby avoids giving the student erroneous bug reports. However, PROUST's top-down approach allows it to identify possibly buggy code, even when it does not understand the program completely. If, for example, PROUST understands the implementation of all the goals in the problem description save one, and it understands the intent of every line in the program save one, then the uninterpreted line is probably a buggy implementation of the unimplemented goal. In this way PROUST can localize bugs even when its understanding of the program is incomplete.

1.4.2 Program synthesis knowledge and bug knowledge

Knowledge about programming is required in order to make predictions about the intent underlying the students' programs. Furthermore, this knowledge must be related to the knowledge that programmers actually use. Otherwise there can be no assurance that the predictions that PROUST makes bear any relation to what the

14

student actually did. It was therefore necessary to make explicit the kinds of knowledge that people use in writing programs, and encode it in PROUST. To the extent that it was possible, I have tried to use knowledge representations which have a sound psychological basis. For example, a major portion of this knowledge consists of programming plans, which are stereotypic methods for implementing requirements in programs. Extensive empirical evidence has been accumulated indicating that programmers make use of programming plans when writing programs [60].

As the development of PROUST proceeded, it became evident that other kinds of programming knowledge were needed in addition to programming plans. For example, it was necessary to determine how to represent programming goals, and how to relate them to plans. Another issue that arose was how to codify and use domain knowledge. The basis for such knowledge representations was introspection and anecdotal evidence. PROUST was then tested on hundreds of novice programs, to ensure that its knowledge was adequate for modeling the intentions underlying these programs. Rigorous psychological investigation is required to ensure that PROUST's knowledge representations really reflect programmers' knowledge. However, the tests of PROUST conducted so far give reason for optimism that such psychological tests will support PROUST's knowledge representations.

The other principal kind of knowledge in PROUST is knowledge about bugs. Bug knowledge in PROUST takes two forms. Most bugs are identified when differences are found between an expected implementation and the code. Bugs in these cases are codified as rules which trigger on certain types of mismatches, and suggest interpretations for these mismatches. Bugs are also incorporated into the program synthesis knowledge bases, as "buggy plans". This is useful when bugs are common enough that they can be predicted.

1.5 Relationship to other work

Because intention-based diagnosis involves both analysis of intentions and analysis of the program, it is a complex analysis technique. Most other debugging systems avoid the intention-based approach in favor of simpler analysis techniques. Some tutoring systems for programming avoid program analysis altogether. On the other hand, intention modeling is relatively common in ICAI systems for domains other than programming. The following is a brief overview of how PROUST's approach relates to other approaches to program analysis. PROUST will also be compared against other systems which perform diagnostic modeling of students, in various domains.

1.5.1 Programming tutors which do not diagnose errors

Some attempts have been made to build programming tutors which do not have diagnostic capabilities. For example, conventional frame-based computer-aided instruction techniques have been used. The Unix *learn* tutorial for the C programming language is an example of a frame-based CAI system for programming [44]. In this system, each lesson frame includes a programming problem which the student must solve. The student enters his or her solution, whereupon the system attempts to execute the student's program. If the program runs correctly, the system proceeds to the next lesson frame. If the program does not run correctly, the system either repeats the problem or goes to some different frame.

Frame-based CAI systems may work in some domains, but they are ill-suited for teaching programming, as Kernighan and Lesk, the authors of *learn*, freely admit.[4] Learning to program involves acquiring a variety of knowledge and skills. It is difficult to determine how to sequence lesson frames so that the necessary skills are acquired, without wasting the students' time on redundant exercises.

The curriculum sequencing problem has been addressed in systems such as BIP [69]. In BIP, the programming knowledge to be taught is made explicit, so that lesson frames can be sequenced dynamically to focus on the knowledge that the student appears to lack. However, without a diagnostic component such as PROUST, a system cannot tell what knowledge the student lacks, or where the student has misconceptions. Two techniques are available in systems such as *learn* and BIP for determining where the student is having difficulties. One method is to have the course author supply a number of buggy solutions to the problem, so that the CAI system can compare the input/output behavior of the supplied solutions against the input/output behavior of the student's solution. The other method is to have the

---

[4]Kernighan and Lesk 1979, p. 5.

16

student try to solve a simpler programming problem, to see whether or not the student is capable of solving the simpler problem. Supplying buggy solutions, or buggy input/output pairs, only works if the problems are simple enough that only a small number of bugs are likely. More complex problems such as the Rainfall Problem, which have a number of inputs and outputs, can exhibit too many different kinds of bugs for enumeration of input/output behavior to be practical. Assigning additional programming problems slows the student down unnecessarily.

1.5.2 Non-intention-based diagnosis systems

In more recent work on intelligent help systems for programming, bug diagnosis has played a more prominent role. Most of these bug diagnosis systems are not intention-based, however. Instead, they try to identify program structures or program behavior which is clearly anomalous. Some systems look for anomalous data flow [29], computations that may not terminate [68], or compare the code against a catalog of common novice mistakes [59]. Others try to interpret run-time errors [36, 67]. Still others analyze program traces for surprising behavior [65]. These systems may be effective for finding certain classes of bugs, but they will not work when the program has no obvious anomalies. Furthermore, they are not very good at pinpointing where the error occurred and why. We saw this in the `while-for-if` bug in the previous section: there it was necessary not only to identify the anomalous `while` loop, but to explain what exactly was wrong with it. The bug-catalog method breaks down as programs become more complex, so that it is harder to tell out of context whether or not a particular fragment of code is buggy.

Another way to find bugs without knowledge of the programmer's intentions is to have the programmer say what is wrong with the program, and have the system try to trace the cause of the bug. The user describes the error by supplying test data which causes the program to generate incorrect output, and indicating the discrepancies between the desired output and the actual output. This approach is used in Eisenstadt's Prolog Trace Package [25], and in troubleshooting systems such as FALOSY [53], E. Shapiro's debugger [55], and D. Shapiro's SNIFFER system [54]. These systems all assume that the programmer is competent enough to spot any and all incorrect behavior. This assumption is not valid for novice programmers; in fact part of what novice programmers must learn is how to test their programs systematically. A debugging system for novices should be smart enough to find bugs without depending upon the user for assistance.

1.5.3 Intention-based systems

Although most diagnostic systems for programming are not intention-based, many ICAI systems in other domains are. The DEBUGGY system [15], which infers students' subtraction procedures by analyzing their solutions to subtraction problems, can be considered intention-based. The PIXIE system in the algebra domain [58] and the Geometry Tutor [3] in the geometry domain can also be considered intention-based. These domains all share the property that problems can be formally stated, and a series of formal operations are applied in order to arrive at a solution. In subtraction, the problem is to subtract one number from another. In geometry, the problem is to construct a formal proof for a given theorem. In algebra, the task is to solve a given equation. In programming, on the other hand, non-trivial problems are not stated formally. The problem requirements are stated in words, and the student has to think about the problem in order to determine what is really required for a solution. Furthermore, in algebra and geometry the student's solution provides information about the student's intentions at intermediate points in the solution process. Algebra problems are solved by performing transformations on the given equation, and a tutoring system can inspect the intermediate steps to infer what those transformations were. Geometry problems are solved by constructing a sequence of statements, each of which contributes to the solution. In programming, in contrast, only the final solution is visible. The student may plan out the solution mentally before writing any code at all. Thus intention-based analysis of non-trivial programming problems is inherently more difficult than intention-based analysis in more formal domains.

Nevertheless, a small number of intention-based systems have been developed for programming. One such system is Miller's SPADE system, which helps students write small LOGO programs, by encouraging them to make explicit their plan for implementing the program. The system can use this information about the student's intentions to guide the student when he or she runs into difficulties. Although a promising approach, the SPADE approach was only tested on relatively small

18

programming problems, in which relatively few planning steps are required. PROUST, on the other hand, is designed to analyze programs in which a number of goals are being satisfied at once, and where the programmer must carry out a number of planning steps. SPADE's model of program planning would have to be extended significantly to handle these more complex problems.

Two other intention-based systems in domains related to PROUST's are the Lisp Tutor [27] and the MACSYMA Advisor [31]. The Lisp Tutor monitors beginning Lisp programmers as they write Lisp programs, simulating their goal state and working memory. When the student makes a mistake, the system is able to intervene immediately, using its model of the student's goal state to determine what the student was trying to do. On-line monitoring of the student makes bug identification easier than would be the case if the system had to take a completed program and analyze it for bugs. It is tractable because the Lisp Tutor mainly assigns small problems whose requirements are clear and unambiguous, such as to write a program which reverses a list. Difficulties arise, however, when the student has a number of active goals, or where the student needs to elaborate on the problem requirements. If the student does something that the Tutor cannot relate to the any of the active goals, the Tutor immediately rejects the student's action. The student is forced to solve the problem in a manner that the Tutor can understand. PROUST, on the other hand, is designed to deal with the actual variability in novice solutions, and therefore does not risk constraining the students' behavior in some unnecessary or unintended way. PROUST thus risks being too lenient, allowing students to write programs which PROUST cannot analyze. It remains to be seen which approach does a better job of helping students learn to program.

The MACSYMA Advisor, on the other hand, performs a task more like PROUST's. It takes a sequence of MACSYMA commands, tries to infer the student's intentions in using these commands, and then suggests misconceptions about MACSYMA that the student might have. The MACSYMA Advisor must make strong assumptions about the students in order to do this: it assumes that the students' errors all stem from misconceptions about MACSYMA commands. PROUST is designed to handle a full range of novice bugs, only some of which result from misconceptions about Pascal statements. It therefore cannot make the same kinds of assumptions about student bugs.

1.6 The status of PROUST's model

PROUST's model of a student's intentions must be able to assign an intent to each line of the program, explain how the problem requirements are satisfied by the program, and describe the bugs. Note, however, that this does not mean that PROUST simulates student behavior in writing the program. PROUST's knowledge about programming is different from novices' knowledge about programming. Furthermore, the process of understanding a program is different from the process of writing a program, even if the same knowledge were used in both cases.

PROUST relies upon program synthesis knowledge to relate problem descriptions to programs, but it does not analyze program components in the same order that the student synthesized them. PROUST must infer the plan that the student had in mind for satisfying each goal, and then determine whether or not the plan was successfully realized. Yet it may be necessary to analyze a number of different parts of the program before it becomes clear what plan was actually being carried out.

PROUST's analysis process is not a simulation of how people debug programs any more than it is a simulation of how people write programs. Human debuggers rely only partly on analysis by synthesis. One reason for the difference appears to be that PROUST is not faced with the same working-memory limitations as people are. People tend to lose track of which parts of the program have been analyzed and which have not been, unless they perform a line-by-line scan of the code. PROUST, on the other hand, can afford to apply analysis-by-synthesis techniques more systematically, skipping through the code to find implementations for particular goals.

1.6.1 The status of the implementation

Although preliminary results with PROUST have been encouraging, PROUST is in many ways incomplete. The account of programming knowledge and bug knowledge that underlies it is also incomplete. Before proceeding, it should be made clear what ideally would be desired of PROUST, and what in fact has been achieved. Likewise, we must make clear which parts of the underlying theory are well worked out, and which parts are sketchy.

The ultimate goal is to give PROUST the ability to analyze arbitrary programming problems. All that should be necessary to make PROUST work on a new programming problem is to write a description of that problem in PROUST's problem description language. Furthermore, the problem description language should be easy enough to use that teachers can write the problem descriptions themselves. PROUST's descriptions of programming intentions and bugs should be rich enough to pinpoint exactly what the students are doing wrong, and why it is wrong. This would enable an automatic programming tutor to make immediate use of PROUST's analysis in instructing the students.

PROUST is currently far from achieving all of the above goals. The main emphasis of the work behind PROUST has been on one part of the task, namely developing methods for understanding and debugging novice programs. The first task that had to be achieved with PROUST was to demonstrate that the intention-based approach to program debugging is feasible. That effort has been reasonably successful. Given the relevant plan and bug knowledge, PROUST is able to understand arbitrary novice programs and find their bugs. Tests of PROUST on hundreds of novice solutions demonstrate PROUST's robust diagnostic capability.

Although the range of programs that PROUST can analyze is quite wide, the range of programming problems that PROUST currently can analyze is narrow. Work on generalizing PROUST to analyze arbitrary programming problems did not really begin until after diagnostic robustness was demonstrated. As a result, the model of programming knowledge underlying PROUST is still limited. PROUST's knowledge base at this point only contains the knowledge sufficient to analyze the two programming problems that it has been tested on. Although these knowledge representations are applicable to a broad class of programming problems, it is to be expected that gaps will appear as PROUST is applied to new problems. Incompleteness of PROUST's knowledge base is the major obstacle preventing teachers from using PROUST's problem description language.

PROUST's descriptions of intentions and bugs are currently less detailed than a programming tutor would need. The reason for this is simple: there is a limit to the amount of information about a programmer's intentions that can be inferred by inspecting a single program. There are two ways in which PROUST could acquire additional information about the programmer's thinking: ask the student questions about the program, and by comparing consecutive versions of the program. Both of these extensions would best be performed by a tutoring module, which could conduct a dialogue with the student, and monitor the student's progress. The construction of such a tutoring module is a matter for future research. Once a tutoring module has been built, we will be able to extend PROUST's student model to take advantage of what the tutor knows about the student.

1.7 Guide to the reader

The subsequent chapters are organized as follows. Chapters 2 and 3 provide background, describing how PROUST works and why its diagnostic method is the method of choice. Chapter 2 presents some examples of PROUST analyzing some novice programs. These examples are intended to provide an understanding of the mechanisms that PROUST uses, and of the kinds of problems that PROUST runs into. Chapter 3 compares intention-based diagnosis against other approaches to diagnosis.

Chapters 4 through 8 describe in detail PROUST's knowledge representation and processing techniques. Chapter 4 discusses knowledge about plans, the role that this knowledge plays, and the mechanisms for matching plans against programs. Chapter 5 discusses problem descriptions and their content. Chapter 6 describes how goal decompositions are created for programs, relating the problem description to the student's program implementation. Chapter 7 is concerned with knowledge about bugs, and how it is used. Chapter 8 is a discussion of the analysis strategies and analysis evaluation techniques that PROUST uses, showing how the various kinds of knowledge are brought into play.

Chapter 9 presents the results of empirical evaluations of PROUST. Finally, Chapter 10 will present concluding remarks, and discuss further directions.

Two appendices have been included for the reader's reference. Appendix I shows a transcript of a student session with PROUST, showing how students and PROUST tend to interact. Appendix II is a listing of the principal components of PROUST's programming knowledge bases.

2 Examples of PROUST's Analysis

This chapter presents some examples of PROUST analyzing buggy novice programs. The aim of these examples is to illustrate the kinds of processing that PROUST performs, and to give a sense of how intention-based diagnosis of program bugs works. The first example is a short program which averages a sequence of numbers. We do not ordinarily run PROUST on programs as short as this, but its size makes the discussion of PROUST's analysis simpler. The second example is of a size which is more typical of what PROUST usually analyzes. This makes it possible to discuss some of the issues that arise when analyzing larger, more complex programs. The third example involves some much more complex processing; it is included to show the kinds of reasoning which is required when the causes of a bug are unclear.

The account of PROUST's processing which is presented here is somewhat simplified. Less important details are omitted at first from the discussion, until the overall framework of PROUST's analysis is laid out. Some of this detail is then reintroduced in succeeding examples; the rest will wait until later chapters which address specific aspects of intention-based diagnosis.

2.1 Example 1: a simple averaging program

Our first example is a solution to a simplified version of the Rainfall Problem, called the Averaging Problem. This problem requires that the student write a program that reads in a series of numbers until the value 99999 is read, and then output the average of these numbers. The problem solution that will be discussed here appears in Figure 2-1; an excerpt of PROUST's bug report for this program is shown in Figure 2-2. The bug which we will focus on in this program is at line 12: `New := New + 1`. `New` is being used as a variable to hold the input data, but line 12 updates it using a counter increment statement rather than a `read` statement. This is a bug which we have encountered on more than one occasion in novice programs: the student appears to have overgeneralized the use of the counter update statement. Students learn that statements that increment variables can be used to compute successive values of counters; they then use this same technique elsewhere to generate new values. Thus the student apparently thinks that incrementing New will serve to get the next value of New! This example will be used to illustrate the following points:

- how programming problems are described to PROUST,

- how predictions about the programmer's intentions are made,

- how predictions are tested, and

- how prediction failures are used to identify bugs.

Problem: Read in numbers until the number 99999 is seen. Report the average. Do not include the final 99999 in the average.

```
1     program Average( input, output );
2     var Sum, Count, New: integer;
3         Avg: real;
4     begin
5       Sum := 0;
6       Count := 0;
7       read( New );
8       while New <> 99999 do
9         begin
10          Sum := Sum + New;
11          Count := Count + 1;
12          New := New + 1
13        end;
14      if Count <> 0 then
15        begin
16          Avg := Sum / Count;
17          writeln( 'The average is ', Avg );
18        end;
19    end.
```

Figure 2-1: A buggy averaging program

It appears that you were trying to use line 12 to read the
next input value. Incrementing NEW will not cause the next
value to be read in. You need to use a READ statement here.
The statement in question is:

      NEW := NEW + 1

Figure 2-2: Excerpt of PROUST's output for Figure 2-1

2.1.1 Defining the problem

PROUST needs a description of the programming problem that the students are
working on, so it has a starting point for identifying the students' intentions. Figure
2-3 shows a representation of the Averaging Problem in PROUST's problem description
language.[5] The aim of such problem descriptions is to render the requirements listed
in the natural-language problem description in a form which is usable by PROUST. I
will first describe briefly PROUST's problem-description notation, and then show how
it is used in the problem description in Figure 2-3.

```
DefProgram Average;

DefObject ?Avg:Input;

DefGoal Sentinel-Controlled Input Sequence(?Avg:Input, 99999);
DefGoal Output(Average(?Avg:Input));
```

Figure 2-3: The Averaging Problem in PROUST's problem description language

PROUST's problem descriptions consist of the following components:

1. the name of the problem,

2. object definitions, and

3. goal definitions.

DefProgram statements are used to declare the names of problems. The
DefProgram statement in this example, DefProgram Average, gives the problem
the name "Average". Object definitions and goal definitions are described below.

---

[5]This problem statement has been syntactically sugared to make it easier to read. The actual
representation that PROUST uses is a Lisp-like notation.

Goals are the requirements which must be satisfied by the program. *Average*(`?Avg:Input`), for example, is the requirement that the average of `?Avg:Input` be computed. Goals are defined in problem descriptions using `DefGoal` statements. Goal names will always appear in this book in *italics*, whereas other components of problem statements will appear in `typewriter` font. The Averaging Problem statement refers to three goals:

- *Sentinel-Controlled Input Sequence*, i.e., input a sequence of values, stopping when a sentinel value is reached,

- *Average*, i.e., compute an average, and

- *Output*, i.e., output a value.

A complete listing of PROUST's goals appears in Appendix II.

Each goal takes a list of data quantities as arguments. For example, the goal *Sentinel-Controlled Input Sequence*(`?Avg:Input, 99999`) has two arguments: the set of inputs to be averaged, denoted by `?Avg:Input`, and the sentinel value, 99999. If goals are nested, as in *Output*(*Average*(`?Avg:Input`)), the outer goal refers implicitly to the data generated by the inner goal. Thus the above goal expression denotes the requirement that the average of the input data be output.

Objects in PROUST parlance are the data quantities which programs manipulate. A natural-language problem statement typically refers to a number of objects. For example, when the Averaging Problem statement says "Read in numbers", it is referring to an object, namely the set of input data being averaged. In natural-language problem statements the references to objects can be either explicit or implicit. An example of an implicit reference is "Report the average", which really means "Report the average of the set of numbers just mentioned."

Objects in PROUST's problem descriptions can also be either explicit or implicit. Explicit declarations are performed using `DefObject` statements. There is one `DefObject` statement in the Averaging Problem description: `DefObject ?Avg:Input`. The object declared here is the set of input data to be read by the averaging program. Object names are preceded by question marks to indicate that they are pattern variables, not constants. By convention, object names have a prefix indicating the problem description that they are part of, e.g., the `Avg` in `Avg:Input`.

The colon has no special significance; it is just part of the object name, separating "Avg" from "Input". Implicit object definitions arise in nested goal expressions such as *Output*(*Average*(?Avg:Input)). Here the *Average* goal implicitly defines a data object, the average; the argument of the *Output* goal is this implicit object, not the *Average* goal itself.

PROUST's problem descriptions are similar in content to the original natural-language descriptions. The requirements in the English description have been regrouped; e.g., "read in numbers until the number 99999 is seen" and "do not include the final 99999" are combined into the form *Sentinel-Controlled Input Sequence*(?Avg:Input, 99999). Nevertheless, as little as possible is added to the problem descriptions. There are two reasons for this. First, it makes PROUST's problem descriptions easy to write. Second, it means that PROUST has to go through a similar set of decisions in deriving an implementation as a programmer does. This makes it possible for PROUST to predict a range of novice interpretations of the problem requirements.

2.1.2 Making predictions about the student's intentions

I will now describe the process whereby PROUST finds the counter overgeneralization bug in this program example. The method presented here is used over and over in PROUST:

- select a goal for analysis,

- generate different realizations of this goal,

- match each realization against the program, and

- interpret the match failures in order to discover and identify bugs.

PROUST takes the list of goals in the problem description and places them on a goal agenda. This agenda is used throughout the analysis of the program to keep track of what program requirements have yet to be analyzed. PROUST selects goals from the agenda, one at a time, and uses its knowledge about program synthesis to predict how each goal might be implemented in the program. These predictions can then be tested against the student's code.

The process of selecting goals and predicting how the programmer might realize them is illustrated in Figure 2-4. The top of the figure shows the goal agenda just after it is loaded with the goals from the problem description. The goal *Sentinel-Controlled Input Sequence* is selected from the goal agenda. PROUST checks its database of goals and plans, and retrieves a plan for implementing *Sentinel-Controlled Input Sequence*. The plan constitutes a prediction of how the student might choose to implement the goal.

The plan shown in this diagram is the SENTINEL-CONTROLLED PROCESS-READ WHILE LOOP PLAN, or in somewhat abbreviated form the SENTINEL PROCESS-READ WHILE PLAN. This plan consists of a `while` loop which reads input, stopping at when the sentinel value is read. There is an initial input statement above the loop, to read the first value, and another input statement at the bottom of the body of the loop to read succeeding values. This plan is called "process-read" because each pass through the loop first processes the current value, and then reads the next value.

Plans are represented in PROUST as frames containing a collection of slots. The most important slot is the `Template` slot; this gives the form that a realization of the plan in Pascal will ordinarily take. As we see in the example, parts of the plan, such as `while ?New <> ?Stop do ...`, are Pascal expressions. Other parts, such as *subgoal Input*`(?New)`, are goals which are added to the goal agenda, and then implemented. Because plans can contain as subcomponents other goals, which in turn may be realized using a variety of different plans, a single plan can be used in a wide variety of different programs.

Although the overall structure of plans is described explicitly in the plan templates, the variables and constants that the plans manipulate are usually unspecified. Instead, pattern variables are inserted into the template in place of variables and constants. The SENTINEL PROCESS-READ WHILE PLAN has two pattern variables: `?New`, which represents the new-value variable, and `?Stop`, which represents the stop value. When PROUST uses a plan, it substitutes these pattern variables with the objects listed in the goal. In this case the goal is *Sentinel-Controlled Input Sequence*`(?Avg:Input, 99999)`, so `?Stop` is replaced by

AGENDA OF GOALS

Sentinel-Controlled Input Sequence (`?Avg:Input, 99999`)
Output (*Average* (`?Avg:Input`))

goal selection

Sentinel-Controlled Input Sequence (`?Avg:Input, 99999`)

plan retrieval

SENTINEL PROCESS-READ WHILE PLAN

Constants:
       `?Stop`
Variables:
       `?New`
Template:

```
InitInput:   subgoal Input(?New)
MainLoop:    while ?New <> ?Stop do
             begin
Process:         ?*
Next:        subgoal Input(?New)
               end
```

variable binding

SENTINEL PROCESS-READ WHILE PLAN

```
InitInput:   subgoal Input(?Avg:Input)
MainLoop:    while ?Avg:Input <> 99999 do
             begin
Process:         ?*
Next:        subgoal Input(?Avg:Input)
               end
```

Figure 2-4: Goal selection and plan instantiation

99999, and `?New` is replaced by `?Avg:Input`.[6] This results in the template at the bottom of Figure 2-4. The resulting plan instantiation is a detailed prediction of what the student's code will look like.

2.1.3 Identifying the counter overgeneralization bug

Let us now examine how the plan instantiation in Figure 2-4 is matched against the program, and how this in turn helps to identify the student's error. Figure 2-5 shows the process of matching the plan against the program. Each Pascal statement in the plan is mapped onto a line of the program. For example, the plan component `while ?Avg:Input <> 99999 do ...` is mapped onto line 8, `while New <> 99999 do`. In this example all of the Pascal components of the SENTINEL PROCESS-READ WHILE PLAN match the program. Next PROUST turns to the *Input* subgoals. For each subgoal, PROUST retrieves from the goal-plan database a plan which implements it. In this case the READ PLAN is chosen; this plan is simply a `read` statement. Although a `read` statement can be found above the loop, at line 7, none can be found inside the loop. There is thus exactly one discrepancy, or *plan difference*, between the SENTINEL PROCESS-READ WHILE PLAN and the code; this plan difference is the missing *Input* subgoal. PROUST must either explain the presence of this plan difference, or else conclude that the plan does not fit the program.

PROUST's method for resolving plan differences is to apply rules, called *plan-difference rules*, which explain their occurrence. Figure 2-6 shows the plan-difference rule that is used in this example. The rule is called the Input-is-Counter Bug Rule. Plan-difference rules are written as frames, just as plans are. Each plan-difference rule contains a test part, which examines the plan difference, and an action part, which either repairs the difference or explains it. The test parts in turn are usually subdivided into component tests, each of which appears as a separate slot in the rule frame. Each component test examines a different aspect of the context in which the plan difference arose. A rule fires if the conjunction of all of its component tests are satisfied.

---

[6]Replacing `?New` by `?Avg:Input` provides no new information about the pattern, since it is not yet known what Pascal variable corresponds to `?Avg:Input`. The pattern variable is still effectively unbound; whatever variable it does match will be bound to `?Avg:Input`. In this way the plan matching process will determine what quantity in the program `?Avg:Input` refers to.

```
1    program Average(input, output);        READ PLAN
2    var Sum, Count, New: integer;
3        Avg: real;                         read(?Avg:Input)
4    BEGIN
5      Sum := 0;                            SENTINEL PROCESS-READ WHILE
6      Count := 0;
7      read(New);                           subgoal Input(?Avg:Input)
8      while New <> 99999 do  ←────── while ?Avg:Input <> 99999 do
9        begin          ←─────────────────── begin
10         Sum := Sum + New;                    ?*
11         Count := Count + 1;
12         New := New + 1;        ?←──────── subgoal Input(?Avg:Input)
13       end;         ←─────────── end
14       if Count<>0 then
15         begin
16           Avg := Sum / Count;
17           writeln( 'The average is ', Avg );
18         end;
19     end;
```

Plan difference: the *Input* subgoal at the bottom of the loop cannot be matched against the program.

Figure 2-5:   Matching a plan against the program

The test part of the rule in Figure 2-6 consists of two parts, a `Goal` slot and a `TestCode` slot. The `Goal` slot names the goal which the rule can explain plan differences for. In the Input-is-Counter Bug Rule the `Goal` slot's filler is *Input*, indicating that the rule is capable of explaining plan differences that arise when *Input* goals are being analyzed. Since the plan difference in Figure 2-5 arose when the *Input* subgoal of the SENTINEL PROCESS-READ WHILE PLAN was being matched, the goal slot of the rule fits the plan difference. The `TestCode` slot contains a test procedure, a piece of Lisp code, which the rule can execute; if the procedure returns without error, the test succeeds. In the Input-is-Counter Bug Rule, the test procedure matches a new statement pattern, `?New := ?New + 1`, against the program. This new statement pattern matches line 12 in the program, `New := New + 1`. The test conditions are satisfied in this example, so the action part of the rule is executed. The action part declares that the counter update that was found implements the *Input* goal, and declares that a bug has been found. The rule generates a *bug description* , which is a frame structure that describes the bug in an intention-oriented fashion. The bug description generated here is a `Wrong Component for`

Plan bug: the programmer's plan for implementing the *Input* goal has a component that in fact implements a *Count* goal.

Input-1s-Counter Bug Rule

> **Goal**: *Input*
> **TestCode**: *try matching the pattern* `?New := ?New + 1`
> **Action**: map the *Input* goal onto code that matches
> `?New := ?New + 1`; declare a
> **Wrong Component for Plan** bug:
> the intended plan really implements
> a *Count* goal

Figure 2-6: The plan-difference rule for recognizing a counter overgeneralization

Once the analysis of the program is complete, the bugs are reported to the student, as follows. The list of bug descriptions that PROUST produced is passed to PROUST's bug-reporting mechanism. The bug-reporting mechanism orders the bugs according to severity, and groups together similar bugs. It then generates English text to describe the bugs, as was shown in Figure 2-2. When the programming tutor for PROUST is constructed, it will be inserted in place of the current bug-reporting mechanism, so that it can decide how best to describe the bugs to the student.

2.2 Example 2: a larger example

The previous example illustrated how PROUST analyzes small programs. However, small programs do not provide sufficient motivation for PROUST's approach. Bugs in small programs can be found by a variety of means; analysis by synthesis is not essential. The next example, however, is a larger program; the importance of intention-based diagnosis will be clearer. In particular, the issues of refining informal problem descriptions and choosing among alternative program interpretations will be discussed.

The English description of the next problem that we will discuss is shown in Figure 2-7. This problem, called the Bank Problem, requires that the students write a program which simulates an automatic bank teller machine. The program shown in Figure 2-8 is a student solution to this problem. Only part of the program is shown

34

here, the entire program being to large to fit on one page. Figure 2-9 shows PROUST's output for the program; four bugs are listed. One of them is a missing `read` statement, resulting in an infinite loop. This bug, often indicating a misconception about how iterations are constructed in Pascal, is one which we have encountered in a number of looping programs. Another bug is that the program does not test the account number and initial balance, to make sure that they are legal values. The other two bugs have to do with the question of what constitutes a well-formed banking transaction. The student's program has permitted zero transactions, but such transactions should really be excluded as invalid.

> Write a Pascal program that processes three types of bank transactions: withdrawals, deposits, and a special transaction that says: no more transactions are to follow. Your program should start by asking the user to input his/her account id and his/her initial balance. Then your program should prompt the user to input
>
> 1. the transaction type, and
>
> 2. if it is an END-PROCESSING transaction the program should print out the (a) final balance of the user's account, (b) the total number of transactions, and (c) total number of each type of transaction, and (d) the total amount of the service charges, and stop;
>
> 3. if it is a DEPOSIT or a WITHDRAWAL, the program should ask for the amount of the transaction and then post it appropriately.
>
> Use a variable of type CHAR to encode the transaction types. To encourage saving, charge the user 20 cents per withdrawal, but nothing for a deposit.

Figure 2-7: The Bank Problem

2.2.1 Identifying the missing-input bug

I will first discuss the process of identifying the missing-input bug in this example. This process is similar to the one which identified the counter-overgeneralization bug in the previous example. In this discussion, the process of differentiating between alternative plans will be highlighted.

Figure 2-10 shows the problem description for the Bank Problem which PROUST uses. As the reader can readily see, much more information is required to specify the

```
1   program BankA(input, output);
2   const    Srvc = 0.20;
3   var Number, TypeW, TypeD, Acct: integer;
4       Deposit, Withdrawal, Balance: real;
5       TransType: char;
6   begin
7     TypeD   := 0;
8     TypeW := 0;
9     writeln('Enter account number, please');
10    readln(Acct);
11    writeln('Enter initial balance');
12    readln(Balance);
13    writeln('Enter type of transaction, w for withdrawal');
14    writeln('d for deposit and e for end-processing');
15    readln(TransType);
16    while(TransType <> 'e') do begin
17      if TransType= 'w' then
18        begin
19          writeln('Enter amount of withdrawal:');
20          readln(Withdrawal);
21          if (Withdrawal >= 0) and (Withdrawal <= Balance - Srvc) then
22            begin
23              TypeW:= TypeW + 1;
24              Balance:= (Balance - Withdrawal) - Srvc;
25              writeln('New balance:', Balance:1:2);
26            end
27          else
28            if Withdrawal > Balance
29            then writeln('Sorry, short of funds')
30              else
31                writeln('No negative withdrawals');
32        end
33      else  if TransType= 'd' then
34        begin
35          writeln('Enter amount of deposit:');
36          readln(Deposit);
37          if Deposit >= 0 then
38            begin
39              typed:= typed + 1;
40              Balance:= Balance + Deposit;
41              writeln('New balance:', Balance:1:2);
42            end
43          else
44            writeln('No negative deposits');
45        end
46      else writeln('sorry, type must be w, d or e');
47      end;
48    writeln('Transactions completed');
...
```

Figure 2-8:   An example solution to the Bank Problem

```
NOW BEGINNING BUG REPORT:

(TO CONTINUE, PLEASE PRESS CARRIAGE RETURN)

 >>> Now Reporting MINOR Bugs in the SETUP part:

There is no input validation for the variables ACCT and
BALANCE.

(TO CONTINUE, PLEASE PRESS CARRIAGE RETURN)

 >>> Now Reporting CRITICAL Bugs in the CONTROL part:

There is no input validation for the variable TRANSTYPE.

Your main loop is missing a READ statement.  As it stands
your loop will process the same input value over and over.

(TO CONTINUE, PLEASE PRESS CARRIAGE RETURN)

 >>> Now Reporting MINOR Bugs in the CONTROL part:

You test at line 24 permits zero transactions.  You may
disagree, but I think they should be excluded.
The statement in question is:
     IF AMOUNT >= 0 AND AMOUNT <= BALANCE THEN ... ELSE ...

You test at line 41 permits zero transactions.  You may
disagree, but I think they should be excluded.
The statement in question is:
     IF AMOUNT >= 0 THEN ... ELSE ...

BUG REPORT NOW COMPLETE.
```

Figure 2-9: PROUST's output for the program in Figure 2-8

Bank Problem than was required to specify the Averaging Problem. This problem
description is quite complex and lengthy; it includes 13 object definitions and 10 goal
definitions, whereas the Averaging Problem description has only one object definition
and two goal definitions. I will only discuss portions of the Bank Problem description
in this section; further discussion will be conducted in Chapter 5. The full problem
description is presented here so that the reader can get a sense of how the parts of the
problem description that I will discuss relate to the problem description as a whole.

```
DefProgram Bank;
DefObject ?Bank:InData
    Type char, ObjectClass SingleLetterCommand,
    Range MultiValued, Values (?Bank:DTrans, ?Bank:WTrans, ?Bank:ETrans);
DefObject ?Bank:DTrans Value 'd';
DefObject ?Bank:WTrans Value 'w';
DefObject ?Bank:ETrans Value 'e';
DefObject ?Bank:AcctID ObjectClass AccountNumber, Range MultiValued;
DefObject ?Bank:Balance ObjectClass AccountBalance, Range MultiValued;
DefObject ?Bank:Deposit ObjectClass TransactionAmount,
                        Range MultiValued;
DefObject ?Bank:Withdrawal ObjectClass WithdrawalAmount,
                        Range MultiValued;
DefObject ?Bank:Charge ObjectClass DollarAmount, Value 0.20;
DefObject ?Bank:WithdrawalCount ObjectClass NaturalNumber,
                        Range MultiValued;
DefObject ?Bank:DepositCount ObjectClass NaturalNumber,
                        Range MultiValued;
DefObject ?Bank:TotalCharge ObjectClass DollarAmount,
                        Range MultiValued;
DefObject ?Bank:TotalCount ObjectClass NaturalNumber,
                        Range MultiValued;

DefGoal Input1 = Input(?Bank:AcctID);
DefGoal Input2 = Input(?Bank:Balance);
DefGoal Loop1 = Sentinel-Controlled Input Sequence (?Bank:InData,
                                                    ?Bank:ETrans);
Input1 Precedes Loop1;
Input2 Precedes Loop1;
DefGoal When(?Bank:InData=?Bank:DTrans,
            GoalBlock(Input(?Bank:Deposit);
                        Accumulate(?Bank:Balance, ?Bank:Deposit);
                        Bind ?Bank:DepositCount = Count(?Bank:InData)));
DefGoal When(?Bank:InData=?Bank:WTrans, GoalBlock(
            Input( ?Bank:Withdrawal);
            CompoundDeduct(?Bank:Withdrawal, ?Bank:Charge, ?Bank:Balance);
            GuardException(Update: component of CompoundDeduct,
                        ?Bank:Withdrawal >= ?Bank:Balance - ?Bank:Charge);
            Bind ?Bank:TotalCharge = ConstantSum(?Bank:Charge);
            Bind ?Bank:WithdrawalCount = Count(?Bank:InData));
Bind ?Bank:TotalCount = Count(?Bank:InData);
DefGoal Output(?Bank:TotalCharge);
DefGoal Output(?Bank:TotalCount);
DefGoal Output(?Bank:DepositCount);
DefGoal Output(?Bank:WithdrawalCount);
```

Figure 2-10: A description of the Bank Problem

Although the Bank Problem description has many more goals than the problem description for the Averaging Problem, the main loop goals in the problem descriptions are similar. The main loop goal in the Bank Problem description is as follows:

DefGoal Loop1 = *Sentinel-Controlled Input Sequence*(?Bank:InData,
                                                ?Bank:ETrans).

The main loop goal in the Averaging Problem is as follows:

DefGoal *Sentinel-Controlled Input Sequence*(?Avg:Input, 99999).

There are two principal differences between the two goals. First, there is a syntactic difference. In the Bank Problem goal expression the phrase "Loop1 =" follows immediately after the DefGoal keyword. This serves merely to assign a unique name to the goal form, so that other parts of the problem description can refer to the goal form by name. One place where this name is used is in the statement Input1 Precedes Loop1, which indicates that the code which implements a goal named Input1, the input of the account number, should precede the code which implements the looping goal. The second difference between the two looping goals is that the sentinel value in the Averaging Problem is 99999, whereas the sentinel value in the Bank Problem is the object ?Bank:ETrans, which has the value 'e'. Characters are equally good sentinel values as integers, so there is no problem with using 'e' as a sentinel value.

Analysis of the Bank Problem example in Figure 2-8 proceeds as follows. As in the Averaging Problem example, PROUST sets up a goal agenda and selects a goal for analysis. Now that we are considering a problem description with numerous goals, however, the question of which goal to analyze first becomes more significant. PROUST does not simply process goals in the order in which they are listed. If it did, it would pick the first goal in the problem description, *Input*(?Bank:AcctID), first. This goal would be a poor choice, because PROUST does not yet know how ?Bank:AcctID is realized in the program; PROUST would therefore have no basis for deciding among the various read statements in the program. PROUST therefore applies heuristics for determining in what order to analyze goals. The heuristic which is applied here is to analyze major goals, those which affect large parts of the

39

program, before analyzing minor goals. This leads to the choice of the *Sentinel-Controlled Input Sequence* for analysis.

PROUST selects the SENTINEL PROCESS-READ WHILE PLAN for instantiation, as before. Figure 2-11 shows how this plan is matched against the program. The result of the matching is the same as in Figure 2-5: the *Input* subgoal at the bottom of the loop cannot be mapped onto the code. As before, PROUST must explain the plan differences.

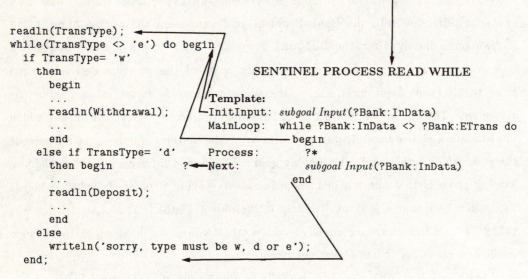

Plan difference: the *Input* subgoal at the bottom of the loop cannot be matched against the program.

Figure 2-11: Relating a goal to the code

`TransType` is used as the new-value variable in each component of the SENTINEL PROCESS-READ WHILE PLAN that matches. Therefore the Input-is-Counter Bug Rule cannot be used this time to explain the plan difference; although there are counter updates in the loop, they operate on variables other than `TransType`. The rule which does fire has the following test and action: if the *Input* subgoal in the `Next:` step of the loop is missing, and the loop initialization is present, then accept the `Next:` step as missing, and declare the bug to be a possible misconception about how loops work. PROUST is thus able to postulate an explanation for the student's code.

40

Now I will introduce a further complication: PROUST must not only construct an interpretation of the code, it must determine that it is the best interpretation. The analysis of the bug described above makes the assumption that SENTINEL PROCESS-READ WHILE is the right plan to use. But given that a component of the plan is missing, how certain can we be that this is the appropriate plan to match against the program? Perhaps if we matched a different plan, which has different plan components, we would find that it fits the program better. The only way to determine this is to check how alternative plans match against the program, and compare the bug analyses that result against the one that has already been derived. This is precisely what PROUST does.

Figure 2-12 shows the result of matching a different plan, the SENTINEL READ-PROCESS WHILE PLAN, against the program. This program differs from the SENTINEL PROCESS-READ PLAN in that an input statement appears at the top of the loop body instead of at the bottom. Each pass through the loop first reads a value, then processes it, hence the "read-process" in the name. Three plan differences result from matching this plan against the example program:

- the input step inside the loop cannot be found;

- the initialization of the new-value variable cannot be found; and

- the additional test for the sentinel value inside of the loop, required in order to break out of the loop when the sentinel value is encountered, is also missing.

One might think that the number of plan differences clearly indicates that this is the wrong plan to match. However, it is not the number of plan differences that is important; that is too syntactic a description of the bugs to be reliable. The question is whether or not the plan differences are explainable as bugs, and if so, which plan results in the best bug description. The plan differences in the SENTINEL READ-PROCESS WHILE PLAN are all explainable. The initialization of a new-value variable is often mistakenly written as an input statement rather than as an assignment. The input statement inside of the loop is often omitted; this is true if the loop is read-process as well as if it is process-read. Finally, the internal guard step is frequently left out by novices, and in any case it is likely to be missing if the input is missing.

```
writeln('Enter type of transaction, w for withdrawal');
writeln('d for deposit and e for end-processing');
readln(TransType);
while(TransType <> 'e') do begin
  if TransType= 'w'
    then                              SENTINEL READ PROCESS WHILE
      begin
      ...                    Template:
      readln(Withdrawal);  ?←Init:        ?Bank:InData := ?Seedval
      ...                    —MainLoop:    while ?Bank:InData <> ?Bank:ETrans do
      end                                    begin
    else  if TransType= 'd' ?←Next:          subgoal Input(?Bank:InData)
      then begin            ?←InternalGuard: subgoal Sent. Guard(?Bank:InData,
      ...                                                        ?Bank:ETrans,
      readln(Deposit);                                          Process: ?*)
      ...                                        end
      end
    else
      ...
  end;
```

Plan differences:

    (1) the *Input* subgoal at the top of the loop cannot
        be matched against the program.
    (2) the Init: step cannot be matched.
    (3) the InternalGuard: step cannot be matched.

Figure 2-12: Relating a goal to the code via a different plan

Only when we compare the two explanations of the bugs is it evident which account of the code is better. The bug in the account based on the process-read plan is also in the account based on the read-process plan, but the other bugs in the read-process account are absent in the process-read account. PROUST applies the following heuristic: if one bug description is a proper subset of another bug description, the shorter bug description is better. Thus the bug description based upon the SENTINEL PROCESS-READ PLAN is accepted as the correct bug description.

There are two observations to be made from this discussion. First, the issues of what is the correct description of the bugs in a program and what is the correct description of the intended implementation are interconnected. Second, bug analysis requires differential diagnosis; one must decide what the competing accounts of the bugs might be, and compare them against each other, in order to determine which is better. Since plans and bugs are differentiated simultaneously, and program analysis and bug diagnosis are intertwined, I will frequently call this process differential analysis, rather than differential diagnosis.

2.2.2 Interpreting imprecise problem descriptions

Let us now focus attention on bugs in PROUST's bug report relating to zero deposits and withdrawals. These bug descriptions indicate that the program should check to make sure that zero deposits and withdrawals are rejected. The original problem statement says nothing about rejecting zero deposits and withdrawals; nevertheless, we expect programmers to infer what the boundary conditions are likely to be on deposits and withdrawals. These bug descriptions illustrate an important fact about programming: problem descriptions are often incomplete, and the programmer must be prepared to resolve such incompleteness. This may involve applying knowledge about the application domain to the problem. A bug recognition system must be prepared to handle variability resulting from alternative interpretations of problem descriptions.

There are two attitudes which one could take toward the role of domain knowledge in a system such as PROUST. One is that PROUST should have knowledge only about programming; whatever domain knowledge is required for analysis should be encoded explicitly in the problem description. The other is that domain knowledge should be codified in PROUST's knowledge base just as programming knowledge is. I favor the latter view. Programmers make errors in applying domain knowledge just as they make errors in applying programming knowledge. If we made domain knowledge explicit in the problem description, we would also have to make explicit the bugs associated with the domain knowledge, thus cluttering the problem description. I have endeavored instead to construct a mechanism in PROUST for applying certain kinds of domain knowledge during program analysis. This reduces the amount of clutter in the problem description and makes it possible to reuse the same domain knowledge in other programming problems.

To see how PROUST employs domain knowledge in identifying the zero-transaction bugs, let us first examine how the transaction requirements are indicated in the problem description. The following definitions appear in the problem statement describing the deposit amounts and the withdrawal amounts:

- DefObject ?Bank:Deposit ObjectClass TransactionAmount;

- DefObject ?Bank:Withdrawal ObjectClass WithdrawalAmount.

These objects are members of *object classes*, i.e., classes of objects sharing common properties. Object classes are similar to data types, except that they correspond to real-world concepts, not just to abstract programming concepts. By indicating that deposits are members of the class `TransactionAmount`, and withdrawals are members of the class `WithdrawalAmount`, we are leaving it up to PROUST to determine what implications this may have on the program. Programmers have to do an exactly analogous thing when told in a natural-language problem description that a quantity is a bank transaction. In order to be able to analyze programs that manipulate bank transactions, we must determine what facts about bank transactions are relevant to programming, and how these facts are called into play.

The following two facts about bank transaction amounts are of potential relevance to programming: transactions are dollar amounts, and they must be positive. The fact that transaction amounts are dollar amounts helps to determine what datatype to use: dollar amounts can be represented as real numbers, or as integral numbers of cents. If a value is a dollar amount we can infer a boundary condition for the value, namely that it ordinarily cannot be negative. These two issues, selecting representations for data and determining boundary conditions, are commonplace in programming. PROUST's knowledge base therefore contains information about data representations and boundary conditions associated with bank transactions.

Figure 2-13 shows PROUST's current representation for transaction amounts. Under each object class in PROUST's knowledge base is a list of possible implementations for that object class. PROUST currently "knows" about one implementation of bank transaction amounts, namely the implementation as a real-valued variable. Each implementation has a `Type` slot, indicating the Pascal type of an instance of this implementation. Two other properties may be associated with each object: an exception condition, and a list of plan-difference rules. These properties will be described below.

The descriptive power of PROUST's object class language currently has some weaknesses. For example, it is not possible to describe the following general property

```
Implementations: RealTransactionAmount
Exception Condition: ?? <= 0
Plan-Difference Rules: SloppyTransactionGuard
```

REAL TRANSACTION AMOUNT

Type: real

Figure 2-13: PROUST's representation for transaction amounts

of withdrawal amounts: that they should not exceed the current balance minus the service charge. The problem is in defining a semantics for the phrases "current balance" and "service charge" which do not refer to the specific balance and service charge objects mentioned in the Bank Problem. This particular property currently is mentioned explicitly in the problem description, as a *Guard Exception* goal, rather than being retrieved from object class knowledge.

PROUST employs object class information in the following manner in dealing with transaction amounts. Each time PROUST processes a goal, it checks the objects which are the arguments of that goal to see if they have special object-class information associated with them. The goals *Input*(?Bank:Deposit) and *Input*(?Bank:Withdrawal) both manipulate objects which are defined as being members of the TransactionAmount object class. At that point PROUST examines the TransactionAmount entry and extracts from it information relevant to the analysis. The datatype associated with bank transactions, real, does not help identify any bugs in this program; the variables Deposit and Withdrawal are both declared real. The other properties, the exception condition property and the bug rule property, are of significance here.

The exception condition property of an object class is an expression specifying the range of values which are illegal for the object class. In the case of the TransactionAmount class, the exception condition is ?? <= 0, indicating that all values less than or equal to zero must be excluded. Whenever an object which has an exception condition is referred to, PROUST adds a *Guard Exception* goal to the goal agenda. This goal serves to check that the exception condition is met. In our example, PROUST examines the goal agenda for goals which refer to the `?Bank:Withdrawal` and `?Bank:Deposit`. It finds two: *Accumulate*(`?Bank:Balance`, `?Bank:Deposit`), and *Deduct*(`?Bank:Balance`, `?Bank:Withdrawal`). It therefore adds two goals to the goal agenda:

- *GuardException*(`Update`: *component of Accumulate*, `?Bank:Deposit <= 0`) and

- *GuardException*(`Update`: *component of Deduct*, `?Bank:Withdrawal <= 0`).

Guard Exception goals are typically implemented using the GUARD EXCEPTION PLAN, which consists of an `if` statement which tests for the exception condition. The process of matching the instantiation of GUARD EXCEPTION PLAN implementing *GuardException*(`Update`: *component of Accumulate*, `?Bank:Deposit <= 0`) is shown in Figure 2-14. A plan difference is discovered when this plan is matched; the `if` statement tests that `Deposit` is nonnegative, when the plan indicates that it should test that it is positive.

```
writeln('Enter amount of deposit:');
readln(Deposit);                          GUARD EXCEPTION PLAN
if Deposit >= 0
   then                                   if Deposit>0 then
     begin                                   contains Update: component of Accumulate
     typed:= typed + 1;                    else
     Balance:= Balance + Deposit;            subgoal OutputDiagnostic()
     writeln('New balance:', Balance);
     end
   else
     writeln('No negative deposits');
end
```

Plan difference:

   1) test of `if` is `>=` rather than `>`

Figure 2-14: Matching the GUARD EXCEPTION PLAN

In order to see what happens with this plan difference, let us now discuss the plan-difference-rule list associated with the `TransactionAmount` object class. Plan-difference-rule lists of object classes are plan-difference rules which interpret plan mismatches that may arise the object class is used in a program. The plan-difference-rule list is added to the plan-difference rule pool when an object class is referenced. The `TransactionAmount` object class has a single rule in its plan-difference-rule list, called the Sloppy Transaction Guard Rule. A paraphrased version of this rule is shown in Figure 2-15. The Sloppy Transaction Guard Bug Rule declares that the responsible bug is an `Implements Wrong Goal Argument` bug, i.e., the student's intended *Guard Exception* goal has an incorrect parameter. The incorrect parameter is the exception condition being tested. In other words, the student is guarding against a different boundary condition from what the situation really calls for.

```
Goal: GuardException
Plan difference patterns:
    ">=" instead of ">",
    ">" instead of "<",
    "<=" instead of "<", and
    "<" instead of "<="
TestCode: check whether the GuardException goal arises from an object
          class exception condition, and whether the object class is
          TransactionAmount or WithdrawalAmount
Action: declare the presence of an Implements Wrong Goal Argument Bug.
```

Figure 2-15:   The Sloppy Transaction Guard Bug Rule

2.2.3 Summary

This example has introduced some augmentations to the basic PROUST approach to bug analysis. Let us review what they are. First, larger problem descriptions require a means to choose among goals to analyze in the program. Second, differential analysis, i.e., comparison of alternative explanations of the student's code, is often necessary in order to determine which is the correct account of the student's bugs. Third, informality in problem descriptions plays a role in PROUST's analysis; it results in new goals being added to the goal agenda, and new plan-difference rules being added to the plan-difference rule pool.

2.3 Example 3: causal reasoning about bugs

Analysis of the next example is rather more complex than that of the previous examples. This next example will further illustrate how PROUST's goal agenda changes during analysis, reflecting the elaboration and development of the program requirements. It will show how PROUST derives detailed models of the student's intentions in order to establish the causes of bugs.

The example that will be discussed here is a solution to the Rainfall Problem, which was introduced in Chapter 1, Figure 1-1. The example program appears in Figure 2-16. Figure 2-17 shows PROUST's output for this program.

Figure 2-17 shows three different bugs. One is a failure to check for division by zero when the average is computed. Another involves attempting to output the average and maximum of a set of integers when the set is empty. These bugs are both boundary-condition bugs; i.e., they involve the use of data outside of their legal range. We have already seen examples of boundary-condition bugs; the zero transaction bugs in the previous example are also boundary condition bugs. The boundary-condition bugs in this example are handled in a similar way to the other boundary-condition bugs.

The third bug is an altogether different type of bug from the others. PROUST is criticizing both the specific bug in the program and the implementation decision that led to the occurrence of the bug. The specific bug involved is as follows. Line 20, `Total := Total + Rainfall`, is executed both when the input is valid and when it is invalid. That is, if `Rainfall` is negative, it is invalid, and should not be added into `Total`, yet line 20 adds `Rainfall` into `Total`, regardless of the value of `Rainfall`. The student's implementation decision which led to the bug is as follows. The student could have chosen a plan for validating input which tests the input as soon as it is read. Instead, he or she decided to examine each individual computation in the loop, determine the effects of negative data on the computation, and filter the data only when it is necessary. The bug at line 20 arose because the student did not catch all the effects of negative input. If the student had instead tested the input as soon as it was read, he or she would not have to worry about which computations are affected by bad input, since the input would be filtered once and for all.

```
1 program Rainfall (input , output);
2 var
3    Total, Rainfall, Highest, Average : real;
4    Number, Days : integer;
5 begin
6    writeln ('Enter your rainfall data, one at a time');
7    readln;
8    read(Rainfall);
9    Number := 0;
10   Highest := 0;
11   Days := 0;
12   Total := 0;
13   while Rainfall <> 99999 do
14     begin
15       Number := Number + 1;
16       if Rainfall > 0 then
17         Days := Days + 1;
18       if Rainfall > Highest then
19         Highest := Rainfall;
20       Total := Total + Rainfall;
21       if Rainfall < 0    then
22         begin
23           writeln ('Impossible, try again');
24           Number := Number - 1;
25         end;
26       readln;
27       read ( Rainfall)
28     end;
29   Average := Total / Number;
30   writeln ( Number:3,  ' valid rainfalls were entered.');
31   writeln ('The average rainfall was', Average:3:2);
32   writeln ('The highest rainfall was', Highest:3:2);
33   writeln ('There were', Days:3, ' rainy days')
34 end.
```

Figure 2-16: an example solution to the Rainfall Rroblem

2.3.1 Identifying the division-by-zero bug

I will start by discussing the division-by-zero bug in this program. The specific manifestation of this bug is as follows. If the first value that the user inputs is 99999, the input loop will be skipped, and the value of the variable Count will be zero. Thus the average computation at line 29 will result in division by zero, and the program will abort. This bug is different from the bugs considered so far in that it is

```
NOW BEGINNING BUG REPORT:

(TO CONTINUE, PLEASE PRESS CARRIAGE RETURN)

 >>> Now Reporting MINOR Bugs in the CONTROL part:

Some of your code is not shielded against invalid input.
The statement in question is:
        TOTAL := TOTAL + RAINFALL
You appear to test for bad input elsewhere, using the
following code:
NUMBER := NUMBER - 1
IF RAINFALL < 0 THEN ...
Your program would really be simpler if it tested
the input in one place, before it is used anywhere.  That
way bugs like this would not crop up.

(TO CONTINUE, PLEASE PRESS CARRIAGE RETURN)

 >>> Now Reporting CRITICAL Bugs in the OUTPUT part:

The maximum and the average are undefined if there is no
valid input.  But lines 32 and 31 output them anyway.  You
should always check whether your code will work when there
is no input!  This is a common cause of bugs.

You need a test to check that at least one valid data point
has been input before line 29 is executed.  The average will
bomb when there is no input.

BUG REPORT NOW COMPLETE.
```

Figure 2-17: PROUST's output for the program in Figure 2-16

not an example of a malformed or missing plan component. Instead, a goal has been
omitted altogether from the program.

Figure 2-18 shows the problem description for the Rainfall Problem. This
problem description is an elaboration of the Averaging Problem; two of the goals,

- *Sentinel-Controlled Input Sequence*(`?Rainfall:DailyRain, 99999`)
  and

- *Output*(*Average*(`?Rainfall:DailyRain`)),

are equivalent to the goals in the Averaging Problem description. In order to see how

PROUST identifies the division-by-zero bug, let us start by examining how PROUST deals with the *Average* goal.

```
DefProgram Rainfall;

DefObject ?Rainfall:DailyRain ObjectClass ScalarMeasurement;
```

DefGoal *Sentinel-Controlled Input Sequence*(?Rainfall:DailyRain, 99999);
DefGoal *Loop Input Validation*(?Rainfall:DailyRain, ?Rainfall:DailyRain < 0);
DefGoal *Output*(*Average*(?Rainfall:DailyRain));
DefGoal *Output*(*Count*(?Rainfall:DailyRain));
DefGoal *Output*(*Guarded Count*(?Rainfall:DailyRain, ?Rainfall:DailyRain > 0));
DefGoal *Output*(*Maximum*(?Rainfall:DailyRain));

Figure 2-18: The Rainfall Problem in PROUST's problem description notation

When PROUST selects the goal *Output*(*Average*(?Avg:Input)) for analysis, it finds that it is a combination of two goals, an *Average* goal and an *Output* goal. PROUST therefore breaks up the expression and considers the *Average* goal first. PROUST goes to the goal-plan database, looking for implementations of *Average*. One plan, called the AVERAGE PLAN, is shown in Figure 2-19.

AVERAGE PLAN

Variables: ?Avg, ?Sum, ?Count, ?New
Exception condition: (?Count *in goal Count*) = 0
Posterior goals:
    Count(?New, ?Count)
    Sum(?New, ?Sum)
    Guard Exception(Update: *component of goal Average*,
                (?Count = 0))
Template:
    Update: ?Avg := (?Sum / ?Count)

Figure 2-19: A plan for implementing *Average*

The template of the AVERAGE PLAN indicates simply that the average should be computed by dividing a variable ?Sum by another variable, ?Count. The content of this plan is not so much in the plan template itself, but in the other slots in the plan frame. One important slot is the Posterior Goals slot; this is a list of goals which must be added to the goal agenda as a consequence of matching the plan. Added goals are one means of elaborating the model of the programmer's intentions as the program is analyzed.

Three goals are listed in the `Posterior Goals` slot of the AVERAGE PLAN: a *Count* goal, a *Sum* goal, and a *Guard Exception* goal. The *Count* goal expression indicates that the denominator variable in the AVERAGE PLAN template, `?Count`, is a counter. The *Sum* goal expression indicates that the numerator variable is a sum. The *Guard Exception* goal guards against a boundary condition; it requires that the `Update:` component of the AVERAGE PLAN be protected against the case where the counter variable is zero. Thus the *Guard Exception* goal protects against division by zero. The `Update:` component is the only component in the AVERAGE PLAN template, which is just one line of Pascal. Thus the *Guard Exception* goal makes sure that the counter variable is non-zero before the average update is executed.

The three posterior goals have as arguments pattern variables from the AVERAGE PLAN. For example, the goal *Count*`(?New, ?Count)` refers to two pattern variables, `?New` and `?Count`. This ensures that the data being averaged is the same as the data being counted, and that the counter that satisfies the *Count* goal is the same as the counter in the AVERAGE PLAN. The `Update:` component argument to the *Guard Exception* goal is an example of a goal parameter that is bound to a line of code in the program. In general, goals can apply to data in a program as well as to other parts of the program.

The *Count* goal and the *Sum* goal are mapped onto lines 15 and 20, respectively, of the program. The *Guard Exception* goal, on the other hand, cannot be mapped onto the code. PROUST tries various plan-difference rules, looking for some way of accounting for the match failure. No rule is applicable, so a different pool of rules is consulted, a pool which indicates when it is plausible that students might fail to implement programming goals. *Guard Exception* is mentioned in one such rule as a goal that is likely to be omitted. PROUST therefore deletes the goal from the agenda, and generates a bug description indicating that the student left out the *Guard Exception* goal. When English is generated describing this bug, we get the output shown in Figure 2-17.

2.3.2 Bugs involving undefined variables

The second bug listed in the bug report in Figure 2-17 has to do with attempting to use undefined values, in this case to output them. The problem arises when the user fails to type in any input data, and instead simply types 99999. The program as written will output values for the average and the maximum, even though these quantities are undefined when there is no input data. The situation is complicated here because these values would probably never be output; on most computers the program would abort when division by zero is attempted at line 29, before the outputs are ever performed. I have adopted the position that it is best to inform the student of all the errors in the student's solution, rather than just the ones that are manifested in incorrect behavior. That way the student can correct the errors in a systematic fashion.

In order to see how these bugs are recognized, consider the AVERAGE PLAN again. This plan has an additional slot which was not discussed earlier: the `Exception Condition` slot. This slot describes the conditions under which the plan will not generate valid values. It thus serves a role similar to the exception condition slots on object class definitions. The exception condition on the AVERAGE PLAN indicates that whenever the variable `?Count` in the plan is zero, the result of the AVERAGE PLAN computation is undefined.

When PROUST instantiates the AVERAGE PLAN it scans the goal agenda, and for each goal which refers to the result computed by the AVERAGE PLAN it adds a *GuardException* goal which checks for the boundary condition. In order to see what the goal agenda will be at that point, take a look at the problem description for the Rainfall Problem in Figure 2-18. The *Average* goal is defined in the statement

DefGoal *Output* (*Average* (`?Rainfall:DailyRain`)).

No other goal refers to *Average*. Thus exactly one *GuardException* goal must be added, which guards the *Output* goal which outputs the average. This *GuardException* goal cannot be matched against the program, so the goal is declared missing.

The maximum boundary condition is treated in a similar way. The MAXIMUM PLAN has an exception condition associated with it, which results in the creation of a *Guard Exception* goal. PROUST concludes that the student failed to realize the *Guard Exception* goal in the program.

When PROUST is done analyzing the program, it inspects the list of bugs that were found, looking for systematic occurrences of bugs. Such systematic bugs are often good indicators of student difficulties. If a student makes a mistake once, it may be an accidental error; if the student makes the same mistake whenever the opportunity for making the mistake presents itself, the error cannot be accidental. In this case, PROUST discovers that none of the *Guard Exception* goals resulting from undefined variables are implemented in the student's program. There is thus suggestive evidence for a gap in the student's programming knowledge: he may not realize that the null-input boundary condition is a common source of bugs. PROUST therefore groups the null-input bugs together, and mentions that null-input boundary conditions should be checked for:

> You should always check whether your code will work when there is no input! This is a common cause of bugs.

This is one example of how PROUST is able to reason backwards from individual bugs to the causes of those bugs.

2.3.3 Causal reasoning about the origin of bugs

I will now describe how the first bug in Figure 2-17 is discovered. First, let us examine carefully the nature of PROUST's criticism here. As you recall, PROUST's criticism was this:

```
Some of your code is not shielded against invalid input.
The statement in question is:
        TOTAL := TOTAL + RAINFALL
You appear to test for bad input elsewhere, using the following code:
        IF RAINFALL < 0 THEN ...
        NUMBER := NUMBER - 1
Your program would really be simpler if it tested
the input in one place, before it is used anywhere.  That way bugs
like this would not crop up.
```

PROUST is claiming here that the student's bug is in the way that he or she is dealing with the possibility of invalid input. The problem statement requires that the programmer make sure that negative input is excluded from the computation. Most competent programmers guarantee this by inserting a plan which filters the input before any of the computations on the input are performed. An example of a program with such a plan is shown in Figure 2-20. Here an `if` statement has been inserted into the body of the loop, and all the computations have been inserted inside of the `if` statement.

```
            while Rainfall <> 99999 do
              begin
                if Rainfall < 0 then
                  writeln ('Impossible, try again')
                else
                  begin
                  Number := Number + 1;
                    if Rainfall > 0 then
                    Days := Days + 1;
                    if Rainfall > Highest then
                    Highest := Rainfall;
                    Total := Total + Rainfall;
                  end;
                readln;
                read( Rainfall )
              end;
```

Figure 2-20:   A well-structured loop for the Rainfall Problem

2.3.3.1 Motivating the analysis

The student who wrote the program in Figure 2-16 evidently intended that negative input be excluded. The program tests whether or not input is negative, and if so it outputs "Impossible, try again". However, this program does not test the input before computations are performed; it tests the input *after* they are performed. At that point the negative input has already entered into the computation, so its effect must be undone; therefore the student adds a line `Number := Number - 1` to undo it. Unfortunately the sum is also affected by the negative input; there should be a line of the form `Total := Total - Rainfall`, but there is not. That is the only line that is missing; the other computations are unaffected by negative input. The maximum update has a test, `if Rainfall > Highest`, which excludes negative input, owing to the fact that `Highest` is initialized to zero and hence is always non-negative. The rainy day counter is unaffected by bad input because its test, `if Rainfall > 0`, also excludes negative values.

I claim that the student made a strategic decision to undo the effects of bad input

55

on each computation individually. That is, instead of inserting code into the loop which guards all of the computations against bad input, the student decided to examine each computation, and insert code to undo the effects of bad input where needed. The alternative is to suppose that there is a single input validation plan at work here. Let us examine what such a plan would look like. Figure 2-21 shows the plan that was used to validate the input in the well-structured loop in Figure 2-20. This plan indicates that the section of the loop that performs the computations should be spanned by an `if-then-else` statement which tests whether the input is valid. This plan can be used in any loop, regardless of the function of the loop. Figure 2-22 shows what a plan would look like which undoes the effect of invalid input in the program in Figure 2-16. This "plan" indicates explicitly that one variable, `?Count`, is decremented, and another variable, `?Sum`, has a value `?Val` subtracted from it. Such a plan can be used in few programs other than solutions to the Rainfall Problem. Instead of presuming such problem-specific plans, it is better to describe the programming knowledge involved in terms of plans that are smaller and problem-independent.

Variables:
        `?Val, ?Pred`
Template:
        (*in component* `Process:` *of goal Read & process*)
        spanned by:
`Test:`   `if ?Pred then`
           `subgoal` *Output Diagnostic*`()`
           `else`
`Process:`   `?*`

Figure 2-21: The BAD INPUT SKIP GUARD PLAN

Although the effects of bad input were accounted for here by undoing the computation, this is not the only way that we see students take care of bad input in such cases. Another method which students use is to add additional guards for validity of input where needed in the loop. Figure 2-23 shows an excerpt of a student program that is similar to the example in Figure 2-16, but where an additional guard has been added to guard the running total update.

56

Variables:
      ?Pred, ?Count, ?Sum, ?Val
Template:
      (*in component* Process: *of goal Read & process*)
      spanned by:
         ?*
Test: if ?Pred then
               begin
                  subgoal Output diagnostic()
                  ?Count := ?Count - 1;
                  ?Sum := ?Sum - ?Val;
               end

Figure 2-22: The "BAD INPUT UNDO PLAN"

```
while Rainfall <> Sentinel do
  begin
    if Rainfall >= 0 then
      if Rainfall > 0 then
        begin
          RainyDays := RainyDays + 1;
          Valins := Valins + 1
        end
        else Valins := Valins + 1
      else
        writeln(Rainfall, ' is a bad value, try again');
    if Rainfall > Highrain then
      Highrain := Rainfall;
    if (Rainfall >= 0) and (Valins <> 0) then
      begin
        Sum := Sum + Rainfall;
        Averain := Sum / Valins
      end;
    writeln('Enter rainfall');
    readln;
    read(Rainfall)
  end;
```

Figure 2-23: An excerpt of a program with supplemental input guards

The following is the account of the intentions underlying Example 3 that we will use here. These may not fit the student's intentions in precise detail, but they are close enough to allow us to account properly for the origin of the bug. First, the input validation goal, *Loop Input Validation*(?Rainfall:DailyRain, ?Rainfall:DailyRain < 0), is reformulated as a *contingent goal*:

57

$$Contingency(Affected\text{-}By(\texttt{?Code, (?Rainfall:DailyRain < 0)}),$$
$$Compensate(\texttt{?Code, (?Rainfall:DailyRain < 0)})).$$

This goal indicates that if there is any code which is affected by `?Rainfall:DailyRain` being less than zero, then a goal should be added to compensate for the effect. The goal is contingent in the sense that it has an effect on the goal agenda only if the right kind of plan is added to the program. *Affected-By*(`?Code, (?Rainfall:DailyRain < 0)`) means that data satisfying the predicate `?Rainfall:DailyRain < 0`, when operated on by the program text bound to `?Code`, can cause `?Code` to function differently than would be the case if the predicate were not satisfied. *Compensate*(`?Code, (?Rainfall:DailyRain < 0)`) is the goal to add something to `?Code` so that it will not be so affected.

In the example program, the student recognized that the *Affected-By* condition was met by the valid input counter; therefore a *Compensate* goal had to be satisfied. The student did not recognize that the running total also met the *Affected-By* condition, so no *Compensate* goal was added there. *Compensate* is implemented differently depending upon the plan that is affected. In the case of a counter update, *Compensate* is realized as a goal *Individual Fix-Up*, which in turn can be implemented either as a *Guard Exception* goal to test for the *Affected-By* condition, or as an update to decrement the counter by one. The process which PROUST uses for going from the contingent goal to the *Compensate* goals to the implementations of the *Compensate* goals will be described later in this section.

2.3.3.2 Alternative diagnoses

Now let us examine what is required in order to get PROUST to choose the interpretation described above. The difficulty in deriving this interpretation is that it consists of more than one step, and the effects of some of the steps cannot be discerned directly in the program. If the *Loop Input Validation* goal had been realized using a single plan, such as BAD INPUT SKIP GUARD, then all that would be necessary to verify the intention model would be to try to match that plan against the program. The reformulation of *Loop Input Validation* as a contingent goal, on the other hand, has no immediate effect; it depends upon what other plans are introduced into the program. The `?Code` parameter in the *Contingency* goal may

58

contain code that has not yet been analyzed. As a consequence, there is no way to determine immediately when the *Loop Input Validation* goal is analyzed whether or not a contingent goal reformulation has taken place. As a consequence, PROUST first presumes that no such reformulation has taken place. PROUST first tries direct plan implementations, in case one of them matches the code exactly. Only if they do not, as in this case, is the contingent-goal possibility considered.

The BAD INPUT SKIP GUARD PLAN is one of the direct plan implementations that PROUST considers. The result of matching BAD INPUT SKIP GUARD against the program is shown in Figure 2-24. The BAD INPUT SKIP GUARD matches the test for negative input partially, but there are three plan differences. First, the supposed match, `if Rainfall<0 then ...` at line 21, has no `else` branch. Second, it only covers part of the `Process:` part of the loop. Third, there is an unexpected update, `Number := Number - 1`, inside the `if` statement.

```
begin                                    BAD INPUT SKIP GUARD
  Number := Number + 1;
  if Rainfall > 0 then          Variables:  ?Val, ?Pred
    DAYS := DAYS + 1;           Template:
  if Rainfall > Highest then               (in component Process: of goal
    Highest := Rainfall;                      Read & Process)
  Total := Total + Rainfall;             spanned by:
  if Rainfall < 0 then  ◄────── Test:         if ?Pred then
    begin                                ─────── subgoal Output Diagnostic ()
      writeln ('Try again');  ◄───  /        ? ◄──else
      Number := Number - 1;          Process:     ?*
    end;
  readln;
  read(Rainfall)
end;
```

Plan differences:

    (1) Plan too far down in loop
    (2) `else` branch missing
    (3) Unexpected code in plan: `Number := Number - 1`

Figure 2-24: Matching BAD INPUT SKIP GUARD against the program

The contingent goal model is suggested by a rule which fires when there is a missing `else` branch on a plan which implements *Input Validation*.[7] This rule, called the Contingent Realization Rule, constructs a new interpretation, and sets up the machinery for verifying the new interpretation. Let us examine what this requires.

Given that an `else` branch has been found to be missing from a BAD INPUT SKIP GUARD, there are two possible conclusions that can be drawn:

- the student reformulated the *Loop Input Validation* goal as a contingent goal;

- the student does not even realize that guarding input is necessary, but instead thinks that an error message is sufficient.

The latter hypothesis attributes a misconception to the student, which I call the Filtering Error Message Misconception. In order to see what the implication of this misconception is, look at Figure 2-25. This is the same loop as in the student program in Figure 2-16, but with one modification, namely that the line `Number := Number - 1` is missing. This one modification is very significant, though; it removes all evidence that the *Loop Input Validation* goal has been reformulated as a contingent goal. Instead, it looks as if the student thinks that all that is necessary to guard against bad input is to print an error message.[8] The only way to be certain that the *Loop Input Validation* goal has been reformulated as a contingent goal is if bad input has been compensated for in at least one case.

Actually, the criterion is more severe than that; we must be sure that at least one compensation for bad input has been performed, and that no alternative interpretation of the code that affects the compensation is possible. To see this, consider the loop in Figure 2-26. Here the running total update, `Total := Total + Rainfall`, has been inserted into the code which updates the rainy day counter, `if Rainfall > 0 then Days := Days + 1`. The question here is whether this insertion was done in order to guard against negative input, or for some other reason.

---

[7]The most general representation of the rule would have it fire on any plan with an `if` statement inside of a loop, but the current formulation is adequate for now.

[8]Alternatively, the student may realize that more must be done than to output the error message, but does not know how to integrate the test into the loop.

```
while Rainfall <> 99999 do
   begin
      Number := Number + 1;
      if Rainfall > 0 then
      Days := Days + 1;
      if Rainfall > Highest then
      Highest := Rainfall;
      Total := Total + Rainfall;
      if Rainfall < 0 then
         writeln ('Impossible, try again');
      readln;
      read ( Rainfall )
   end;
```

Figure 2-25: An example with the Filtering Error Message Misconception

There is another possible reason: the student thought that he or she was writing a more efficient program by excluding zero values from the running total. Therefore the code is ambiguous, and it is necessary to query the student to determine with certainty which was the correct interpretation.

```
while Rainfall <> 99999 do
   begin
      Number := Number + 1;
      if Rainfall > 0 then
         begin
            Days := Days + 1;
            Total := Total + Rainfall;
         end;
      if Rainfall > Highest then
         Highest := Rainfall;
      if Rainfall < 0 then
         writeln ('Impossible, try again');
      readln;
      read(Rainfall)
   end;
```

Figure 2-26: An ambiguous example

For reference, Figure 2-27 shows the output that PROUST currently generates for each of these three kinds of student programs. Note that PROUST does not currently ask the student for an explanation of the ambiguous case; this will wait until a tutoring module has been built for PROUST.

61

```
Some of your code is not shielded against invalid input.
    The   statement in question is:
        TOTAL := TOTAL + RAINFALL
You appear to test for bad input elsewhere, using the following code:
        IF RAINFALL < 0 THEN ...
        NUMBER := NUMBER - 1
Your  program  would  really  be  simpler  if it tested the input in one
place, before it is used anywhere.  That way bugs like  this  would  not
crop up.

You have not implemented your input validation correctly.  Some of your
code is executed when it should not be.
The statements in question are:
        TOTAL := TOTAL + RAINFALL
        NUMBER := NUMBER + 1
Printing out an error message such as this is not enough:
        WRITELN('IMPOSSIBLE, TRY AGAIN')
You must structure your code so that line 15 and other code like it will
not be executed when the input is invalid.

Your program does not perform input validation properly.  The following
code executes when it should not:
        NUMBER := NUMBER + 1
Yet the following code is guarded:
        IF RAINFALL>0 THEN ...
        TOTAL := TOTAL+RAINFALL
Was this intended to guard against bad input?  If so, it would be better
to test the input once, before it is used.
```

Figure 2-27:   Three kinds of diagnostic messages from PROUST

2.3.3.3 Differentiating the interpretations

Given that there are three possible interpretations of the input validation step in Example 3, and distinguishing these interpretations hinges upon details of how different parts of the loop are guarded, there is no good way to determine at first which realization of the *Loop Input Validation* goal is appropriate. PROUST makes the final decision about the interpretation after the entire program has been analyzed, so that all available evidence about the programmer's intentions can be brought to bear on the decision. The technique used in such cases is as follows:

1. Provisionally assume that the contingent goal hypothesis is correct.

2. Keep a record of the fate of each goal which is added to the goal agenda as a result of the contingent goal.

3. At the end of the analysis, examine what happened to each goal, and on the basis of this determine whether or not there is really evidence for contingent realization of *Loop Input Validation*.

In accordance with the first step, the *Loop Input Validation* goal is presumed to be realized as a contingent goal. Currently this is not done by taking the *Contingency* form shown in the previous section and adding it to the goal agenda. Instead, a demon is activated which has the same effect, looking for plans which are affected by the boundary condition. When an affected plan is found, the demon inserts into the goal agenda a realization of *Compensate* appropriate for the particular plan being affected. This realization takes the form of a goal whose implementations are the various ways of compensating for the effects on the particular plan. In the case of the affected counter update, the goal added is

Individual Fix-Up(?Code, (?Rainfall:DailyRain < 0), ?Var, 1),

where ?Code is bound to the counter update statement and ?Var is bound to the counter variable. The 1 in the argument list is the amount to subtract from ?Var in order to undo an update. This goal in turn can be implemented either as a *GuardException* goal checking for negative input, or as an update which decrements 1 from ?Var. The appropriate reformulation for *Compensate* is currently determined from a table relating each plan in PROUST's database to the corresponding fix-up goal. All plans which can be affected by bad input in the problems considered so far can be fixed by adding or subtracting some value. When that is no longer the case the process of selecting a fix-up plan will have to be generalized.

The fate of each *Compensate* goal must be tracked in order to determine whether or not it was appropriate to reformulate *Input Validation* contingently. In order to do so, whenever a *Compensate* goal is created by the contingent goal demon, a new demon is created which waits for the *Compensate* goal to be disposed of, and then records the disposition. This demon looks to see whether (a) the *Compensate* goal was implemented, (b) the *Compensate* goal was omitted, or (c) the *Compensate* goal was not implemented, but the code to be guarded happens to be guarded by some other guard which serves to prevent invalid data from reaching the update. The demon then adds its findings to a table which keeps a record of the ways in which the *Compensate* goals have been disposed.

Once the analysis is complete, the interpretation of the *Loop Input Validation* goal is reconsidered. At this point there is hopefully enough information available that the alternative hypotheses about the *Loop Input Validation* goal can be differentiated.

Upon examining the record of the disposition of the *Compensate* goals in the example program, PROUST finds that one *Compensate* goal was definitely implemented in the program, and one *Compensate* goal was definitely omitted. This is sufficient to establish that the contingent goal hypothesis is valid. PROUST therefore generates the output indicated for the example.

2.4 Summary

Three examples of PROUST's analysis have been presented. These examples give some idea of how PROUST goes about diagnosing bugs in novice programs. They show how analysis of plans and goals in programs provides the context for bug recognition. They also show that the variety of plans and bugs makes it necessary to compare alternative interpretations of the program's bugs in order to determine which fits most closely. The next chapter will provide further motivation for the intention-based approach to debugging, and will contrast this approach against other approaches for identifying bugs.

3 Why Intention-Based Diagnosis is Needed

3.1 Introduction

The examples in Chapter 2 illustrated a number of details of PROUST's analysis of novice programs. Motivation of many of these details will wait until subsequent chapters. In this chapter I am concerned with motivating PROUST's basic approach. The discussion is intended to support the following claim:

> accurate bug identification must be based upon analysis of the programmer's intentions, i.e., the intended function of the program (goals) and the intended implementation of this function (plans).

Any method which focuses on the actual structure and/or function of the program, rather than the intended structure and function, will not work as well on larger or buggier novice programs.

In order to motivate PROUST's approach, I will describe the principal non-intention-based methods for program analysis, and show where they fall short. Analysis of run-time errors and input/output behavior will be discussed first. Then approaches which analyze the internal functioning of programs will be considered. Once each of these techniques are shown to be inadequate, I will examine an approach which attempts to combine analysis of program behavior with analysis of program function, namely heuristic software troubleshooting. This method works better than the others, but it still is limited because it analyzes the actual function of the program instead of the intended function, and therefore is ineffective when intended function and actual function disagree. The approach of finding bugs by matching patterns of buggy code against the program will also be considered. This approach only works adequately on very small programs.

Next, some systems with limited ability to identify and reason about intentions will be considered. These systems can recognize patterns of correct code in programs, i.e., plans, thereby inferring programmers' goals. Some of these systems also recognize patterns of buggy code in programs, in order to identify bugs. These plan-based systems are are limited in their ability to reason about the resulting goals to see whether they give a coherent picture of what the programmer is trying to do. Such a coherent picture of goals and plans is called a *goal decomposition* in PROUST. PROUST's ability to construct goal decompositions, and employ them in program and bug analysis, results in superior understanding and bug-diagnosis capabilities than plan analysis alone provides.

3.2 Heuristic classification of input/output behavior

Let us first compare intention-based diagnosis of program bugs against systems which diagnose bugs by analyzing the input/output behavior of buggy programs. These systems attempt to identify and classify faulty program behavior, and relate the faulty behavior to probable causes. They thus fall within the category of heuristic classification diagnosis systems.

Heuristic classification problem solving, as defined by Clancey [17], is a problem solving technique common to a variety of diagnostic systems. In heuristic classification problem solving, the diagnostician has a pre-enumerated set of disease types to choose from. The diagnostician first collects data about the symptoms of the faulty artifact, and classifies the data, extracting salient features. Diagnosis is then performed via heuristic matching rules which relate features of the symptom data to one or more of the pre-enumerated disease types. The diagnostic power of the system stems mainly from the heuristic matching rules.

A paradigmatic example of a diagnosis system which performs heuristic classification is MYCIN [57]. MYCIN contains heuristic rules which associate data about the patient with classes of diseases. An example of such a rule is "If the patient is a compromised host, there is suggestive evidence that the patient has a Gram-negative infection." "Compromised host" is a characterization of the patient, and "Gram-negative" is a characterization of the organism causing the disease. The association between the two is a heuristic one. Determination that the patient is a compromised host can be inferred directly from lab data such as the white blood cell count, so no heuristic matching is involved. Likewise heuristic matching is unnecessary for determining which particular strain of Gram-negative organism is involved; well-defined tests exist for discriminating among Gram-negative organisms.

Heuristic classification can be applied to the analysis of program input/output behavior in the same way that it can be applied to medical diagnosis. Figure 3-1 shows an example of how this might be done. Suppose that we are given a solution to the Averaging Problem, and are told to check it for bugs. We run the program and discover that it aborts, printing the message "FLOATING POINT EXCEPTION AT PC=028A109E". This behavior serves as the basis for our diagnosis of the bug. We abstract the key features out of the data, observing that the significant information is that a floating point exception occurred, not the value of the program counter when it occurred. We then make a heuristic association: floating point exceptions can be caused by division by zero. Finally, we refine this account of the error, by noting that the average computation might result in division by zero, and conclude that the student failed to check whether the counter variable was zero before the average is computed.

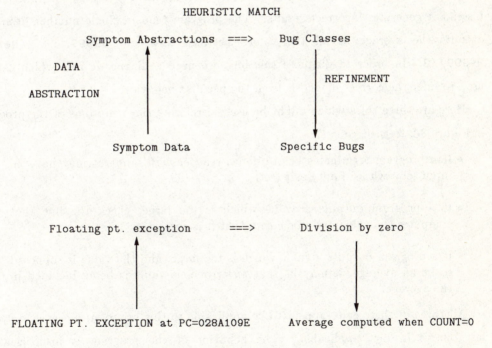

Figure 3-1: Classificatory diagnosis of bugs

Experienced programmers usually know a variety of classificatory rules for diagnosing bugs in programs based upon program malfunctions. It is commonplace for a programmer to observe a program malfunction and know immediately what the cause of the bug is likely to be. Since programmers have such diagnostic expertise, it seems appropriate to try to codify it and build it into a computer system. Harandi, for one, has attempted this [36].

Nevertheless, there are serious problems with basing bug diagnosis on program behavior. Although the relationships between program behavior and bugs are evident in some cases, they are obscure in others. Furthermore the same set of symptoms often can be explained by a variety of different bugs. Information about input/output behavior alone is therefore inadequate for identifying bugs in novice programs.

The Averaging Problem example discussed in Chapter 2 illustrates some of the problems with behavior-based diagnosis. This example is repeated Figure 3-2. Unlike the division-by-zero example above, this program does not abort with run-time errors. Instead it generates incorrect results. The program reads a single number New, and outputs the average of all the values between New and 99999, i.e., (New + 99999)/2. In order to diagnose this bug, we need a diagnostic rule which can be used to infer the correct diagnosis from the peculiar behavior.

Here are three rules which might be used in relating the symptoms of the program in Figure 3-2 to their causes.

- If a program terminates before it has read enough input, it may have an input loop with a faulty exit test.

- If a program outputs a value which is too large, check the line that computes the value and make sure that it is correct.

- If a program outputs a value which is too large, and the value is supposed to be an average, it may be that an erroneous value is being included in the average.

All three of these rules appear to be applicable to this program; however, only the last one is in fact applicable. The behavior of the program is insufficient to determine which rule should apply. Each rule refers to facts about the program other than behavior, such as the intended function of parts of the code. Since the intended function is not known to a behavior-based system, it has no basis for making a decision.

68

```
program Average( input, output );
var Sum, Count, New: integer;
    Avg: real;
begin
  Sum := 0;
  Count := 0;
  read( New );
  while New<>99999 do
    begin
      Sum := Sum+New;
      Count := Count+1;
      New := New+1
    end;
  id Count<>0 then
    begin
      Avg := Sum/Count;
      Writeln( 'The average is ', avg );
    end;
end;
```

Figure 3-2:   A buggy averaging program

The only way that the behavior-based approach can be salvaged is by embedding it in a system which performs other analyses on the program in order to supplement the diagnostic rules. In this sense PROUST's plan-difference rules can be viewed as heuristic classification rules, since they are heuristic relations between symptoms (plan differences) and causes (bugs and misconceptions). However, PROUST's rules classify plan expectation failures, not faulty program behavior.

3.3 Analysis of internal function

Another way of identifying bugs in a program is by analyzing the internal function of the program. Note that this is different from analyzing the *intended* internal function; such an analysis of intentions would be a form of intention-based diagnosis. Rather, let us examine what can be done in the way of analyzing the actual internal workings of a program. This is similar to analyzing the behavior of a program, except that now we are analyzing the behavior of the program's components as well as the behavior of the program as a whole.

3.3.1 Data-flow analysis

A common method for analyzing internal program behavior is to perform data-flow analysis [29]. Data-flow analysis, when used for purposes of error detection, identifies anomalies in the pattern of definition and use of variables. It detects references to undefined variables, and assignments to variables of values which are never used. Global data-flow analysis of a program can also detect anomalies such as unreachable code, a likely indication of buggy control flow. Infinite loops can be detected when the loop control variable is not modified in the body of the loop, which means that the use of the control variable is anomalous.

A bug detection system which is based upon anomaly detection can work only to the extent that program bugs are associated with anomalies. There is a wide range of bugs which produce no data-flow anomalies. Any buggy assignment statement which refers to the proper variables but computes the wrong result will not be anomalous. Any bug resulting from improper implementation of the problem requirements, or failure to check for boundary conditions, will not result in anomalies. The frequency of such bugs is too great in novice programs for us to be able to overlook them.

Data-flow analysis can detect paths through the code which use data incorrectly, but it cannot determine whether or not those paths will ever be executed. If a variable is defined in the body of a WHILE loop, for example, and is used below the loop, then the program has a data-flow anomaly in the case where the loop body is never executed. This would happen if the exit test if the loop is satisfied upon entering the WHILE loop. However, if the body of the loop can be guaranteed to execute at least once, then the program is not buggy. In such cases data-flow analysis would mark as buggy code which is really correct.

Even when a data-flow anomaly results from a bug, it is not sufficient to establish what specific part of the program is buggy. Suppose that a program has an anomaly in which one statement stores a value in a variable, and before the value is used it is overwritten. The error in the program could be in the first assignment to the variable, in the reassignment to the variable, or it could be that the code which was supposed to reference the variable was accidentally omitted. There is no way to localize the error to a single statement, much less suggest an appropriate correction.

70

3.3.2 Matching canonical data-flow structures

Data-flow analysis alone identifies too narrow a range of errors, and does not do a good job of diagnosing the errors that it identifies. I will therefore consider the possibility of supplementing data-flow analysis, or replacing it with a more powerful mechanism for analyzing program function.

One way of supplementing data-flow analysis is to employ a pattern matcher of data-flow descriptions. A representation of the data flow of the program is constructed, and this is compared against the data-flow configuration of a correct program. The correct program is provided by the instructor. Differences between the two data-flow configurations are likely to be bugs. Data-flow analysis then becomes a method of translating programs into a canonical form, in order to aid the matching process. Such an approach is used in the LAURA system [1].

The weakness of data-flow canonicalization is that it only works if the student's algorithm and the instructor's algorithm are the same. Otherwise there will be differences between the data flow of the student's program and that of the instructor's program, which are not caused by bugs. Non-trivial programming problems can be solved in any of a number of ways, so canonicalization can only work if the problems that are assigned are very simple, or the algorithm is supplied beforehand by the instructor. For example, when LAURA is used to analyze sorting routines, the students must be told exactly how to perform the sort. Since our aim is to allow students to solve non-trivial problems on their own, the canonicalization approach is unsuitable.

3.3.3 Symbolic execution

Another method for analyzing program function is symbolic execution [45]. Symbolic execution can be used to determine which paths through a program are executed, and under what circumstances. Thus symbolic execution helps to solve the problem which data-flow analysis has of not being able to determine whether or not anomalous code is buggy. Symbolic execution can detect a wider range of functional anomalies than data-flow analysis can. For example, data-flow analysis can determine that a loop fails to terminate only if the control variable is never referenced. Symbolic execution detects that a loop is infinite when it is able to prove that the control variable never assumes a value which satisfies the exit test. The PHENARETE system [68] is an example of a system which uses symbolic execution for detecting program anomalies.

Symbolic execution may be more effective than data-flow analysis for detecting anomalies, but it still suffers from the shortcoming that bugs do not always result in detectable anomalies. As long as the program generates some plausible result, symbolic execution will not find anything wrong with it. Of course symbolic execution has the advantage that it can be run on any program; no prior knowledge of the programming problem is necessary. In our case, however, we can freely assume that information about the problem is available, so the versatility of symbolic execution is less important.

The PUDSY system [46] illustrates another way that symbolic evaluation can be used in analyzing bugs. It combines symbolic execution with matching against a correct solution, in an analogous fashion to LAURA. PUDSY goes through the following steps:

1. it executes the program symbolically in order to derive a formula relating the outputs of the program to the inputs, keeping track of which part of the program is responsible for which part of this formula;

2. it compares this formula against a similar formula provided by the instructor, in order to identify differences;

3. it identifies the parts of the program which are responsible for the differences in the two formulas.

In the example in Figure 3-2, PUDSY would determine that the program computes New / 2 + 49999.5, and compare this against what it should compute, namely $(\Sigma \text{New})/\text{count}(\text{New})$. It would then examine the parts of the program which compute the erroneous parts of the formula. The main problem here is that it is hard to compare these two expressions and determine which parts are wrong; the two expressions bear little formal resemblance. To make such a comparison requires knowledge of which components of the first expression correspond to which components of the second expression. In general, expression components correspond only if their underlying intentions correspond. Thus some knowledge of the programmer's intentions is necessary in order for PUDSY's approach to generate reliable results.

72

3.4 Troubleshooting

The next debugging method which I will consider is troubleshooting. Troubleshooting has been applied extensively in the electronic circuit domain [22, 21, 32]; there has also been significant interest in applying it to programming [54, 53, 55]. In program troubleshooting, the user is expected to describe the specific symptoms of the fault. The system then traces the flow of information in the program to determine what might have caused the symptoms. Some additional knowledge is usually employed to guide the troubleshooter toward the faulty program component. This can take the form of hints from the user or heuristic rules for generating fault hypotheses.

3.4.1 Oracle-driven troubleshooting

The debugging system described in Ehud Shapiro's thesis [55] is an example of a troubleshooting system which is driven by hints from the user. In Shapiro's approach, the programmer describes the program's symptoms to the debugging system, by supplying an example which causes the program to behave incorrectly. The debugging system then traces the incorrect values back through the program, asking at each point whether or not the intermediate value computed at that point in the program is correct. The programmer thus serves as an "oracle", providing information about whether or not the behavior matches the programmer's intentions. It assumes that the user has identified the program's failure modes, and can provide all necessary information about the correctness of intermediate results. When the system identifies a section of the program where the values entering the section are correct but the values that are computed are incorrect, it flags an error. Shapiro's system focuses quickly on the code which led to the incorrect result, proceeding depth-first until a bug is found. It therefore needs only ask a relatively small number of questions before it identifies the buggy code.

3.4.2 Heuristic troubleshooting

Another way that the troubleshooting process can be guided is by using heuristic rules which suggest hypotheses to account for the program's symptoms. Such a troubleshooting process would go through a cycle of the following steps:

- collecting symptoms,

- suggesting hypotheses to explain the symptoms, and

- analyzing the structure and function of the program in order to verify the hypotheses.

Typically the explanations generated are incomplete, such as "variable FOO's value is too low"; further analysis must be performed in order to elaborate the explanations. The conclusions are therefore added into the collection of symptoms, and the process repeats. Finally the system reaches a point where it can suggest a specific change to the code which remedies the symptoms. Assuming that the program has only a small number of bugs, this will often succeed in tracking down a bug.

Here is how a heuristic troubleshooting approach would work in tracking down the bug in the Averaging Problem example. This scenario is loosely based on what existing troubleshooting programs do, although it incorporates some capabilities that current troubleshooting systems do not appear to have. The troubleshooter is presented with the following facts about the behavior of the program:

1. The program reads only one value and then terminates;

2. it always prints out a terribly large value.

The troubleshooter searches for testable hypotheses which can account for these symptoms. It is hard to do much with the fact that the program outputs terribly large values; this can result from a number of causes. The fact that the program only reads a single value is useful information, however. The following heuristic diagnosis rule can be applied:

If a program is supposed to read in a series of values, and instead reads only one, it may have a loop which should contain an input statement, but for some reason does not.

The troubleshooter checks the program and finds a loop there, and suggests that this loop might be malfunctioning.

The next question is what is wrong with the loop. The following rule can be applied here:

If a loop is supposed to input data but does not, and the input data is used in determining the exit condition of the loop, and the loop does in fact iterate, then there must be a problem with the iteration step.

74

The troubleshooter checks the loop, finds that the loop does in fact iterate. It therefore infers that the line which updates the loop control variable, `New := New + 1`, must be incorrect.

Next, the troubleshooter tries to explain why `New := New + 1` appears in the loop instead of an input statement. A bug rule, similar to PROUST's plan-difference rules, could explain this. The troubleshooter then makes the change, and tests the resulting program. Lo and behold, the program now works correctly. This serves to verify the troubleshooter's analysis of the buggy program.

These diagnostic rules are very similar to the diagnostic rules which we discussed in the context of classificatory diagnosis. In fact, we can view each step in the process of tracking the cause of the bug as a classificatory diagnosis problem. Functional analysis is required in order to collect data about the program and to verify diagnoses, and multiple diagnoses are performed, not just one; nevertheless, the diagnostic decision-making at each step is a form of heuristic classificatory problem solving. This is true of a number of troubleshooting systems, such as SOPHIE III [14, 17]. It seems that classificatory diagnosis combined with functional analysis is more powerful than either technique taken by itself. This approach is the clearest competition with intention-based diagnosis for analyzing novice programs.

In order to be able to evaluate this approach, I will present one more troubleshooting example. Consider the program in Figure 3-3, a novice solution to the Rainfall Problem. This program has the following symptoms:

- if the first input is 99999 the program bombs with a division-by-zero error;

- if a series of positive values is entered, then the output of the program is correct;

- if a combination of positive and zero values is entered, the average is too low and the rainy day counter and valid day counter are both too high;

- if a combination of negative and non-negative values are entered, then the average is too low and the rainy day counter and valid day counter are both too high.

The troubleshooter observes that whenever the average is too low, the valid day counter and the rainy day counter are too high. It therefore hypothesizes that these

```
 1 program Rainfall (input ,output );
 2
 3 const
 4      Sentinal = 99999;
 5 var
 6      Num, Sum, Count1, Count2, Highnum, Total: real;
 7
 8 begin
 9   writeln ('Input rainfall amounts, one day at a time.');
10   readln;
11   read(Num);
12   Count1 := 0;
13   Count2 := 0;
14   Sum := 0;
15   Highnum := 0;
16   while (Num <> Sentinal) do
17     begin
18       if (Num > 0)
19         then
20           Sum := Sum + Num;
21       Count1 := Count1 + 1;
22       if (Num > Highnum)
23         then
24           Highnum := Num;
25       if (Num = 0)
26         then
27           Count2 := Count2 + 1;
28       if (Num < 0)
29         then
30           writeln ('Invalid, please reenter.');
31       readln;
32       read(Num);
33     end;
34   Count2 := Count2 + Count1;
35   if (Num > 0)
36     then
37       Total := Sum/Count2;
38   writeln ('The average rainfall was ',Total:0:2);
39   writeln ('the highest rainfall was ',Highnum:0:2);
40   writeln (Count2:0:2,' valid rainfalls were entered');
41   writeln ('There were ', Count1:0:2,' rainy days.');
42 end.
```

Figure 3-3: A troubleshooting example

errors all stem from a common cause. It examines the code which generates each of these values. The average is generated by line 37, `Total := Sum / Count2;`, the valid day counter is generated by line 34, `Count2 := Count2 + 1;` the rainy day counter is generated by line 21, `Count1 := Count1 + 1`. The bug cannot be in the computation of `Total`, because if that is changed `Count1` and `Count2` are still buggy. Fixing `Count2` also fixes `Total`, but it does not fix `Count1`. Only by fixing `Count1` are all three bugs fixed at once. Assuming that the explanation which assumes the minimum number of bugs is best, the bug has to be in the way that `Count1` is computed. If an `if Num > 0` test is added where `Count1` is computed, then the problem is fixed. There is already such a line in the program, two lines above the `Count1 := Count1 + 1` line. If we add a `begin-end` pair after it, then the bug is fixed. This is therefore the suggested bug fix.

3.4.3 Problems with troubleshooting

Both Shapiro's troubleshooting approach and the heuristic approach can be used for debugging certain kinds of programs. However, both approaches have drawbacks which limit their usefulness on novice programs.

Shapiro's system requires that the programmer identify the failure modes of the program. Since novice programmers are also novice program testers, they usually fail to test all of the relevant cases, and are bound to miss some of the failure conditions. Shapiro's system also assumes that the programmer can tell at all times whether or not the intermediate computations are correct. This is difficult to do if the computation involves many steps. Furthermore, if the student has misconceptions about control flow, the student may not be able to determine correctly what the intermediate results should be.

Heuristic troubleshooting depends even more heavily than the oracle-driven approach on having good descriptions of the program's failure modes. In fact, heuristic troubleshooting is liable to fail unless the description of failure modes is complete. If in the example in Figure 3-3 the troubleshooter did not know the exact conditions under which the various outputs are incorrect, it would not be able to decide whether the computation of `Total`, the computation of `Count1`, or the computation of `Count2` is at fault. It is only by correlating the cases when `Total`,

`Count1`, and `Count2` are incorrect that the proper bug fix becomes apparent. We certainly cannot depend upon novice programmers to perform such exhaustive tests. We might depend upon the instructor to provide test data to run on the student's programs, but if a programming assignment is moderately complex one cannot expect such canned test data to provide an exhaustive test.

Troubleshooters depend upon being able to identify a single cause for a bug. It is assumed that a single part of the program can be identified which is uniquely responsible for the failure. If a program has multiple bugs, then there must be a way to isolate the effects of the bugs. In a typical buggy program only some of the bugs have behavior that can be clearly isolated and traced, and the situation gets worse as programs grow larger.

A serious problem for all troubleshooting approaches is that once the bug is localized, there is a certain amount of guesswork in determining what the fix is. Shapiro avoids the issue by having the user fix the bug, but that is not adequate in the novice domain, since the student may have a misconception and not know how to fix the bug. The heuristic troubleshooter can suggest a fix, but it cannot be very confident of it, since it does not know the intent behind the code. PROUST, on the other hand, constructs a model for the intentions underlying each line of code in the program. This model helps ensure that any proposed bug fix is consistent with the student's intentions.

3.5 Recognizing patterns in buggy code

The analytic techniques which we have discussed up to now focus on analysis of the behavior of the program. Another way of finding bugs is to analyze the structure of a program, looking for code which is visibly buggy. We have already seen one analysis method which involves a kind of analysis of structure; the LAURA system compares the structure of the data flow of the student's program against the structure of the data flow of the instructor's model solution. LAURA matches entire programs against entire programs. The assumption underlying LAURA is that the major part of the analysis is in the functional analysis which resulted in the data-flow representation of the programs in the first place. The approaches which I will discuss here involve matching a library of patterns of code against programs, thus permitting a wider range of program structures to be analyzed.

Two different kinds of code patterns will be discussed here: patterns of buggy code, and patterns of correct code. If the pattern library consists of patterns of buggy code, then we assume that if a pattern matches, a bug has been identified. If we match patterns of correct code, then the purpose of the matching is to acquire information about the intent underlying the code, to support subsequent bug analysis. I will show that neither approach is satisfactory unless it makes explicit the overall intent underlying the program.

3.5.1 Buggy code recognition

Suppose that we were to build a collection of patterns of buggy code. If these patterns depict code which is always buggy, regardless of context, then this method is really equivalent to the methods which look for anomalies in program function, such as data-flow anomaly analysis. The case which I will focus on here is where the code may or may not be buggy, depending upon what the program is intended to do. Such an approach was taken in MENO [59], a precursor to PROUST.

It is not possible to make a bug library sensitive to the programmer's intentions without information about those intentions. Assuming that such information is not available, the next best thing is to make the bug library problem-dependent. A separate collection of buggy code fragments must be constructed for each problem. A collection of buggy code fragments for the Averaging Problem would include a fragment of the example in Figure 3-2 depicting the counter overgeneralization bug. The same bug would not appear in a buggy-fragment library for a problem where a counter-controlled loop is necessary to solve the problem correctly. Problem-dependent bug libraries work acceptably well on simple problems such as the Averaging Problem, as experience with MENO has shown [11].

The buggy-code-library approach begins to break down when it becomes necessary to analyze correct code as well as buggy code. For example, if the bug is that part of the program is missing, then no one line of code is buggy, hence no bug template can be constructed. In order to find division-by-zero bugs, for example, it is necessary to look for a statement that performs a division, and then check to see whether or not the denominator of the division can be zero. There may be arbitrary code which computes the denominator, so there is no general pattern which can be matched to determine whether or not the denominator is zero. In order to write a pattern for division-by-zero bugs, it is necessary to have some prior knowledge of how the denominator is likely to be computed. In the Averaging Problem division by zero can occur whenever the main loop is implemented correctly, and the average computation is after the loop. Therefore the bug patterns for division-by-zero in the Averaging Problem must match the main loop and the average computation. A different pattern is required for each different method of constructing the main loop and computing the average.

Simple problems such as the Averaging Problem are usually solved in one of a limited number of ways. Therefore it is feasible to write problem-specific patterns for bugs in solutions to such problems. As programs become more complex, the number of possible solutions becomes much greater. Thus the number of bug patterns required is much greater, and the bug patterns become increasingly specialized. Even in problems requiring only a page of code to solve, the number of bug patterns required is already too great.

As an example of the difficulties in constructing bug patterns for larger programs, consider the missing `begin-end` bug at line 18 in the program example in Figure 3-3. The bug is that a `begin-end` pair is missing from the `then` clause of an `if` statement. Although this description serves to characterize the bug, it is not specific enough to be used as a bug pattern. In the program in Figure 3-3 there are five different `if` statements which lack `begin-end` pairs. In only two of these cases could the lack of a `begin-end` pair be considered a possible bug. Therefore we need additional contextual information in order to construct a bug pattern. The reason that we know that there should be a `begin-end` pair after line 18 is that the counters generate an implausible result. `Count2` is the sum of the total number of inputs and the number of zero inputs; it is unlikely that the programmer would have intended to compute such a thing. When the `begin-end` pair is added to the program, `Count2` has the proper value. The pattern for the missing-`begin-end` bug thus has to match the counter updates in this program. In other words, it would match if there are two counters, such as `Count1` and `Count2`, where `Count2` is the sum of the number of valid inputs and the number of zero inputs. Such a pattern would be so specific that it would be used very infrequently.

3.5.2 Matching correct code

Since bug pattern recognition requires the ability to recognize patterns of correct code, one might make analysis of correct code an explicit part of the matching process. In other words, one could include a library of correct implementation methods instead of incorporating the correct code patterns into the patterns for buggy code. I will call such implementation methods *programming plans.*

Plans serve various roles in bug diagnosis systems. D. Shapiro's Sniffer system [54] assumes that plan analysis has already been performed by the Programmer's Apprentice [20] before bug analysis is performed. Thus plans are not used in the actual diagnosis process; rather, they allow software troubleshooting to be performed on the plan structure of the program rather than on the code itself. Sedlmeyer and P. Johnson's FALOSY system [53] has a knowledge base of plans used for bug recognition purposes. These plans are used in the error diagnosis process itself; the plans provide context which helps to localize the parts of the program which are faulty.

A major problem with matching patterns of correct code against a program is that it can lead to unexpected results if the program is buggy. A bug can cause a plan to appear to be a different plan from what it is. In the Averaging Problem example discussed earlier, the loop looks like a counter-controlled iteration; diagnosing the bug requires the realization that the loop was not intended to be counter-controlled. Without an overall model of the student's intentions, there is no way of predicting which plans are relevant to the program. FALOSY resorts to unconstrained plan recognition when its troubleshooting tactics fail to isolate a bug, and thus risks falling into this trap. The Programmer's Apprentice is geared toward recognizing correct plans in programs, so it also risks being misled by bugs, unless it is provided with information about the programmer's intended goals.

Another problem with plan analysis is that bugs can arise not in plans themselves, but in the way that they interact or in the manner that the programmer has employed them. Plan analysis alone is insufficient to identify division-by-zero bugs, for example. The code which performs the division and the code which computes the value in the denominator of the division will be separate plans. It is only by analyzing the effects of the plans together that the boundary-condition error can be detected. In such cases a better understanding of the programmer's intentions is needed than what plan recognition alone provides.

3.5.3 Making plan recognition work

In order to make plan recognition an effective tool, we must constrain its use. We need to avoid matching plans which are not relevant to the program, and recognize when plans did not match which should have been relevant. One way of constraining the set of plans to match against a program is to provide for each programming problem a list of plans which can be matched against problem solutions. I will show that constraining plan application in this fashion is inadequate, unless the plans are organized around the goals that they implement. In other words, plan application is best constrained through reference to the goals or intentions that underlie the choice of plans.

Simply to list plans which a program should use, and then require that every plan appear in the program, is clearly too simplistic an approach. Some plans are frequently interchangeable with other plans; for example, the Averaging Problem can be solved by using a SENTINEL PROCESS-READ WHILE PLAN, a SENTINEL READ-PROCESS WHILE PLAN, or some other plan altogether. We therefore cannot insist on a unique plan decomposition even for solutions of simple problems. On the other hand, if the plan list is simply a list of suggestions of plans which might appear in the program, then it would be impossible to recognize bugs resulting from missing plans. In order to make the plan-enumeration approach work, it is necessary to indicate choices among plans. For example, SENTINEL PROCESS-READ WHILE PLAN and SENTINEL READ-PROCESS WHILE PLAN must be marked as equivalent; one of these two, or else some other equivalent plan, must be present in any correct solution of the Averaging Problem.

Assuming that plan lists are marked to indicate interchangeable plans, it is possible to analyze simple problems such as the Averaging Problem. For example, consider the example solution to the Averaging Problem shown in Figure 3-2. The program contains a `while` loop, but it does not match either the SENTINEL PROCESS-READ WHILE PLAN or the SENTINEL READ-PROCESS WHILE PLAN. There are no alternative plans which match the code, so there must be a bug in the loop. After comparing the two plans, it becomes clear that the process-read plan fits the program better. This leads to the discovery of the counter overgeneralization bug. Such an approach has been used in Micro-PROUST [41].

The reason why the plan-enumeration approach works for the Averaging Problem is that virtually every solution to this problem has the same overall structure. Most solutions compute the sum and count of the input, divide the sum by the count, and print out the result. When we mark plans as being equivalent, we really are saying that they satisfy the same goals, and that the goals which the program implements are fixed. The goals which a program implements, the relationships between those goals, and the plans and subgoals that implement these goals is called the *goal decomposition* of the program. Different students may choose different plans to implement the goals in the Averaging Problem, but they rarely come up with a different set of goals to implement. They may use a process-read plan or a read-process plan, but whatever plan is chosen will be a sentinel-controlled looping plan. Therefore the range of possible plans in solutions to the Averaging Problem is strictly limited.

As programming problems become more complex, the variation in the goal decompositions of the solutions increases. Suppose, for example, that we augment the Averaging Problem slightly and require that the program count the number of positive inputs as well as the total number of inputs. This change is sufficient to cause variation in the decomposition of problem goals. Figure 3-4 shows excerpts of solutions with different goal decompositions, and illustrates the kinds of variation that arise in novice goal decompositions. Some novice programmers, when presented with a problem such as this, will write separate code for counting the total number of inputs and for counting the positive inputs. An example of such a program is Example A in Figure 3-4. Others, as in Example B, count the positive values and the non-positive values, and then add the two counts in order to get the total count.

Example A (correct goal decomposition)

```
while N <> 99999 do
  begin
    Count := Count + 1;
    Sum := Sum + N;
    if N > 0 then
      Pos := Pos + 1;
    writeln('Enter next value:');
    read(N);
  end;
```

Example B (correct goal decomposition)

```
while N <> 99999 do
  begin
    Sum := Sum + N;
    if N > 0 then
      Pos := Pos + 1
    else
      NonPos := NonPos + 1;
    writeln('Enter next value:');
    read(N);
  end;
Total := Pos + NonPos;
```

Example C (buggy goal decomposition)

```
while N <> 99999 do
  begin
    Sum := Sum + N;
    if N > 0 then
      Pos := Pos + 1
    else
      Count := Count + 1;
    writeln('Enter next value:');
    read(N);
  end;
```

Figure 3-4: Programs with different goal decompositions

Example C in Figure 3-4 is a program with a buggy goal decomposition. It counts the positive inputs, using the line `Pos := Pos + 1`. It also counts the non-positive inputs, using the line `Count := Count + 1`. However, it never adds the two counters together, so it fails to compute the count of all the inputs. In other words, the goal to combine the partial counts is not implemented. Simply listing plans and their equivalents is not sufficient to determine that `Count` and `Pos` must be added together; `Count` and `Pos` are not added together in Example A, yet Example A is correct. Example C can be debugged only if the system has knowledge of what the alternative goal decompositions are, and how they are likely to be realized in terms of plans.

3.6 Summary

This chapter has discussed a number of different methods for finding bugs in programs. Some work adequately on small programs, but less well on large programs. Others require detailed information about the program's behavior, which novices cannot provide. Some work when there are a limited number of bugs, but are unreliable when programs are extremely buggy. Some are able to localize the buggy part of a program, but have difficulty determining what the proper bug fix is. None of these approaches are as reliable as an approach based upon analysis of the programmer's goals and plans, such as intention-based diagnosis. In the following chapters I will discuss in detail the roles that goals, plans, and other knowledge structures play in the analysis of novice programs, and show how these knowledge structures are used in PROUST.

4 The Role of Plans

Intention-based diagnosis requires the ability to make accurate predictions about how artifacts are likely to be constructed. In PROUST these predictions are derived using a knowledge base of programming plans. This chapter describes the representation and use of plans in intention-based diagnosis of novice programs. First the psychological basis of plans in programming will be described. Then I will discuss how plans can be used in an intention-based diagnosis system. Issues relating to the proper choice of plan representation and plan contents will be discussed. Then the particular plan representation that PROUST uses, and the mechanisms for matching plans against programs, will be described.

4.1 The psychological basis for plans

The notion of plans in PROUST is derived from the psychological theory of programming plans being developed at Yale. Programming plans describe stereotypic action sequences in programs. This notion draws on the concept of a *schema* in text understanding research (e.g., [9, 52, 12, 34]):

> Schemata are generic knowledge structures that guide the comprehender's interpretations, inferences, expectations, and attention when passages are comprehended [34].

Likewise, programming plans facilitate the understanding of programs by providing background knowledge or context. When a person reading a program recognizes a plan, his/her knowledge about the plan aids in determining the intended function of the code which implements the plan.

There is already empirical evidence that provides support for the above hypothesis. Shneiderman [56], Adelson [2], and McKeithen et al. [48] used techniques similar to those of DeGroot [23] and Chase & Simon [16] to show that expert programmers recalled meaningful programs better than did novice programmers, but that both groups performed about the same on nonsense programs (randomly composed lines of code).

We make a further claim: programmers use programming plans not only in understanding programs, but also in writing programs. Programmers write programs by determining what goals must be satisfied, and then selecting plans which satisfy those goals. Empirical studies have uncovered evidence for the use of specific plans in programming [62, 61, 24, 60].

Figure 4-1 shows one way of dividing a program into plans. Three plans are listed. The RUNNING TOTAL VARIABLE PLAN and the COUNTER VARIABLE PLAN are the standard methods for computing totals and counts. The third plan, referred to here as a SENTINEL READ-PROCESS WHILE PLAN, is the main looping plan. This plan reads the input, and stops reading input when 99999 is entered. It also insures that 99999 is not used in computing the sum and count. PROUST's representation for this plan was shown in Figure 2-12.

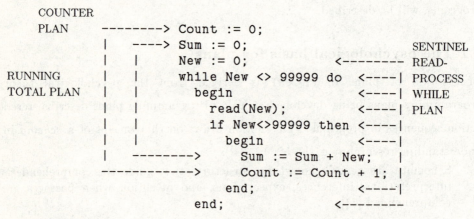

```
COUNTER
PLAN        --------> Count := 0;
        |   ----> Sum := 0;                        SENTINEL
        |   |     New := 0;            <--------   READ-
RUNNING |   |     while New <> 99999 do <----|  PROCESS
TOTAL PLAN |   |     begin                <----|  WHILE
        |   |         read(New);         <----|  PLAN
        |   |         if New<>99999 then <----|
        |   |           begin            <----|
        |   -------->       Sum := Sum + New;   |
        -------------->     Count := Count + 1; |
                    end;                <----|
                end;                    <--------
```

Figure 4-1: Plan annotations on a fragment of Pascal code

Programming plans are not immutable knowledge structures. Rather, programming plans are adapted and modified by programmers as needed. These modifications include such things as making two plans share a common component, or performing optimizing transformations on plans. Some modifications retain the original intent of the program, while others tend to obscure it. Programmers learn *discourse rules*, i.e., they learn which transformations result in readable programs and which do not, and avoid using plans in a way that would make it hard for a reader to understand the code [60].

4.2 Plans in intention-based diagnosis

The dual nature of programming plans as synthesis knowledge structures and understanding knowledge structures makes plans ideally suited for analysis by synthesis. Programmers use plans to map their intended goals into code. The program understander's task can be viewed as trying to invert this mapping, to map code back into the programmer's goals. However, it is not always possible to inspect a line of code and determine what the underlying goals are; in other words, there is no unique inverse for the goals-to-code mapping. Analysis by synthesis attempts to recreate the original mapping from goals to code, which in turn provides a unique mapping from code back to goals. The duality of plans is crucial, because it makes it possible to select a plan which maps goals to code, and then use this plan instead for understanding purposes, to map the code back into goals.

Although attractive in principle, the symmetry between plan-based program synthesis and plan-based program understanding can only be pushed so far. Plan theory holds that plans are used both for synthesis and understanding, but this does not imply that the *same* plans are used both for synthesis and understanding. In fact, if the person doing the understanding is an expert programmer and the person doing the programming is a novice programmer, it is almost certain that the same plans will not be used. For example, the fact that the SENTINEL READ-PROCESS WHILE PLAN was used to analyze the averaging program in Figure 4-1 does not necessarily imply that the novice programmer also had a version of the SENTINEL READ-PROCESS WHILE PLAN in his head. What can be inferred from the plan analysis is the intended function of each statement in the program, and how those statements are employed to achieve the programmer's higher-level goals. For example, the plan analysis in Figure 4-1 indicates that the statement `read(New)` is part of the plan SENTINEL READ-PROCESS WHILE PLAN. Our knowledge of the Averaging Problem tells us that this plan is being used to input the data to be averaged. We can therefore infer the function that the programmer intended the `read` statement to have: it inputs values, and it helps to achieve the goal of reading in the set of data to be averaged.

Since the uses of plans in program understanding and program synthesis are not fully symmetrical, we should not expect to design a plan library which is equally useful for synthesis and understanding. In an intention-based diagnosis system the emphasis must be on understanding, because the diagnostic process is primarily an understanding process. This is the case in PROUST. PROUST's knowledge base is probably similar to the plan knowledge of an expert human grader of novice programs. As such it is based upon the knowledge base that one would use to understand expert programs, supplemented with knowledge about the kinds of programs that only novices write. It most definitely is not the same knowledge that a novice programmer has about writing programs. Because it is used in an analysis-by-synthesis system, though, it is useful to be able to retrieve and apply the knowledge in a way that is somewhat similar to the way that novices do.

Plans are used in PROUST as follows. First, PROUST selects a goal to be analyzed. It retrieves a set of plans from a plan database, each of which might be used by novices to implement the goal. Such sets typically contain some expert plans, some novice plans, and some buggy novice plans. PROUST's plan matcher then matches each plan against the program. The plans may contain subgoals as components; if so, plans will have to be retrieved which implement the subgoals, so the plan-matching process can be recursive. If a plan fails to match the program exactly, the plan matcher generates a description of the differences between the plan and the program. These plan differences are then passed to the plan-difference rule applier, which attempts to explain the differences.

The remainder of this chapter will focus on how plan knowledge is represented, how plans are matched against programs, and how plan-difference descriptions are generated. We will not be overly concerned here about how PROUST selects goals for analysis, and how it retrieves plans which implement the goals. We will also not be concerned with what the plan-difference rule applier does with the plan differences which the plan matcher generates. However, since the requirements of goal reasoning and plan-difference analysis have an impact on the representation of plans, we will have to refer in passing to these other processes, in order to motivate PROUST's plan representation.

4.3 Requirements for the plan representation

This section describes the factors which affect the choice of plan representation in PROUST, and the implications of plan representation on the process of matching plans against programs. Two kinds of information go into the description of a plan: a description of the structure of the plan, which will be called the *plan template*, and a set of properties and assertions about the plan. The principal issues in designing a plan representation are determining the right level of abstraction for plan templates and deciding what properties and assertions must be included. The following factors have an impact on these decisions:

- the variability of novice implementations,

- requirements for bug recognition, i.e., the need to generate meaningful plan-difference descriptions,

- the need for parsimony in the plan knowledge base, and

- the kind of reasoning about plans that is required.

4.3.1 Choosing the right level of abstraction for plans

The paramount issue in designing a representation scheme for plans is choosing the right level of abstraction. To see the effect that the choice of level of abstraction has, consider the following example. Figure 4-2 shows an abstract version of a plan to input and process a sequence of values terminated by a sentinel value. Figure 4-3 shows a more concrete version of the same plan. The abstract version simply specifies the order in which operations are performed: each value is input one at a time, tested, and then processed. Nothing is said about the form that this plan takes in Pascal. The concrete version, on the other hand, states explicitly what the plan looks like in Pascal. This is the SENTINEL PROCESS-READ WHILE PLAN introduced in Chapter 2, Figure 2-4. It indicates that a `while` loop should be used, that the processing of data should go at the top of the body of the loop, and the inputs should be performed at the bottom of the loop.

Now consider the two solutions of the Averaging Problem shown in Figure 4-4. Program `Average1` uses a `while` loop which is constructed in a process-read fashion.

1. Input the data one value at a time.

2. Test each datum after it is read; if it is the sentinel value, then quit.

3. Process each datum after it has been tested.

Figure 4-2: An abstract description of a sentinel-controlled input plan

```
input ?X;
while ?X <> ?Sentinel do
begin
    process ?X;
    input ?X;
end;
```

Figure 4-3: A concrete description of a sentinel-controlled input plan

Program `Average2` uses a recursive procedure. The abstract version of the sentinel-controlled input plan fits both programs. The concrete version fits only Program `Average1`. Thus the abstract version of the plan is more generally applicable than the concrete plan. The question is whether this is an advantage or a disadvantage. It is an advantage if our goal is to construct a general knowledge base of programming plans. It is a disadvantage if our goal is to acquire information about the particular method that the student used for implementing the program.

Representation schemes for programming plans have already been developed; the Programmer's Apprentice, for example, has developed a calculus for plans [50]. We could simply adopt one of these representations, and let it dictate the form of the plan templates and the range of programs that each plan matches. However, the criteria which determine an optimal plan representation in PROUST are different from the criteria which have guided other plan representation schemes. PROUST is designed to analyze novice programs, not expert programs. It is intended to analyze buggy programs as well as correct programs. I therefore chose to examine the requirements that PROUST's domain place on a plan representation, and then design my own representation scheme for plans.

There is a parallel issue which arises alongside the issue of the proper abstraction level for plans. This is the question of what the right abstraction level for programs

```
program Average1(input, output);          program Average2(input, output);
var Sum, Count, New: integer;             var Sum, Count: integer;
    Avg: real;                                Avg: real;
begin
  Sum := 0;                                   procedure SumUp();
  Count := 0;                                 var New: integer;
  writeln('Enter a value:');                  begin
  read(New);                                    writeln('Enter a value:');
  while New <> 99999 do                         read( New );
    begin                                       if New <> 99999 then
      Sum := Sum+New;                             begin
      Count := Count+1;                             Sum := Sum+New;
      writeln('Enter a value:');                    Count := Count+1;
      Read(New);                                    SumUp;
    end;                                          end;
  if Count <> 0 then                          end;
    begin
      Avg := Sum / Count;                   begin
      writeln('The average is ', avg);        Sum := 0;
    end;                                      Count := 0;
end;                                          SumUp;
                                              if Count <> 0 then begin
                                              Avg := Sum / Count;
                                              writeln('The average is ', avg);
                                              end;
                                            end;
```

Figure 4-4:   Two different solutions to the Averaging Problem

is. PROUST matches plans against programs; that really means that it matches them
against some *representation* of programs. Such a representation might be a parse
tree, or it might be a data-flow graph, or it might be something else altogether.
Whatever it is, it has to be similar to the representation for plans, otherwise the
matching process turns into a reasoning process. For example, if our plan
representation consisted of an abstract set of assertions about order of execution, such
as in Figure 4-2, and the program representation was a concrete parse tree, then a
theorem prover would be needed to establish whether or not plans fit programs. I
will assume at the outset that it is desirable to use a pattern matcher rather than a
theorem prover to match plans against programs. Otherwise PROUST would be too
slow to use in a classroom. This means that any factor affecting the choice of
program representation also affects the choice of plan representation, and *vice versa*.

4.3.2 Variability in novice implementations

There is a high degree of variability in the program implementations that novices generate. In general this variability is greater than that of expert programmers solving the same programming problems. Consequently it is difficult to come up with a plan representation which can be used to match against any student implementation.

The following rule seems to apply to novice programmers: the more programming constructs they know, the more constructs they will try to apply to a given programming problem. Students who are just a few weeks into a programming course already know enough different programming constructs that they start generating unusual solutions to programming problems. I have not seen recursive solutions to the Averaging Problem, such as Program `Average2` in Figure 4-4, but that is only because the novices which we have studied had not yet learned recursion. We once assigned the Rainfall Problem in a more advanced programming course, in which the students had already learned recursion; many of these students generated recursive solutions. PROUST is currently restricted to novices, and its plan representation is therefore not equipped to interpret recursive programs as variants of iterative programs.

Even without recursion, there is a large amount of variation which PROUST must handle. For example, PROUST must be prepared to understand programs containing a range of different looping constructs. PASCAL has three looping constructs: `while`, `repeat`, and `for`. Of these the `while` loop is best suited for writing sentinel-controlled loops, because it tests data before it is processed. This ensures that the loop will work properly if the first value entered by the users is the sentinel value. Nevertheless, novice programmers may use any one of the three looping constructs to implement a sentinel-controlled loop [62]. The programs in Figure 4-5 show the kind of solutions which novice programmers might write for the Averaging Problem. One uses a `repeat` loop and the other uses a `for` loop. Note that the `for` loop does not meet the problem requirements exactly, since the program first asks the user how many inputs are going to be processed. This may be a result of misunderstanding the problem, or it may be that the programmer decided to use a `for` loop because it was the last construct learned in class.

94

```
program Average3(input, output);        program Average4(input, output);
var Sum, Count, New: integer;           var Sum, Count, New, Max: integer;
    Avg: real;                              Avg: real;
begin                                   begin
  Sum := 0;                               Sum := 0;
  Count := 0;                             Count := 0;
  writeln('Enter a value:');              writeln('How many inputs?');
  read( New );                            read( Max );
  if New <> 99999 then                    for Count := 1 to Max do
    repeat                                  begin
      Sum := Sum + New;                       writeln('Enter next value:');
      Count := Count + 1;                     read(New);
      writeln('Enter a value:');              if New <> 99999 then
      read(New);                                Sum := Sum + New
    until New=99999;                          else
  if Count <> 0 then                            writeln('End of input');
    begin                                   end;
      Avg := Sum/Count;                 if Count <> 0 then
      writeln('The average is ', avg);    begin
    end;                                    Avg := Sum / Count;
end;                                        writeln('The average is ', avg);
                                          end
```

Figure 4-5: Use of alternative looping constructs

Jeffrey Bonar's work has shown that rank novices tend to organize the steps in a program in a sequential fashion [10]; but as students come to understand the principles of control flow and data flow, they start reorganizing their code in unusual ways. This is most evident in loops. Section 2.2.1 showed how sentinel-controlled loops can work either in a process-read fashion or a read-process fashion. There are many other ways in which novices organize loops. Figure 4-6 shows two examples of the kind of unusual code organization that novices generate.

Program Average5 in Figure 4-6 is an example where the read is in the middle of the loop. This example looks like a read-process loop, except that the line Count := Count + 1 appears above the read statement. The program has to decrement the counter further down in the loop when the input is negative. Even though the organization of the loop is peculiar, and the counter updates counteract each other, the program nevertheless works.

Program Average6 in Figure 4-6 is an example which has two read statements in the loop instead of one. Each of these read statements is in a different branch of an if-then-else statement; therefore only one read statement is executed on each pass through the loop. As a consequence, the program works correctly in spite of the duplicated read statements.

95

```
program Average5( input, output );        program Average6( input, output );
var Sum, Count, New: integer;             var Sum, Count, New: integer;
    Avg: real;                                Avg: real;
begin                                     begin
  Sum := 0;                                 Sum := 0;
  Count := 0;                               Count := 0;
  New := 0;                                 writeln( 'Enter a value:' );
  while New <> 99999 do                     read( New );
    begin                                   while New <> 99999 do
      Count := Count + 1;                     begin
      writeln('Enter a value:');                if New >= 0 then
      read(New);                                  begin
      if New < 0 then                               Count := Count + 1;
        begin                                       Sum := Sum + New;
          writeln('Value is invalid');             writeln('Enter a value:');
          Count := Count - 1;                       read(New);
        end                                       end
      else if New <> 99999 then                 else
        Sum := Sum + New;                         begin
    end;                                            writeln('Invalid entry');
  if Count <> 0 then                                read(New);
    begin                                         end
      Avg := Sum / Count;                     end;
      writeln('The average is ', avg);      if Count <> 0 then
    end;                                      begin
end;                                            Avg := Sum / Count;
                                               writeln('Average is ', avg);
                                             end;
                                         end;
```

Figure 4-6: More alternative looping constructs

If we were to have each program example discussed so far in this chapter match the same plan, except for Program **Average4**, which is buggy, we would clearly need a very abstract representation for the sentinel-controlled loop plan, such as the representation in Figure 4-2. We would need a program representation which is abstract enough that all of the variation that we have seen in these programs would be abstracted away. This would require a representation which ignored the particular programming constructs used, so that it would not matter whether the student used a **while** or a **repeat** statement. It would have to combine statements which have the same effect in different parts of the program, such as the two **read** statements in the loop in Program **Average6**. The result is that the only information which would be retained about the program would be the data-flow structure.

4.3.3 Identifying bugs

Although variability in program implementations makes abstract plan representations desirable, such a representation does not facilitate bug recognition. As we saw in Chapter 2, PROUST identifies bugs by analyzing plan-match failures. The mismatches between the expected plan and the actual code, called plan differences, may be characteristic of a particular kind of bug. In order for the bugs responsible for plan differences to be recognizable, detailed information about how the plan failed to match is required. If the plan representation is itself concrete and detailed, then the matching process can provide detailed information about why the match failed. If a plan is very abstract, on the other hand, it is harder to tell exactly which statements in the program are responsible for the match failure.

Figure 4-7 shows a very buggy solution to the Rainfall Problem. The original indentation that the student used has been retained in this example, so that the program structure intended by the student is more apparent. This student clearly has some major misconceptions about how block structuring and looping work. The following evidence leads to this conclusion:

1. The main `while` loop in the program has no `begin-end` pair surrounding the loop body. Instead, the `begin` statement is *above* the `while` statement.

2. The code which tests the input to make sure that it is non-negative appears to be missing a `begin-end` block.

3. The loop at line 26, `repeat until Rainfall = Sentinel`, serves no function. Yet its intended function is clear; the program is supposed to loop back to the beginning, and this line indicates when the looping back should take place. The student expects this line to be interpreted as if it were English, not as if it were Pascal.

Now imagine that PROUST translated the program into an abstract data-flow representation before any bug analysis was performed. The `begin-end` blocks would disappear, so there would be no way of recognizing that the `begin` statement above the `while` statement is supposed to denote the beginning of the loop. The null `repeat` statement would be replaced by an abstract description of its control flow, i.e., it would appear as an infinite loop. The English-language meaning of the statement would not be discernible. Thus translating programs into an abstract representation for plan-matching purposes can obscure the programs' bugs.

```
1    program Rainfall (input, output);
2    const
3      Sentinel = 99999;
4    var
5      Rainfall, Valid, Highest, Average, Total : real;
6      RainDay : integer;
7    begin
8      writeln('Please enter the amount of rainfall for each day');
9      readln;
10     read(Rainfall);
11       if Rainfall < 0 then
13     writeln('the data is impossible please check and reenter data');
14     readln;
15     read(Rainfall);
16     begin
17      while Rainfall <> Sentinel do
18      if Rainfall > Highest then
19       Highest := Rainfall;
20       Total := Rainfall + Total;
21       if Rainfall >= 0 then
22       Valid := valid + 1;
23      if Rainfall > 0 then
24       RainDay := RainDay + 1;
25    end;
26    repeat
27        until Rainfall = Sentinel;
28      Average := (Total / Valid);
29      writeln(' ',Valid:2,'valid rainfalls were entered.');
30      writeln('the average rainfall was',Average:8:2,'inches per day');
31      writeln('the highest rainfall was',Highest:8:2,'inches');
32      writeln('there were',RainDay:2,'rainy days in this period')
33    END.
```

Figure 4-7: A program with major syntactic misconceptions

We see in this example that detailed knowledge about the syntactic structure of programs is often needed for bug-recognition purposes. One needs to know what specific statements were used by the student in the program, e.g., whether they used a `while` statement or `repeat` statement. Furthermore, the more detailed one's expectations are about how a plan is likely to be implemented, the easier it is to interpret plan match failures. For example, one usually expects the bodies of sentinel-controlled `while` loops to be `begin-end` blocks. As written, however, the body of the `while` loop in Figure 4-7 is not a `begin-end` block; it is an `if` statement,

`if Rainfall > Highest then Highest := Rainfall.`

Since the expected `begin-end` pair is missing, it makes sense to inspect the code around the `while` loop to see if the `begin-end` pair is misplaced, as in this example. If the sentinel-controlled-loop plan did not state that a `begin-end` pair was expected, there would be no particular reason to look for a misplaced `begin-end` pair. The student's buggy block structure might therefore be misinterpreted.

Unfortunately, sometimes detailed syntactic information about plan differences does not facilitate bug recognition; it just gets in the way. If a bug is a high-level error, such as a misreading of the problem statement, then translating the program into a high-level representation actually makes the bug easier to find, because it removes syntactic clutter from the program representation. As an example, when novice programmers compute an average they sometimes fail to count zero values in the average. When looking for this bug, it is not relevant what method the student uses for excluding zero values, only that such values are excluded. An abstract representation would reduce the variability in representations of student solutions, thereby making it easier to determine what data is used to compute the average.

Given the choice between a high-level representation of plans and programs and a low-level representation, the low-level representation is preferable from a bug-recognition standpoint. The syntax-oriented representation may be overly cluttered at times, but at least it does not throw valuable information away. If a high-level representation were used, cases will arise where the causes of a plan-match failure cannot be determined, so the quality of PROUST's bug analysis would suffer.

There is a way to avoid making this choice, however; we could construct both high-level and low-level descriptions of the plans and the program, and then use whichever level is best for describing the bugs. The complexity of such a framework would be significantly greater than one based on a single representation. For one thing, the high-level description would frequently have to be dynamically updated or recomputed, as PROUST's view of the intended function of program statements changes. For example, when PROUST detects that the block structure of the program in Figure 4-7 is wrong, it would have to recompute any data-flow analysis of the program that it had previously performed. Such an enhancement of PROUST's plan knowledge is left open as a possibility for the future. PROUST's current plan knowledge base was designed under the assumption that a single level of representation for plans would be used.

4.3.4 Generality and parsimony of the knowledge base

If we observe the requirements that bug recognition places on plan representation, then plans will end up looking like the concrete plan representation in Figure 4-3. This has two unfortunate effects: the generality of individual plans becomes limited, and plans become language-dependent. Generality and parsimony of the plan knowledge base thus suffer a severe blow.

The fact that PROUST's plan representation is Pascal-dependent is a disappointment. One would hope that the same plan knowledge base could be used for different programming languages, and the language dependence guarantees that this cannot be done. However, the fact is that plans, as programmers use them, appear often to be language-dependent. Each programming language has its own set of idioms; the form of these idioms cannot be predicted from a language-independent representation. For example, in Pascal it is preferable to construct a loop with a process-read structure than use a read-process structure, even though the computations are equivalent. Expert program understanders rely upon such idioms to guide their understanding of correct programs, and to identify bugs in buggy programs.

Another consequence of the loss of generality in the plan representation is that more plans must be added to the knowledge base. PROUST's plan knowledge base contains more plans than an abstract plan database would have, but the increase in the number of plans is on the average less than a factor of three. An extreme case is the *Sentinel-Controlled Input Sequence* goal. Instead of there being a single abstract plan for implementing this goal, there are four plans: SENTINEL PROCESS-READ WHILE PLAN, SENTINEL READ-PROCESS WHILE PLAN, SENTINEL PROCESS-READ REPEAT PLAN, and SENTINEL READ-PROCESS REPEAT PLAN.

Yet another consequence of the loss of generality in plans is that transformations must be introduced to produce greater variability of implementations. The programs in Figure 4-6 are examples where transformations are necessary. Program `Average6`, for example, has three input statements; there is no looping plan in PROUST which has three input statements. In fact, it would make no sense to have such a plan in the knowledge base. By adding more `if-then-else` statements to a loop, resulting

100

in more branching, it is possible to construct a loop with any number of input statements in it. This would result in an indefinitely great expansion of the knowledge base. Instead, we apply *transformations* to generate the unusual forms from the standard plans in the knowledge base. The transformation used here, called the Distribution Transformation, duplicates pieces of code and moves them inside of `if-then-else` statements. Transformations are simply a different kind of plan-difference rule, one which accounts for match failures without identifying bugs. Transformations allow PROUST to reason about unusual code without out actually having to codify the unusual code in the plan knowledge base.

The introduction of transformations not only makes it possible to retain a certain amount of parsimony in the knowledge base; it also gives a more realistic model of how plans are used in programs. Plan theory predicts that programmers will occasionally modify plans in order to fit them into a program; transformations can be thought of as a way of modeling these modifications.

4.3.5. Assertions and annotations on plans

The discussion up to this point has focused on the issues governing the choice of plan template representation. I will now describe the kinds of assertions and annotations which must be added to plans in PROUST's framework. These assertions serve two purposes. First, the mechanism which selects goals and plans for analysis needs information about each plan in order to determine when the plan can be used, and what implications such use may have. Second, bug analysis requires plan annotations indicating what role each component of the plan plays. These annotations are used to determine what interpretation should result if a plan component fails to match.

The preconditions and postconditions associated with plans are key to the plan selection process. Such information has an important role in PROUST's plan representation as well as in other plan representations, such as the one used in the Programmer's Apprentice. Conditions on plans can be used either to determine if a plan is appropriate for satisfying a goal, or to determine what additional goals must be satisfied in order to make the plan appropriate. PROUST uses plan conditions for the latter purpose.

Exception conditions are one type of plan condition which is attached to PROUST's plans. An exception condition is a condition under which the plan fails to generate correct results. The AVERAGE PLAN is an example of a plan which has an exception condition; this plan was introduced in Section 2.3, and is shown in expanded form in Figure 4-8. The exception condition of this plan is (?Count *in goal Count*) = 0. This indicates that whenever the plan variable ?Count in the plan implementing the goal *Count* is zero, the output of the AVERAGE PLAN is undefined. If some other goal refers to a value generated by an instance of AVERAGE PLAN, it must ensure that the value is not used when the counter is zero.

AVERAGE PLAN

Variables:
> ?Avg, ?Sum, ?Count

Posterior goals:
> *Count*(?New, ?Count)
> *Sum*(?New, ?Sum)
> *Guard Exception*(Update: *component of goal Average*,
>   (?Count *in goal Count*) = 0)

Exception condition:
> (?Count *in goal Count*) = 0

Template:
> (*component* Mainloop: *of goal Read & Process*)
> *followed by:*

Update: ?Avg := (?Sum / ?Count)

Figure 4-8:   A plan for implementing *Average*

Another way of describing conditions on plans is by defining goals which must be satisfied when the plan is used. The PosteriorGoals slot of the AVERAGE PLAN, for example, contains such a list of goals. These goals are added to the agenda of goals to be analyzed whenever the AVERAGE PLAN is instantiated. There are three goals in the AVERAGE PLAN's PosteriorGoals slot: a *Sum* goal, a *Count* goal, and a *Guard Exception* goal. The *Sum* and *Count* goals define the values that the AVERAGE PLAN uses to compute the average. The *Sum* goal defines the pattern variable ?Sum which appears in the numerator of the average computation; the *Count* goal defines the pattern variable ?Count which appears in the denominator. The *Guard Exception* goal prevents the average update from being executed when the

102

count is zero. Note that the function of this *Guard Exception* goal is slightly different from the function of the exception condition, although both check whether the counter is zero. The *Guard Exception* goal requires that the average update not be executed when the counter is zero, and the exception condition indicates that the plan does not generate a meaningful result when the counter is zero.

Plan components in PROUST must be annotated to indicate the role that they perform. These annotations allow goals to refer to components of other goals. An example of this appears in the *Guard Exception* goal listed in the AVERAGE PLAN. This goal has as one of its arguments the phrase `Update:` *component of goal Average*, which denotes the update component of the plan implementing the goal *Average*, i.e., the AVERAGE PLAN. The update component of a plan is defined to be the part of the plan which computes the final result, as opposed to the initialization, loop exit test, etc. The *Guard Exception* goal in the AVERAGE PLAN serves to prevent the update of the plan from being executed when the counter is zero.

Another use of plan-component annotations is in bug analysis. The plan-component annotations indicate the function of each component in the plan. This knowledge of intended function is useful in understanding bugs that a component might have, and in describing the bug to the student.

4.4. PROUST's representation of plans

The previous section described the factors which determine the appropriate representation for plans in an intention-based diagnosis system. I will now discuss the plan representation which is actually used in PROUST, and show how it takes these considerations into account.

Each plan in PROUST is a frame containing a set of slots. One of these slots, the `Template` slot, describes the structure of the plan template. The other slots provide various additional facts and assertions about the plan. Since the template is the most important part of the plan, I will discuss it first.

4.4.1 Plan template components

PROUST's plan templates are represented in a concrete form, fairly close to the Pascal code that they are matched against. The basic building blocks of plan templates are Pascal statements. Each component of a plan is one of the following:

- a Pascal statement,

- a subgoal which in turn is implemented as one or more Pascal statements, or

- a reference to a component of another plan (i.e., one or more statements in another plan).

Statements were chosen as the primitive unit because in an imperative language such as Pascal each statement usually can be viewed as a primitive unit of action. Plans can be built up in a natural way out of such primitive actions. There are times when statements perform more than one action, in which case decomposition of programs into statements fails to identify the primitive actions. However, in most cases PROUST's decomposition of plans and programs facilitates plan recognition.

The following discussion will make repeated reference to a specific example plan, the by-now-familiar SENTINEL PROCESS-READ WHILE PLAN. PROUST's representation for this plan is shown in Figure 4-9. Figure 4-9 shows both the syntactically sugared form of the plan, such as has appeared in previous examples, and the actual Lisp-like representation that PROUST uses. The present discussion will refer to the unsugared version, so that the reader can see what the notation actually looks like. Figure 4-9 is the only place in this document where the unsugared notation is used, since it is somewhat harder to read. The unsugared notation has the following relationship with the sugared notation.

- Operators such as +, −, and, etc., are written as prefix operators in PROUST's plan notation. These operators appear as infix operators in the sugared form.

- Goal forms are written in prefix notation, i.e., (Goal arg1 arg2 ...). Goals appear as *Goal*(arg1, arg2, ...) in the sugared form.

- Pascal statements are written as lists, where the head of the list is the type of statement, and the tail of the list consists of the subexpressions of the statements. Syntactic delimiters and separators are omitted. Thus a sugared Pascal statement such as

```
        while ?New <> ?Stop do
        begin
            ?*
        end
```

becomes

```
        (while (<> ?New ?Stop)
               (begin ?*))
```

SENTINEL PROCESS READ WHILE

Constants:	?Stop
Variables:	?New
Template:	
InitInput:	*subgoal Input* (?New)
MainLoop:	while ?New <> ?Stop do
	begin
Process:	?*
Next:	*subgoal Input* (?New)
	end

```
(DefinePlan SentinelProcessReadWhile
    Constants (STOP)
    Variables (New)
    Template  ((InitInput: (SUBGOAL (Input ?New)))
              (MainLoop:
                 (while (<> ?New ?STOP)
                     (BEGIN
                       (Process: ?*)
                       (Next: (SUBGOAL (Input ?New)))))))))
```

Figure 4-9: PROUST's representation of a plan

4.4.1.1 Statement patterns

Statement patterns are patterns for specific Pascal statements which a plan must
match. The SENTINEL PROCESS-READ WHILE PLAN has two statement patterns:
(while (<> ?New ?STOP) ...) and (begin ...). The while statement
pattern matches a while statement in the program, and the begin statement
pattern matches some begin-end pair in the program. The arguments of a
statement pattern correspond to the components of the Pascal statements, after
syntactic keywords such as then, do, and end have been removed. Thus in the

105

`while` statement pattern `(<> ?New ?STOP)` matches the test expression of the `while` loop, and the embedded `begin` pattern matches the statement following the `do` keyword in the `while` loop.

Plan components can be combined just as Pascal statements can be combined. In the template in Figure 4-9, the `begin` pattern is embedded inside the `while` pattern. Syntactic delimiters such as semicolons do not appear in the template; successive statement patterns are simply listed one after another.

4.4.1.2 Subgoal expressions

Subgoal expressions are expressions of the form *subgoal goal-expr*, where *goal-expr* is a goal expression. A goal expression consists of a goal name followed by a list of arguments. Each subgoal expression must be implemented via some plan, and the code for that plan must appear where the subgoal expression appears in the plan template. For example, at the bottom of the `begin` pattern in Figure 4-9 there appears a subgoal expression `(SUBGOAL (Input ?New))`; this indicates that at the bottom of the `begin-end` block there should be a plan to satisfy the goal *Input* (`?New`), i.e., to input a value into the input variable, `?New`.

4.4.1.3 Component labels

Plan components are labeled to indicate what role they serve. The labels appear as symbols followed by colons, such as `MainLoop:`. Each label appears in the unsugared notation at the head of a list, where the tail of the list is the set of components to be labeled. In the SENTINEL PROCESS-READ WHILE PLAN there are four labeled plan components:

- the initial input, labeled `InitInput:`,

- the looping statement, labeled `MainLoop:`,

- the part of the loop body where the input is processed, labeled `Process:`, and

- the step which performs the remaining inputs, labeled `Next:`.

A standard classification of plan component roles is used in PROUST's plans. These classes are not mutually exclusive, because a plan component can fulfill more than one role. The component classes are the following:

- **Init:** -- an initialization,

- **Guard:** -- a conditional branch,

- **GuardedCode:** -- one of the branches of a conditional branch,

- **Input:** -- an input,

- **InitInput:** -- an input which serves as an initialization,

- **MainLoop:** -- a loop,

- **Next:** -- a component which gets the next value,

- **Output:** -- something which outputs,

- **Process:** -- a block of code which processes data,

- **Update:** -- something which computes a value, and

- **BoundaryUpdate:** -- an update that is only performed in special cases, unlike **Update:**, which handles the base cases.

4.4.1.4 Wild-card patterns

Some parts of plans can be bound to arbitrary sets of statements; these are gaps in the plan which can be filled in by other plans. Such gaps are called *wild-card patterns*. There are two kinds of wild-card patterns in plan templates: `?*`, which can match an arbitrary sequence of statements, and `??`, which is bound to exactly one statement. In the example in Figure 4-9, a wild-card pattern is used to refer to everything in the loop which precedes the *Input* subgoal at the bottom of the loop. Wild-card patterns can be labeled; thus the wild-card pattern in this plan is assigned the role **Process:**.

4.4.1.5 References to other plans

Plans can make explicit reference to components of other plans. The purpose of such references is to fix the location of a plan component relative to the referred plan component. Such component references make it possible to state, for example, that the update component of a running-total plan should appear within a looping plan that iterates over the data being totaled. References to plan components are denoted using `ComponentOf` directives. A `ComponentOf` directive has two required arguments: the class of goal which is being referred to, and the type of plan component. Thus, for example, a directive (`ComponentOf Read&Process Process:`) refers to the `Process:` component of a plan satisfying a goal in the goal class *Read&Process*.[9] `ComponentOf` directives can have an optional third argument, which is a pattern which must match some part of the code which the `ComponentOf` directive refers to. In sugared notation, (`Component Read&Process Process:`) is written as "*the* `Process:` *component of goal Read&Process*".

Figure 4-10 shows a plan which uses a `ComponentOf` directive. The plan is the RUNNING TOTAL PLAN; this plan has one component, an initialization, which must precede the main loop, and another component, an update, which must be inserted inside of the main loop. The configuration of the plan is indicated with a `ComponentOf` directive referring to the `Process:` label of a *Read&Process* goal. The initialization component precedes the `ComponentOf` directive; this serves to indicate that the initialization must precede the `Process:` component. The update component is contained in the third argument of the `ComponentOf` directive; this indicates that the update must match part of the `Process:` component.

```
(DefinePlan RunningTotal
    Variables   (Total New)
    Template    ((Init: (:= ?Total 0))
                (ComponentOf
                Read&Process
                Process:
                (Update: (:= ?Total (+ ?Total ?New))))))
```

Figure 4-10:   A plan with a `ComponentOf` directive

---

[9]Goal classes will be described in Chapter 6.

108

4.4.2 Expressions within plan components

Expressions within plan components contain, in addition to Pascal expressions, pattern variables and operators on plan variables. I will describe variables and operators briefly below.

4.4.2.1 Pattern variables

Pattern variables are used to parameterize plans. Each has a type associated with it: their values can either be constants, Pascal variables or one or more Pascal statements. The type of a pattern variable is determined by whether it is listed in the `Constants` slot, the `Variables` slot, or the `CodeVars` slot of the plan.

Constant-valued pattern variables must be bound to some Pascal constant or constant-valued expression. An example of a constant pattern variable in SENTINEL PROCESS-READ WHILE is `?Stop`, the sentinel value.

Variable-valued pattern variables are bound to Pascal variables or variable-valued expressions. The variable-valued pattern variable in SENTINEL PROCESS-READ WHILE is `?New`, the new-value variable. In complex arithmetic expressions variable pattern variables can be bound to intermediate results of the computation. For example, in the AVERAGE PLAN the average update is denoted by the expression `(:= ?Avg (/ ?Sum ?Count))`. If this is matched against the Pascal statement `Avg := (Sum - 99999)/(Count - 1)`, then `?Sum` will be bound to `Sum - 99999` and `?Count` will be bound to `Count - 1`. Variable-valued pattern variables can be bound to boolean-valued expressions; it is possible to write a statement pattern such as `(while ?Pred ...)`, where `?Pred` is bound to an expression such as `New > 0`.

The mapping between variable-valued pattern variables and Pascal variables is not one to one. It is possible for two Pascal variables to share the same value; it is also possible for a Pascal variable to take on one role in one part of a program and another role in another part of the program. Therefore variable-valued pattern variables are bound to a list of Pascal variables, together with an indication of the parts of the program in which each Pascal variable matches the pattern variable.

Code-valued pattern variables are bound to some set of statements in the program. These are commonly used when a plan operates on a piece of code which is part of another plan, in which case the code variable is bound to the part of the other plan that is being operated on. A prime example is the GUARD EXCEPTION PLAN, an implementation of the goal *Guard Exception*; this plan is shown in Figure 4-11. The GUARD EXCEPTION PLAN is used to keep a part of a program from executing when a predicate evaluates to true. The GUARD EXCEPTION PLAN has two pattern variables, ?Code and ?Pred. ?Code is a code-valued pattern variable bound to the part of the program which is being guarded. ?Pred, is a variable-valued pattern variable bound to the condition being guarded against. The plan specifies that ?Code will be embedded inside of an if statement which checks that ?Pred is false.

```
(DefinePlan GuardExceptionPlan
    Variables
    (Pred)
    CodeVars
    (Code)
    Template
    (IF (*NOT* ?Pred)
        (Contains ?Code)))
```

Figure 4-11: A plan with a code-valued pattern variable

4.4.2.2 Operators on pattern variables

Expressions within statement patterns sometimes contain operators on pattern variables. One such operator is currently defined, *NOT*. *NOT* takes as an argument a pattern variable bound to a boolean-valued expression, and generates a pattern which matches the complement of that expression. Thus if ?Pred is bound to New < 0, then (*NOT* ?Pred) will match New >= 0.

4.4.3 Configuration and processing directives

Two more elements of plan templates remain to be described: configuration directives and processing directives.

4.4.3.1 Configuration directives

The configuration of plan components usually follows the structure of the plan template. Suppose, for example, that we have a plan template of the form (if ?Pred (begin ...)), where the begin statement is embedded inside of the if statement. The code which matches this pattern must have an `if` statement and a `begin` in exactly the same configuration as the statement pattern configuration. The pattern thus can match code like this:

```
if New > O then
    begin
     ...
    end;
```

but it cannot match code like this:

```
if New > O then
    while I < Max do
        begin
         ...
        end;
```

On the other hand, when a `ComponentOf` directive appears in a plan, and there is a plan pattern embedded inside of it, then the embedded pattern is assumed to match some part of the referred plan component, not the entire plan component. For example, in the RUNNING TOTAL PLAN, in Figure 4-10,

```
(ComponentOf Read&Process
          Process:
          (Update: (:= ?Total (+ ?Total ?New))))
```

indicates that the `Update:` part of the plan should be contained in the `Process:` part of the `Read&Process` loop, not that it should be the only update in the `Process:` part of the loop.

The default assumptions about plan component configuration can be explicitly overridden using `Contains` and `SpannedBy` directives. The `Contains` directive indicates that the plan component can occur anywhere within the region specified by the plan. An example of a `Contains` directive appears in the GUARD EXCEPTION PLAN shown in Figure 4-11. There the `Contains` directive indicates that the guarded code must occur somewhere inside the `then` part of the `if` statement which tests the guard condition. `SpannedBy` directives are just the reverse of `Contains` directives; they indicate that the plan component must be found exactly at the indicated spot. These are used in conjunction with `ComponentOf` directives. If a `ComponentOf` directive contains a statement pattern, as in RUNNING TOTAL PLAN in Figure 4-10, and a `SpannedBy` directive is not used, then the statement pattern is assumed to be only a part of the labeled code region.

111

4.4.3.2 Processing directives

The symbol -> is a processing directive, indicating in what order plan components should be matched against the program. In ordinary cases, PROUST automatically orders components in plans, matching first those components which are likely to match the program unambiguously. The heuristics which govern this ordering are their motivations are described in Chapter 8. The inclusion of an -> overrides the default ordering, and indicates that the designated plan component should be matched before the others in the plan.

4.4.4 Slots defining assertions about plans

As was indicated in Section 4.3.5, assertions and annotations must be added to plans in PROUST. Some of the annotations, the labeling of plan components, are embedded within the plan templates. The remaining assertions are included in separate slots within the plan frame; these slots and their fillers will be discussed below.

4.4.4.1 Slots defining goals and boundary conditions

Four plan slots define goals and boundary conditions. These slots are ExceptionCondition, PriorGoals, AddedBindings, and PosteriorGoals. Exception condition slots have already been described in some detail in Section 4.3.5; the remaining slots require some further elaboration.

PriorGoals and PosteriorGoals are both used to define goals which are required when a plan is used. The difference between the two slots is that the goals in the PosteriorGoals slot are added to the goal agenda after the plan is matched; goals in the PriorGoals slot are added before the plan is matched. Goals are listed as prior goals when other parts of the plan refer to the goals. Goals are listed as posterior goals when the current plan does not refer to them; analysis of these goals can thus be safely postponed until some time after the current plan has been matched. Figure 4-12 shows an example of such a plan, the MAXIMUM PLAN. The MAXIMUM PLAN requires that at least one value be processed by the maximum update; otherwise the maximum is undefined. The method which is used in this plan for ensuring that at least one value is processed is to create a goal *Count*, to count the number of values being processed, and make sure that the counter is non-zero.

112

An exception condition is used to phrase the requirement that the counter be non-zero. However, the exception condition cannot be asserted until after the *Count* goal is analyzed, since the exception condition refers to it. Therefore the *Count* goal is listed as a prior goal, so that it will be processed before the MAXIMUM PLAN is matched.

MAXIMUM PLAN

Variables:
>   ?New, ?Max

Prior goals:
>   *Count*(?New *in goal Read & Process*)

Exception condition:
>   (?Count *in goal Count*) = 0

Template:

Init:	?Max := 0
	(*in* Process: *component of goal Read & Process*)
Guard:	if ?New > ?Max then
Update:	*subgoal Supercede Value*(?Max, ?New)

Figure 4-12:   A plan with a `PriorGoals` slot

`PriorGoals` slots are sometimes accompanied by `AddedBindings` slots. The `AddedBindings` slot indicates what the relationship is between the pattern variables in the prior goals and the pattern variables in the plan being matched.

4.4.4.2 Bug demons

It is sometimes useful to include plans in PROUST's knowledge base that are incorrect implementations of goals. Such plans are called *buggy plans*. Buggy plans are used to describe plans that are radically different from any correct plan, so that is easier to match the buggy plan rather than trying to match a correct plan and then try to explain the plan differences. In order to make a plan into a buggy plan, one or more *bug demons* are associated with the plan.

Bug demons are procedures stored in the `BugDemon` slots of plans. There are two cases in which bug demons are used. If a plan is always buggy, then the bug demon attached to the plan does nothing more than to assert the presence of the bug. This assertion is added to a database of facts about the program, as will be described

113

in chapter 6. In the other possible case, a plan is either correct or buggy depending upon the goal that the plan is being used to implement. In that case the bug demon first checks what goal is being implemented, and then declares the presence of the bug, if necessary. In retrospect, now that the conditions under which plans can be buggy is better understood, it would be desirable to replace most bug-demon procedures with a declarative description of the goal-plan configurations that can cause a plan to be buggy.

The EXCHANGE PLAN, shown in Figure 4-13, is an example of a plan which is buggy only in certain circumstances. The EXCHANGE PLAN exchanges the values of two variables. Novice programmers sometimes erroneously use the EXCHANGE PLAN when all that they need to do is assign the value of one variable to another. This can happen when the novices are trying to compute a maximum. Instead of writing

```
if New > Max then
    Max := New,
```

they write

```
if New > Max then
    begin
        Temp := New;
        New := Max;
        Max := Temp;
    end.
```

Once the exchange has been performed, the value of New is changed; subsequent usage of New can lead to incorrect results.

The bug demon attached to the EXCHANGE PLAN checks to see how the plan is being used, in order to determine whether or not it is buggy. It checks to see if the plan is intended to implement the goal *Supercede Value*. If so, it asserts that the plan is buggy.

4.5 PROUST's program representation

I will now describe the program representation that PROUST uses. Once this is done I will describe the process of matching plans against programs.

The basic program representation that PROUST uses is a syntax tree. PROUST

114

EXCHANGE PLAN

Variables:

```
        ?Var, ?Val, ?Temp
```

Template:

Update:

```
        begin
            ?Temp := ?Val
            ?Val := ?Var
            ?Var := ?Temp
        end
```

Bugdemons:

```
        ((λ (Inst)
            (if (eq? (Goal-Name (HistInst-PlanGoal Inst))
                     'SupercedeValue)
                (let ((NewBug (New-Bug 'WrongPlanForGoal)))
                    (set (Bug-HistInst NewBug) Inst)
                    (set (Bug-FoundStmt NewBug)
                        (car (LocalLabelBinding 'Update:
                                                Inst)))
                    (set (HistInst-BugReport Inst)
                        (cons NewBug
                              (HistInst-BugReport Inst)))))
            T))
```

Figure 4-13:   A bug demon which examines context

parses the program using a conventional lexer and parser.[10] After the syntax tree has been constructed, it is modified in order to make it more usable by PROUST. Recall that primitive components of PROUST's plans are Pascal statements, and the motivation was that statements usually denote what programmers regard as primitive actions. If a statement contains complex arithmetic expressions, the statement is likely to perform more than one action. Therefore complex statements must be broken up in PROUST's program representation in order to make it possible for the parts of such statements to match PROUST's plan components in a one-to-one fashion.

Arithmetic expressions are broken up by adding assignment statements which assign to intermediate variables. Thus a statement such as

---

[10]The particular parser that PROUST uses was generated by a modified version of *yacc* [40] which generates Lisp code.

```
        Avg := (Sum - 99999) / (Count - 1)
```

is translated into a sequence of statements such as

```
        G0001 := Sum - 99999;
        G0002 := Count - 1;
        Avg := G0001 / G0002.
```

There is a problem with breaking up expressions into subexpressions: bugs in the structure of arithmetic expressions can make an expression have different subcomponents than the student intended. For example, suppose that the student wrote

```
        Avg := Sum - 99999 / Count - 1,
```

where the order of precedence of Pascal operators is not observed. This would be rendered by PROUST as

```
        G0001 := 99999 / Count;
        G0002 := Sum - G0001;
        Avg := G0002 - 1.
```

PROUST is not able to make any sense of such a sequence of operations. Even though PROUST's program representation is reasonably low-level, it is too high-level for bugs involving operator precedence.[11]

4.6 Plan matching

Now that the plan representation and the program representation have been described, I will describe the process of matching plans against programs. The process of plan matching must do two things. First, it must identify exact matches of plans. Second, if no exact matches exist, it must identify partial matches, and describe the differences between the plan components and the code which is partially matched. In what follows, a definition of exact matches and partial matches will be given. Then the process which PROUST's plan matcher uses for identifying exact and partial matches will be described.

---

[11]A possible solution to this problem, suggested by Jim Spohrer, is to decompose arithmetic expressions as novice programmers do, rather than as Pascal operator precedence dictates.

4.6.1 Interpretation of plan templates

A plan in PROUST can be regarded as a collection of component patterns, each of which matches one or more Pascal statements. The organization of the plan components dictates the relative position of the statements matching the plan components in the program. Thus a plan expression such as

```
if ?New > ?Max then
    ?Max := ?New
```

consists of two components, an `if` pattern and an assignment statement pattern. Since the assignment statement pattern is enclosed within the `if` statement pattern, the statement which matches the assignment statement pattern must be enclosed within the `if` statement that matches the `if` statement pattern.

Suppose that the `if` pattern in the above expression has been matched against the program, and we are now trying to match the assignment-statement pattern against an assignment statement in the program. There are two reasons why the match might fail. First, the assignment statement being matched might be of the wrong form, e.g., it is something like `Max := Max + 1` instead of `Max := New`. Second, the match could fail because the assignment statement is in the wrong place, i.e., it is not enclosed in the `if` statement that matches the `if` pattern.

Thus there are two questions to answer in defining how plans match against programs. First, when does a statement match a plan component, assuming that it is in the proper place in the program? Second, where must a statement appear in a program in order to be considered to be in the proper place? Each of these questions will be addressed below.

4.6.1.1 Matching statements

The criteria which determine whether or not a pattern matches a statement exactly are just as one would expect. For a pattern to match a statement, the pattern and the statement must be the same type of statement, e.g., `if` statement patterns can match only `if` statements. Each sub-expression in the pattern must match the corresponding sub-expression of the statement. If the pattern contains a pattern variable, and the variable is bound, then the corresponding expression in the statement must match the binding of the pattern variable. If a pattern variable is unbound, it can match any expression, provided that it is of the right type; e.g., if the pattern variable is constant-valued, it can match any constant.

A statement matches a plan component partially if it is conceivably construable as a buggy realization of the plan component. The following definition of "conceivably construable" is built into PROUST's plan matcher. Any statement can be considered a partial match if it is the same type of statement as the statement pattern, e.g., all assignment statements are partial matches of assignment statement patterns. Furthermore, a statement is considered a partial match if it is a type of statement that sometimes is used by novices in place of the statement pattern's statement type. In particular, novices sometimes use `while` statements in place of `if` statements, and counter updates in place of `read` statements. Therefore `while` statements are partial matches of `if` statement patterns, and assignment statements are partial matches of `read` and `readln` statement patterns. This definition of partial match succeeds in identifying all known buggy realizations of plan components. It also includes some statements which could not possibly be buggy realizations of the plan components. However, it is not the job of the plan matcher to determine what is a plausible bug; its job is only to determine where buggy implementations might be found, and match them against the plan component if necessary.

4.6.1.2 Locating statements within a program

A statement is considered to be in the right location to match a plan component if its syntactic position in the program mirrors the location of the plan component in the plan. We saw this in the example of the `if` pattern and the assignment pattern discussed above. In addition, statements outside of the position dictated by the plan are acceptable matches, provided that there are no data-flow conflicts between the expected position and the actual position. That is, it should be possible to move the statement into the position that the plan expects without changing the behavior of the program. Determining with certainty whether or not behavior is affected is difficult in general; however, data-flow conflicts do indicate places where behavior *might* be affected. Subsequent analysis can determine whether or not the data-flow conflicts are significant.

Figure 4-14 shows two different code fragments which one might wish to match

118

against the SENTINEL PROCESS-READ WHILE PLAN. Fragment A matches the plan, even though two of the statements are slightly out of place. There is an assignment statement `Max := New` between the input statement and the loop, which the plan does not call for. The plan also indicates that the other input statement should be at the bottom of the loop, but instead there is a `writeln` statement between the input and the end of the loop. Neither of these differences are significant, because they do not affect the data flow of the loop. Fragment B, however, does not match the plan. There is an assignment `New := Count` between the initial input statement and the loop; this clobbers `New`. Therefore the data-flow constraints of the plan are violated.

Fragment A

```
read( New );
Max := New;
while New<>99999 do
  begin
    Writeln( 'Enter next value' );
    if New>Max then
      Max := New;
    read( New );
    writeln( 'The value entered was ', New )
  end;
```

Fragment B

```
read( New );
New := Count;
while New<>99999 do
  begin
    ...
    read( New );
  end;
```

Figure 4-14: Loops with and without data-flow conflicts

PROUST permits plan components to appear in a variety of different positions in a program, but it always assumes that each plan component appears in exactly one place. Two different statements are not allowed to match the same plan component.

A statement can be considered to match a plan component partially on grounds of

119

location in the program if the statement could conceivably be misplaced by mistake. Novices misplace statements in their programs in a variety of different ways. A common problem is to place above or below a loop code which belongs inside the loop, or to place inside the loop code which belongs outside. As a consequence, most any statement in a program can be considered a partial match on the basis of location in the program.

4.6.2 Plan compilation

Before a plan can be used by the plan matcher, it must be compiled. PROUST's plan compiler breaks each plan apart into its individual components, orders the components, and determines where to look in the program for matches to each plan component.

There are a couple of reasons why plans are compiled before being given to PROUST's plan matcher. One reason is that if the plan matcher were to use use plans directly as they appear in PROUST's plan notation, it would have to decide at run time in what order to match plan components. Some plan component patterns are more ambiguous than others, and matching ambiguous components first can widen the search for the right plan match. For example, the top-most plan component in the RUNNING TOTAL PLAN is `?Total := 0`. If this component were matched first, before the binding of `?Total` is known, then it could match any initialization in the program. If the update step were matched first, however, ambiguous matching is less likely to occur. The plan compiler examines each plan and determines what the optimal ordering of plan components should be, so that ordering need not be performed at run time. The heuristics for optimal ordering of plan components are described in detail in Section 8.2.2.

Another reason why plan compilation is desirable is to support parallel matching of plans. The plan matcher is designed to match a number of plans simultaneously, and to interrupt the matching of one plan and switch to another if match errors occur. Saving the state of the matcher and then restoring it when switching from one plan to another is potentially tricky, particularly since the order in which components are matched does not necessary follow the order in which they appear in the plan. When matching of a plan resumes it would be hard to tell which components have

120

been matched so far and which component should be matched next. Because the plan compiler breaks the plans apart into individual components, and places the components in a linear sequence, it is easy for the plan matcher to interrupt and resume matching. In order to resume matching the plan the plan matcher need only maintain a pointer into the list of plan components, and start matching where the pointer indicates.

As we have seen, the relative position of each statement matching a component of a plan is determined by the configuration of the components in the plan. When the components are pulled apart, this information is lost. The plan compiler therefore creates for each plan component an explicit description of the region of the program which should be searched for a match. Suppose, for example, that a plan has two components, an initialization and a loop, and the plan compiler decides that the loop should be matched first. Then the plan compiler would indicate that the loop can appear anywhere in the program, and the initialization should appear immediately above the loop just found.

4.6.3 The plan matcher

PROUST's plan matcher works as follows. It creates a vector of the same length as the number of plan components in the plan. This vector will hold the results of the match. The plan components are then matched one at a time. A set of possible matches for each plan component are collected, and the plan component is matched against each match candidate in turn. The exact and partial matches are then stored in the vector of match results. For each partial match, a list of the differences between the plan and the match candidate is also stored.

Ordinarily the plan matcher will process one component after another, until all of the components have been matched. There are two reasons why matching might be interrupted. First, if no exact match is found for a component, the matching stops and the partial matches and their corresponding plan differences are passed to the plan-difference rule applier. It must decide which partial match is the correct one, after which the matching can resume. Second, if a plan component is a subgoal, plan matching is interrupted so that the subgoal can be analyzed and mapped onto the program.

121

Candidates for matching against a plan component are selected as follows. At first, the plan matcher considers only those candidates which might possibly be exact matches. In other words, it focuses on those statements which are in the region of the program dictated by the plan component, and only those which are the same type of statement as the statement pattern. Thus if the plan component is an assignment statement which should appear above a loop, the plan matcher will first consider all assignment statements above the loop. If none of these statements match exactly, the plan matcher will consider any statement which might be a partial match. This includes statements which are in the wrong place in the program, as well as `while` statements in place of `if` statements and assignments in place of input statements.

A table is constructed for each program at parse time listing where each type of statement occurs in the program. This table is used by the plan matcher to look up candidate matches.

If the plan matcher finds mismatches while matching a statement against a plan component, it records it in a list of errors which is saved in the record of the match. These errors are denoted as dotted pairs, where the `car` of the pair is the expected pattern, and the `cdr` is the portion of the statement which it corresponds to. The matching process does not stop when it encounters an error, but continues and tries to match the subcomponents of the pattern if this is possible. Thus for example if the plan component pattern is (`while` (<> ?New ?Stop) ??), and the statement is `if 99999 > Rain then ...`, then, assuming that ?New is bound to `Rain` and ?Stop is bound to 99999, the following list of match errors will be generated:

```
(while . if)
(<> . <)
(?New . 99999)
(?Stop . Rain)
```

4.7 Problems with PROUST's plan and program representations

PROUST's plan representation and plan matching mechanism do a fairly good job of analyzing student programs and collecting the information that is required in order to find their bugs. Unfortunately there are limits to effectiveness of any one representation for plans. PROUST's representation is too literal in some circumstances,

122

and too abstract in others. Changing the representation to work better with some programs will make the representation harder to use on other programs.

One type of problematic case involves missing parentheses, as described earlier. If the student types `Sum - 99999/ Count - 1` instead of `(Sum - 99999) / (Count - 1)`, then PROUST becomes confused. In these cases PROUST makes unwarranted assumptions about the kinds of bugs which can occur; its representation for arithmetic expressions is not literal enough.

In other cases, however, PROUST's representation of arithmetic expressions is too literal. By breaking up complex expressions into component computations, PROUST fails to recognize equivalent reorderings of arithmetic operators. The expressions `A + B +C + D` and `D + C + B + A` would look very different to PROUST, even though they are equivalent. The reader will encounter several plans in Appendix II which are equivalent except that computations are performed in different orders.

The ultimate solution will have to be to abandon the notion of a unique plan, program, and plan-difference program representation. PROUST will have to use a higher-level representation in ordinary cases, to keep from being thrown off by irrelevant variability. When a match fails, the plan differences will have to be described both in terms of syntactic differences and functional differences. Then bug analysis of the plan differences could make use of whatever level of description is useful.

4.8 Summary

The chapter has discussed the role of plans in an intention-based diagnosis system such as PROUST. The requirements for a plan representation for novice programs was presented. PROUST's actual representation was then presented, and related to the requirements for the representation. The mechanisms for matching plans against programs were then described. Although this chapter describes how plans are represented and manipulated in PROUST, it does not describe how PROUST chooses which plans to match against a program. This will be discussed in the next two chapters.

5 Problem Descriptions

Earlier chapters have indicated that effective diagnosis of errors in programs requires the ability to analyze the programmer's intentions, i.e., the programmer's goals and the programmer's plans for realizing those goals. The previous chapter gave an overview of plans in PROUST. This chapter will begin to discuss goals, in particular how goals are stated in problem descriptions. PROUST starts out with a description of the problem that the programmer is working on. Assuming that the programmer intends to solve the stated problem, the problem statement provides information about the programmer's intentions. PROUST must then relate the problem to the student's solution, to determine the programmer's goal decomposition, and its realization in the code. This chapter describes PROUST's problem descriptions. The next chapter describes the process of deriving goal decompositions from problem descriptions and relating them to the students' programs.

The ultimate goal would be to have the instructor enter a problem statement, in English, and have PROUST automatically extract information which it needs to analyze solutions. This goal is far from being achieved at the present time. What is described here are some intermediate steps: a) determining what information is needed by PROUST in order to interpret student programs, b) deriving a description language which encapsulates this information, and c) exploring how such problem descriptions can be derived by hand from English problem statements. The work presented here is exploratory; PROUST's vocabulary for describing intentions is still quite limited. The principles motivating PROUST's problem description language appear to apply to a wide range of introductory programming assignments. However, analysis of student solutions to a wider range of programming problems must be done in order to test this.

The discussion in this chapter will proceed as follows. First I will explain why it is necessary to describe programming problems to PROUST. I will show how knowledge of the problem can be used to predict the variety of goal decompositions in novice programs. Important characteristics of a problem description language for intention-based analysis will be described. An example will be presented of how problem descriptions are derived from natural-language problem statements. Then I will describe PROUST's problem description language, and discuss the assumptions underlying the design of this language, and the generality of the language.

Before proceeding, I will define some terminology which will be used throughout the discussion. *Goal decompositions*, first described in Section 3.5.3, are accounts of the goals underlying a program and their realization. They relate goals to the means by which the goals are implemented, i.e., subgoals and plans. They also describe the operations that are performed on goals in the process of program design, e.g., refinement, elaboration, reformulation, and recombination. *Problem statements* will always be taken to mean the natural-language problem statement which is given to the students. "Problem descriptions" will be taken to mean the problem descriptions which are given to PROUST in PROUST's special problem description language.

5.1 Why problem descriptions are necessary

As was indicated in Section 3.5.3, a major problem for program error diagnosis systems is accounting for variations in goal decompositions of programs. The problem arises when a system is trying to analyze a fragment of code for bugs, and there are no obvious anomalies in the code. In such a case the system can be certain that the code is buggy only if the system knows what the code fragment is supposed to do, how it is supposed to relate to other parts of the program, and whether the intended design is correct. Then the code can be shown to be buggy either if the programmer's intentions are incorrect or if the code fails to realize the programmer's intentions. If different goal decompositions are possible for a program, one cannot know *a priori* how the program is intended to work, so it is not possible to determine with assurance whether or not there is a bug.

An intention-based diagnosis system such as PROUST therefore needs a way of determining what the possible goal decompositions are. PROUST predicts possible goal decompositions automatically from the problem description. The advantage of this

126

approach is that it is the best way of getting a handle on the variability in novice programs. Novice programmers may solve programming problems in a variety of different ways, and their programs may exhibit a variety of different bugs, but the problem that they are working on is fixed. Novices sometimes deviate from the stated problem in certain ways. They may write the program incrementally, in which case the program satisfies a subset of the problem requirements. They may misinterpret the problem, or they may ignore some of the problem requirements in order to use a programming construct that they have just learned. Even in these cases, however, most of the student's intentions can be related back to the problem requirements. Thus the problem statement is a good place to start in trying to understand what a program is supposed to do. The disadvantage of deriving goal decompositions automatically from problem descriptions is that it requires a much richer knowledge base describing program requirements and their realizations than otherwise would be necessary.

5.1.1 The alternative: enumerating goal decompositions

In order to justify problem descriptions as a basis for program analysis, let us examine the alternative, namely to enumerate explicitly the possible goal decompositions for the problem. A restricted form of goal-decomposition enumeration has been used as a basis for hand analyses of program bugs [64, 63]. In order for enumeration of be effective in an automatic bug diagnosis system, the debugging system would have to determine which goal decomposition is applicable to the student's program. Once this is done, however, the goal decomposition would provide the basis for predicting the plans that the student used in his/her program.

Enumerating possible goal decompositions for a problem is a non-trivial task. We must consider not only the range of correct goal decompositions, but also the range of buggy goal decompositions resulting from misinterpretations of the problem. A simple misinterpretation of the problem can result in a goal decomposition that is radically different from any correct goal decomposition. A complete enumeration of goal decompositions requires careful analysis of the programming problem, and of students' programs, in order to identify misinterpretations that the students are likely to make.

Figure 5-1 shows how a single misinterpretation of a programming problem can result in a goal decomposition which differs significantly from correct goal decompositions. This program is supposed to be a solution to the Rainfall Problem. It has the following bugs:

1. there is an error in the code which checks input for validity -- instead of checking the input to see if it is nonnegative, it checks the input to see if it is positive;

2. there should be two counters, one to count positive values and one to count nonnegative values; instead there is only one;

3. the average is computed using the count of positive inputs, instead of the count of nonnegative inputs (which does not exist, due to the fact that there is only one counter);

4. there is an output statement missing (only one counter is output).

The probable cause for these errors is that the student believed that both zero input and negative input are invalid, instead of just negative input. Therefore there is no distinction between valid input and positive input, so there is only need for one counter instead of two, and likewise one fewer output statement is needed. Thus a single misinterpretation of the problem statement can result in a radically different goal decomposition for the problem.

The number of goal decompositions resulting from misinterpretations of requirements, together with those resulting correct interpretations of requirements, can be quite large. Enumerating the possible goal decompositions beforehand might save PROUST some work, but it would be a laborious task, and not one which could be performed by class instructors. Furthermore, minor changes in problem requirements might make it necessary to derive a completely new set of goal decompositions. In order to make sure that the enumeration of goal decompositions is complete, and in order to avoid duplicating effort when new problems are assigned, a program which automatically generates goal decompositions would be desirable. That of course would simply consist of taking PROUST's goal decomposition generator and making it an off-line program. Either way automatic generation of goal decompositions from problem descriptions is necessary.

128

```
        while New <> 99999 do
          begin
            if New <= 0 then
              writeln('This input is in error')
            else
              begin
                Count := Count + 1;
                Sum := Sum + New;
                if Max < New then
                  Max := New;
              end;
            read(New);
          end;
        if Count > 0 then
          begin
            Avg := Sum / Count;
            Writeln('The average is ', Avg);
            Writeln('The maximum is ', Max);
            Writeln('The number of valid inputs is ', Count);
          end;
```

Figure 5-1:   A program with bugs resulting from problem misinterpretation

5.2 Requirements for a problem description language

The problem descriptions which PROUST uses must provide sufficient information so that PROUST can predict the likely goal decompositions of problem solutions. The problem statement itself certainly provides such information. Given a good enough model of program synthesis, one could predict goal decompositions by modeling the entire process which people go through in solving a programming problem. However, many of the steps in understanding and solving a programming problem, such as parsing the natural-language problem statements, do not account for significant variability in goal decompositions. As we shall see later in this chapter, it is the meaning of the problem statement which is important; the wording of the problem statement plays a very limited role. PROUST's problem descriptions therefore are paraphrases of the original problem statements, in a language which is easier for PROUST to manipulate than English. They preserve the content of the problem statement, as well as much of the informality of the problem statement. This information, and its informality, enables PROUST to predict both correct and buggy goal decompositions of problem solutions.

Various formal languages have been developed for specifying programming problems [5, 33, 37, 38, 71]. These existing specification languages are unsuitable as a basis for intention-based diagnosis. Formal specification languages are designed to enable one to carry out a rigorous derivation process, frequently using transformation rules, resulting in some program which is guaranteed to fit the specification. Intention-based diagnosis, on the other hand, requires a language which makes it possible to predict the range of solutions which programmers actually generate, both correct and incorrect. Formal specification languages support the use of formal inference mechanisms in deriving a program. PROUST's problem description language supports reasoning which is modeled after what people actually do in writing programs.

There are two kinds of informality which can appear in problem statements. One type of informality, analyzed by Balzer, Goldman, and Wile, [4], is *linguistic informality*. This kind of informality results from the use of linguistic devices such as ellipsis and anaphoric reference which result in incomplete descriptions of the requirements. The second type of informality, which might be called *semantic informality*, results when requirements are incomplete or ambiguous. If a set of requirements are semantically informal, the programmer will have to draw on his own knowledge to fill in the gaps in the requirements. PROUST's problem description language does not address the issue of linguistic informality, because it sidesteps the issue of natural language interpretation altogether. Instead, PROUST's problem description language attempts to capture the semantic informality of problem statements.

There is nothing new in designing an informal problem description language such as PROUST's. Specification languages which lack a formal semantics tend by default to have the kind of informal characteristics that are needed by PROUST. The difference in PROUST's case is that this informality is considered a virtue, not a vice.

In order to understand the role of semantic informality in requirements descriptions, let us examine closely a requirements description in an existing informal specification language, PSL [66]. Figure 5-2 shows the description of a module which is supposed to interpret time cards and produce a pay statement.[12] This description is specified in too much detail for a typical programming problem, since a sketch of the procedure is included as well as a summary of the requirements. However, note how this description uses informal means to describe the problem. It uses names for the input and output data, such as `time-card` and `hourly-employee-report`, which are never defined; the implementor must either go find out what the form of these should be, or else must design something appropriate. Parts of the input-output description are missing; for example, the procedure refers to a "department record" which is not listed among the inputs and outputs. Other parts of the problem require world knowledge to be elaborated. For example, when the requirements say to "compute tax", nothing is said about what taxes are actually to be computed. This does not mean that the implementor has the freedom to design a tax to apply to the employee's pay. Relations between objects are sometimes left unspecified; for example, a status code is mentioned, but nowhere is it indicated where that status code is to be found. Clearly a large measure of the work of implementing these requirements would be involved in interpreting and elaborating them. Errors in requirements analysis would also be responsible for a large portion of the bugs in implementations of these requirements.

5.3 Derivation of problem descriptions

In order to illustrate the properties of PROUST's problem descriptions, I will now present an example of constructing a problem description from a problem statement. The problem statement which I will analyze is the Rainfall Problem, the text of which appears in Figure 5-3. This example will give some sense of what information is retained, what information is discarded, and how the information is rendered into an appropriate form. It will also show what kinds of informality are retained in problem descriptions, and what kinds are discarded. The process of constructing problem

---

[12]This example is taken from (Teichreow and Hershey 1977), p.45, with the permission of the publisher.

```
PROCESS hourly-employee-processing;
    DESCRIPTION:
        this process performs those actions needed to interpret
        time cards to produce a pay statement for each hourly
        employee.;
    KEYWORDS:    independent;
    ATTRIBUTES ARE:
        complexity-level high;
    GENERATES:       pay-statement, error-listing,
                     hourly-employee-report;
    RECEIVES:        time-card;
    SUBPARTS ARE:    hourly-paycheck-validation, hourly-emp-update,
                     h-report-entry-generation,
                     hourly-paycheck-production;
    PART OF:         payroll-processing;
    DERIVES:         pay-statement
        USING:       time-card, hourly-employee-record;
    DERIVES:         hourly-employee-report
        USING:       time-card, hourly-employee-record;
    DERIVES:         error-listing
        USING:       time-card, hourly-employee-record;
    PROCEDURE:
        1. compute gross pay from time card data.
        2. compute tax from gross pay.
        3. subtract tax from gross pay to obtain net pay.
        4. update hourly employee record accordingly.
        5. update department record accordingly.
        6. generate paycheck.
      note: if status code specifies that the employee did not work
        this week, no processing will be done for this employee.;
    HAPPENS:
        number-of-payments TIMES-PER pay-period;
    TRIGGERED BY:    hourly-emp-processing-event;
    TERMINATION-CAUSES:
                     new-employee-processing-event;
    SECURITY IS:     company-only;
```

Figure 5-2: An example of a PSL/PSA problem description

descriptions is currently done by hand. However, there has been some effort to make the process as methodical as possible, so as to avoid producing problem descriptions which do not properly reflect the problem statement.

The first step in analyzing a problem statement is to break up the problem statement into individual propositions. A sentence such as "Noah needs to keep track

132

Noah needs to keep track of rainfall in the New Haven area in order to determine when to launch his ark. Write a Pascal program that will help him do this. The program should prompt the user to input numbers from the terminal; each input stands for the amount of rainfall in New Haven for a day. Note: since rainfall cannot be negative, the program should reject negative input. Your program should compute the following statistics from this data:

1. the average rainfall per day;

2. the number of rainy days.

3. the number of valid inputs (excluding any invalid data that might have been read in);

4. the maximum amount of rain that fell on any one day.

The program should read data until the user types 99999; this is a sentinel value signaling the end of input. Do not include the 99999 in the calculations. Assume that if the input value is non-negative, and not equal to 99999, then it is valid input data.

Figure 5-3: The Rainfall Problem

of rainfall in the New Haven area in order to determine when to launch his ark" consists of several propositions:

- Noah needs to keep track of rainfall.

- The location where the rainfall is being measured is in New Haven.

- This will enable Noah to determine when to launch his ark.

Splitting a problem statement into propositions makes it easier to see what information is really being conveyed by the problem statement.

The next step is to sort out the propositions which novices are likely to use in solving the problem. Information such as "the location of the rainfall is New Haven" will not affect the form of the novices' solutions, so such information is dropped. Some experience with novice programs is required to know what information will be used by novices, and what role it will play. Nevertheless, I find that as long as the problem statement is reasonably clear, it is fairly easy to tell what the novices will regard as relevant. The significant propositions, or groups of propositions, in the Rainfall Problem are shown in Figure 5-4.

1. Read the rainfall for each day.

2. Rainfall cannot be negative.

3. The program should reject negative input.

4. Print out the average rainfall per day.

5. Print out the number of rainy days.

6. Print out the number of valid inputs.

7. Print out the maximum amount of rainfall that fell on any one day.

8. Read the data until "99999" is read.

9. "99999" is a sentinel indicating the end of input.

10. Do not include the "99999" in the calculations.

11. If the data is not negative or 99999, it is valid.

Figure 5-4: Individual requirements in the Rainfall Problem

The next step in the analysis process is to classify and sort the various propositions, in order to identify those which define properties of data, and those which describe program goals. Redundant statements are removed. Many of the propositions contain pronouns and make oblique references to data objects; these must be made explicit. This can be done by giving names to some of the data objects. The Rainfall Problem makes frequent reference to the rain data, for example; this data is given the name `?Rainfall:DailyRain`. `"Rainfall"` indicates that this is the Rainfall Problem, and `"DailyRain"` is the name of the particular data object in the Rainfall Problem. Once these steps are done, we have something such as in Figure 5-5.

In order to complete the problem description, the goals have to be translated into instances of PROUST's goals, and the objects have to be translated into instances of PROUST's object classes. The mapping onto PROUST's goals may be many-to-one. For example, *Sentinel-Controlled Input Sequence* subsumes both the proposition `"read ?Rainfall:DailyRain repeatedly"` and `"stop when ?Rainfall:DailyRain`

134

- Data Objects:

    1. ?Rainfall:DailyRain is a scalar measurement.

    2. 99999 is a sentinel indicating the end of input.

- Goals:

    1. Read ?Rainfall:DailyRain repeatedly.

    2. Stop when ?Rainfall:DailyRain = 99999.

    3. If ?Rainfall:DailyRain is negative, reject it.

    4. Print out the average rainfall per day over the period.

    5. Print out the number of rainy days.

    6. Print out the number of valid days.

    7. Print out the maximum amount of rainfall that fell on any one day.

Figure 5-5:   Sorted requirements

= 99999". The important thing is that the goals which are selected out of PROUST's repertoire convey similar information to what was in the original wording of the goals. The object classes are intended to represent the real-world concepts which the data objects are instances of. Programmers use their knowledge of the world to determine the role these concepts play in a programming context. Likewise, PROUST should be able to use its knowledge about a concept in order to determine how the data is likely to be manipulated in the student's program. For example, the important fact about rainfall for this program is that it is a scalar measurement; it is real-valued and non-negative. Therefore ?Rainfall:DailyRain is declared to be a member of the object class ScalarMeasurement. PROUST can then apply its knowledge about the ScalarMeasurement class to determine how the rainfall data is likely to be represented in novices' programs. The result of the translation of the Rainfall Problem into PROUST's notation appears in Figure 5-6.

There is relatively little informality in the problem description for the Rainfall Problem; this is because the original problem statement was fairly precise and

```
DefProgram Rainfall;

DefObject ?Rainfall:DailyRain ObjectClass ScalarMeasurement;

DefGoal Sentinel-Controlled Input Sequence(?Rainfall:DailyRain, 99999);
DefGoal Loop Input Validation(?Rainfall:DailyRain, ?Rainfall:DailyRain<0);
DefGoal Output(Average(?Rainfall:DailyRain));
DefGoal Output(Count( ?Rainfall:DailyRain ));
DefGoal Output(Guarded Count(?Rainfall:DailyRain, ?Rainfall:DailyRain>0));
DefGoal Output(Maximum(?Rainfall:DailyRain));
```

Figure 5-6: The Rainfall Problem in PROUST's notation

unambiguous. However, we can identify one kind of informality in this example: absence of detail. The problem statement and the problem description do not say anything about what happens when the number of valid inputs is zero, for example. The output which a solution to this problem would produce would be meaningless in this case, and solutions to the problem should make provision for this. Object classes are another potential source of informality. If a real-world concept has a variety of information associated with it, it may be unclear what information is really relevant to the programming problem. However, the object class used in the Rainfall Problem, `ScalarMeasurement`, is unambiguous. I will consider more informal object class descriptions later in this chapter.

5.4 Goals in problem statements and problem descriptions

As we saw in the previous example, problem descriptions in PROUST consist of two parts:

- a set of descriptions of objects which the program must manipulate, and

- a set of goals which must be satisfied.

This section discusses programming goals and their representation in PROUST's problem description language. Section 5.5 will discuss object descriptions.

I will start by describing the goal description notation, and show how it relates to natural-language descriptions of goals. Then I will discuss some of the assumptions underlying the representation. The process of translating a problem statement into a problem description for PROUST causes some information in the problem statement to be modified or elaborated, and some information to be lost. The underlying

136

assumptions concerning what information is safe to modify and what information is safe to delete must be explained and justified. I will also discuss the kinds of variability that PROUST's goal descriptions can and cannot support. There is some evidence that problem statements affect novices' solutions in ways that PROUST's problem description language cannot make allowances for. However, in each case, the evidence is either inconclusive, or else the problem can be avoided, given a certain amount of care in constructing problem statements.

5.4.1 Goals in problem descriptions

The following discussion will draw numerous examples from the Rainfall Problem and the Bank Problem. The Rainfall Problem statement appeared in Figure 5-3, and PROUST's description of the problem appeared in Figure 5-6. The Bank Problem statement appears in Figure 5-7, and PROUST's description of it is in Figure 5-8.[13]

Write a Pascal program that processes three types of bank transactions: withdrawals, deposits, and a special transaction that says: no more transactions are to follow. Your program should start by asking the user to input his/her account id and his/her initial balance. Then your program should prompt the user to input

1. the transaction type, and

2. If it is an END-PROCESSING transaction the program should print out the (a) final balance of the user's account, (b) the total number of transactions, and (c) total number of each type of transaction, and (d) the total amount of the service charges, and stop;

3. if it is a DEPOSIT or a WITHDRAWAL, the program should ask for the amount of the transaction and then post it appropriately.

Use a variable of type CHAR to encode the transaction types. To encourage saving, charge the user 20 cents per withdrawal, but nothing for a deposit.

Figure 5-7: The Bank Problem

Each goal is a name followed by a set of arguments. For example, in the goal

---

[13]The actual representation used in PROUST is an S-Expression notation. I have added syntactic sugar to the description in order to make it easier to read.

137

```
DefProgram Bank;
DefObject ?Bank:InData
     Type char, ObjectClass SingleLetterCommand,
     Range MultiValued, Values (?Bank:DTrans, ?Bank:WTrans, ?Bank:ETrans);
DefObject ?Bank:DTrans Value 'd';
DefObject ?Bank:WTrans Value 'w';
DefObject ?Bank:ETrans Value 'e';
DefObject ?Bank:AcctID ObjectClass AccountNumber, Range MultiValued;
DefObject ?Bank:Balance ObjectClass AccountBalance, Range MultiValued;
DefObject ?Bank:Deposit ObjectClass TransactionAmount,
                         Range MultiValued;
DefObject ?Bank:Withdrawal ObjectClass WithdrawalAmount,
                           Range MultiValued;
DefObject ?Bank:Charge ObjectClass DollarAmount, Value 0.20;
DefObject ?Bank:WithdrawalCount ObjectClass NaturalNumber,
                                Range MultiValued;
DefObject ?Bank:DepositCount ObjectClass NaturalNumber,
                             Range MultiValued;
DefObject ?Bank:TotalCharge ObjectClass DollarAmount,
                            Range MultiValued;
DefObject ?Bank:TotalCount ObjectClass NaturalNumber,
                           Range MultiValued;


DefGoal Input1 = Input(?Bank:AcctID);
DefGoal Input2 = Input(?Bank:Balance);
DefGoal Loop1 = Sentinel-Controlled Input Sequence (?Bank:InData,
                                                    ?Bank:ETrans);
Input1 Precedes Loop1;
Input2 Precedes Loop1;
DefGoal When(?Bank:InData=?Bank:DTrans,
             GoalBlock(Input(?Bank:Deposit);
                       Accumulate(?Bank:Balance, ?Bank:Deposit);
                       Bind ?Bank:DepositCount = Count(?Bank:InData)));
DefGoal When(?Bank:InData=?Bank:WTrans, GoalBlock(
          Input( ?Bank:Withdrawal);
          CompoundDeduct(?Bank:Withdrawal, ?Bank:Charge, ?Bank:Balance);
          GuardException(Update: component of CompoundDeduct,
                         ?Bank:Withdrawal >= ?Bank:Balance - ?Bank:Charge);
          Bind ?Bank:TotalCharge = ConstantSum(?Bank:Charge);
          Bind ?Bank:WithdrawalCount = Count(?Bank:InData));
Bind ?Bank:TotalCount = Count(?Bank:InData);
DefGoal Output(?Bank:TotalCharge);
DefGoal Output(?Bank:TotalCount);
DefGoal Output(?Bank:DepositCount);
DefGoal Output(?Bank:WithdrawalCount);
```

Figure 5-8:   PROUST's description of the Bank Problem

$$Average(\text{?Rainfall:DailyRain}),$$

the name of the goal is *Average* and the argument is `?Rainfall:DailyRain`. This goal corresponds to the English phrase "compute the average rainfall per day over the period", where `?Rainfall:DailyRain` denotes the rainfall per day.

`DefGoal` statements are used to declare goals in problem descriptions. They either contain just a goal expression, as in

$$\text{DefGoal } Average(\text{?Rainfall:DailyRain}),$$

or they also include a name to give to the goal expression, as in

$$\text{DefGoal Input1} = Input(\text{?Bank:AcctId}).$$

This latter statement, taken from the Bank Problem description, declares the goal *Input*(`?Bank:AcctId`), and gives it the name `Input1`. Since there are several *Input* goals in the Bank Problem description, the unique name is needed to allow other goals and statements in the problem description to refer uniquely to the account-ID input goal.

The arguments in goal expressions can be data objects, expressions, code, and other goals. A particularly complex goal expression, which contains various types of arguments, is the following:

```
DefGoal When(?Bank:InData=?Bank:DTrans,
             GoalBlock(Input(?Bank:Deposit);
                       Accumulate(?Bank:Balance, ?Bank:Deposit);
                       Bind ?Bank:DepositCount = Count(?Bank:InData)));
```

This is a paraphrase of the following:

> If the transaction is a DEPOSIT, the program should ask for the amount of the transaction and then post it appropriately.

When is a goal specifying that a requirement be asserted whenever a condition holds true. It thus is a test-action pair, similar to demons in GIST [5]. *When* takes two arguments: the first is a predicate describing the condition under which the requirements are asserted; the second argument is the requirement which is asserted. The second argument of *When* goals are themselves goals; in this example the argument is a *GoalBlock* goal. *GoalBlock* is simply a means for grouping a list of goals together; each of its arguments must be goals. Thus the goals which are really asserted when the predicate is true are the *Input* goal, the *Accumulate* goal, and the *Count* goal.

139

Goals in problem descriptions are usually unordered. Although *Output* (?Bank:DepositCount) precedes *Output* (?Bank:WithdrawalCount) in the Bank Problem description, the codes which satisfy these two goals could be in either order in a program. Sometimes, however, an explicit ordering is required by the problem statement. In the Bank Problem the program must first ask the user to input his/her account id and his/her initial balance, and then input the transactions. In such cases Precedes statements are added to make the ordering explicit. The Bank Problem description uses two Precedes statements, Input1 Precedes Loop1 and Input2 Precedes Loop1.

Some goals involve the generation of values; goals which refer to these goals either refer to the goal itself or to the value generated by the goal, depending upon the goal. Or to put it another way, we use a convenient shorthand of writing a goal form instead of writing the value which that goal form generates, if no other goal refers to the value. Thus, for example, the form *Output* (*Count* (?Bank:InData)) uses this notation. The *Output* goal refers not to the *Count* goal itself but to the value which this goal generates, namely the count of values of ?Bank:InData.

Conversely, if we want to give a name to the value which is generated by a goal, we use the Bind statement. This has the form

Bind \<name\> = \<goal\>.

This defines a data object whose value is generated by the goal. For example, the data object denoting the count of withdrawal transactions in the Bank Problem is defined using the statement Bind ?Bank:WithdrawalCount = *Count* (?Bank:InData).

5.4.2 Assumptions underlying the goal representation

Let us now examine some of the assumptions underlying the design of PROUST's problem description language. This will show why PROUST's problem descriptions provide sufficient information for predicting variability in novice programs.

5.4.2.1 Problem description lists only explicitly mentioned goals

An important characteristic of PROUST's problem descriptions is that, whenever possible, goals are not listed in the problem description unless they are explicitly mentioned in the problem statement. PROUST must be able to predict which goals are likely to be included in a novice's goal decomposition and which may be omitted. Novice programmers are not very good at recognizing when implicit goals need to be added. This is particularly true if the implicit goal is a boundary condition check. Consequently, if a goal is inferrable from the problem description, I have attempted to build sufficient knowledge into PROUST so that it would be possible for PROUST to make the same inferences. When PROUST makes such an inference it can be prepared for the possibility that the novice has failed to make the same inference.

5.4.2.2 Ordered vs. unordered goals

PROUST's problem descriptions do not indicate ordering relations between goals unless those ordering relations are indicated explicitly in the problem statement. However, novices do tend to follow implicit orderings in problem statements. An example of an implicit ordering in a problem statement is the following:

Your program should compute the following statistics from the data:

- the average rainfall per day;

- the number of rainy days;

- the number of valid inputs (excluding any invalid data that might have been read in);

- the maximum amount of rain that fell on any one day.

The four goals listed here have been presented in a particular order. Although expert programmers ignore such orderings, novice programmers are more likely to write code which mirrors the ordering of statements in the problem statement.

Although novices tend to order the plans in their program in the same order as the goals are mentioned in the problem statement, this does not lead to bugs. If ordering the plans in the same way that they appear in the problem statement would result in bugs, novices generally reorder the plans. The one exception which I have seen is the following. In the Rainfall Problem statement, the goal to check the input for validity appears after the goal to read in the input. Three students in one class, out of a total of 143, wrote process-read loops and placed their plan to check the input after the plan for reading the input, even though this results in a bug. Such a construction is buggy because it does not check the initial input for validity. Of the 143 students, 80 used process-read loops. 3 out of 80 is a high enough frequency of buggy programs to require explanation, and the correlation with problem statement order may be such an explanation. Nevertheless, this is still not a very significant phenomenon; until it is established that these students really order their plans according to the goal order, implicit goal ordering will be ignored in PROUST.

5.4.2.3 Wording of goals is unimportant

Goals are specified in a single uniform manner in PROUST's problem descriptions: the type of goal is named, followed by a list of arguments. In problem statements, however, goals can be specified in a variety of different ways. Some goals are described explicitly:

Your program should print out the number of valid days typed in.

Other goals are described indirectly:

How many months will it take until the fish population is one-tenth the original size? Write a program to solve this problem.

The latter goal is indirect in the sense that it does not specify what the program should do; rather, it states only that there is a problem, and the program must solve it. The implication of PROUST's uniform goal description is that wording of the goals in the problem statement is irrelevant. No matter what wording appears in the problem statement, the same range of goal implementations in novice programs will result.

It might seem obvious that the wording of goals is unimportant, as long as the wording is clear and unambiguous. Expert programmers have no trouble getting past the wording of requirements and determining what the requirements really are. For novices, however, the distinction between natural language and programming language is blurred, particularly if the novices are rank beginners [10]. Thus it could not be taken for granted that wording is unimportant. In order to determine the extent to which PROUST would have to be sensitive to wording, I analyzed a number of solutions to the Rainfall Problem and similar problems. I was looking for correlations between the wording of goals and the program constructions and bugs that appear in novice programs. No such correlations were found.

One way in which the wording of goal descriptions appeared to have an effect on variability was the extent to which knowledge was required to interpret the goal descriptions. Consider the following goal in the Rainfall Problem: "if the user types in a negative value, reject it." The novice might not understand what is involved in rejecting erroneous data. A common misconception among novices is that once a bad data value has been rejected by the program, the program need not check anymore whether the data is valid. Once the program prints an error message, the user presumably will make note of it and enter only valid data thereafter. As a result, novice programs frequently test input data just once, using an `if` statement, while experts use a `while` loop, testing the input repeatedly until the data is correct. If the problem statement explained how input is to be validated, then the students might not produce this type of solution, and the variability in the students' solutions would be decreased.

Suppose, however, that the Rainfall Problem statement explained exactly what "reject input" meant. That would mean including a statement such as the following:

by rejecting input we mean that the program should print an error message, reread the input, and then test it again, until a valid value has been read.

In that case the "reject input" goal is redundant! As we saw in the problem description derivation in Section 5.3, redundant goals are not included in the problem description. The definition of rejecting input which appears in the problem statement would be included in the problem description instead. Thus if the wording of the "reject input" goal is changed as in this case, this change in wording changes the list of goals which are being described. It is the change in the list of mentioned goals which affects variability of solutions, not the wording itself.

More recently, Spohrer *et al.* [63] have turned up an example where wording of goals can really affect novices' solutions. They cite a case where novices were shown examples of what their program was supposed to do, and misinterpreted the examples. The students apparently interpreted the examples too narrowly. PROUST's goal descriptions name data objects directly; instead of describing the examples, the problem description simply states the generalization. Therefore PROUST is unable to predict variability resulting from students' inability to generalize properly from examples. Current programming curricula make no attempt to teach programmers how to perform proper generalizations; PROUST is no different in this respect.

5.5 Objects in problem descriptions

An object, or data object, is some quantity, either a variable or a constant, which a program manipulates. Some objects are defined implicitly by goals; whenever a goal involves generating a value, that value is an object. For example, in the expression

$$Output(Average(\texttt{?Rainfall:DailyRain})),$$

the *Average* goal defines an object, the average of the daily rainfalls, which the *Output* goal refers to. More commonly, however, objects are explicitly declared. Objects are declared in problem descriptions either via `DefObject` statements or `Bind` statements. `DefObject` statements are used in order to associate specific properties with objects. `Bind` statements are used when the properties of the objects are determined by the goal which generates it. Examples of `Bind` statements appear in Section 5.4.

An example of an object which is declared using a `DefObject` statement is the transaction code in the Bank Problem. The following declaration is used to define the transaction code object.

```
DefObject ?Bank:InData
    Type char, ObjectClass SingleLetterCommand,
    Range MultiValued,
    Values (?Bank:DTrans, ?Bank:WTrans, ?Bank:ETrans);
```

This statement defines an object `?Bank:InData`, which represents the set of processing commands, DEPOSIT, WITHDRAWAL, and END-PROCESSING, which the program processes. It associates the following properties with this object.

- `?Bank:InData` should be implemented in Pascal using the `char` datatype (the problem statement stipulates this explicitly).

- It belongs to the class of objects called `SingleLetterCommand`'s. An object is a `SingleLetterCommand` if it is part of a command language in which only the first letter of each command is significant.

- `?Bank:InData` is multi-valued. That is, the object can have different values at different times during the execution of the program.

144

- The value of `?Bank:InData` at any one time must be a member of the set

  {`?Bank:DTrans, ?Bank:WTrans, ?Bank:ETrans`}.

  These objects denote the deposit transaction, the withdrawal transaction, and the end-processing transaction.

The transaction code is described in the problem statement via the following statements:

Write a Pascal program that processes three types of bank transactions: withdrawals, deposits, and a special transaction that says: no more transactions are to follow... Your program should prompt the user to input the transaction type...

There is a relatively small number of properties which can be given to objects. The current list is as follows:

- `Type`

- `ObjectClass`

- `Range`

- `Value`

- `Values`

The number of properties is small because, as we shall see, the `ObjectClass` property makes it possible for objects to inherit a variety of properties which are not listed directly in the object definition.

The `Value` slot is used when the object being defined is a constant. For example in the Bank Problem the service charge is defined as follows:

```
DefObject ?Bank:Charge ObjectClass DollarAmount;
DefObject ?Bank:Charge Value 0.20;
```

The `Values` slot is used when an object can take one of a finite set of values. An example of a `Values` slot appears in the definition of `?Bank:InData` shown above.

The `Range` slot of an object indicates whether the object assumes a unique value throughout the program, or whether the object can take on a series of values.

The object class of an object determines most of the properties which an object has. The object classes that appear in the Bank Problem specification are `SingleLetterCommand`, `AccountNumber`, `AccountBalance`,

145

`TransactionAmount`, `WithdrawalAmount`, `DollarAmount`, and `NaturalNumber`. Each object class has a set of properties associated with it, which members of that class inherit. One of these properties is the range of values which objects can take. Thus, for example, if an object is of class `NaturalNumber` then it can only assume natural numbers as values. If an object is of class `DollarAmount` its value must be some integral number of dollars and cents. If an object is a `SingleLetterCommand` its values must be single alphabetic characters. While some properties of object classes hold for all instances of the class, others hold most of the time, but not always. For example, if an object is a `SingleLetterCommand`, it is probably irrelevant whether it is in upper or lower case. However, if the application runs under the Unix operating system, the command may have to be supplied in lower case.[14] If an object is an `AccountBalance`, it cannot be negative, unless overdraft privileges have been granted. These default properties for objects allow PROUST to elaborate specifications that have been imprecisely specified, and hence allow it understand programs in which the programmer has elaborated the specification in similar ways. PROUST's object class definitions are stored in a knowledge base, the organization of which will be described in the next chapter.

Object classes may appear to be like abstract datatypes. However, the intent of object classes is quite different. First, the properties of object classes may or may not hold in a given student's interpretation of a programming problem. PROUST is thus prepared for a range of possible implementations of a given object. Second, abstract datatypes such as stacks are generally viewed only as programming constructs. Object classes, on the other hand, usually denote domain-dependent concepts.[15]

Types, as opposed to object classes, indicate the specific Pascal datatype that is being used to implement the object. Types are usually inferred from the object class. However, if a Pascal datatype is included as an implementation hint, then the type is specified directly in the object definition. Such a hint appears in the case of the object `?Bank:InData`, which is specified as being of type `char`.

---

[14] This distinction is not currently supported in PROUST.

[15] Other researchers have emphasized the importance of domain concepts in program synthesis and understanding, e.g., Barstow [8] and Brooks [13].

146

5.5.1 Assumptions underlying object definitions

There is a set of assumptions which were made in designing the representation for object descriptions. These assumptions are fairly similar to those made in the design of goal descriptions.

5.5.1.1 Implicit properties of data are omitted

PROUST's problem descriptions do not list properties of objects which are not explicitly mentioned in the problem statement, just as they do not list goals which are not explicitly mentioned. The motivation is the same in both cases: properties which are not explicitly mentioned can be a source of error in novice programs. For example, solutions to the Bank Problem differ widely as to what properties are attributed to bank transactions and account balances. Some students treat bank transactions and account balances simply as real numbers; they do not perform any validity checks on these quantities. Other students check whether the deposits and withdrawals are negative, but do not check whether or not they are zero. Still others make sure that every transaction is positive, and that the resulting balance is also always positive.

The advantage of using object classes to describe objects is that it makes it easy to avoid mentioning implicit properties of data. One need only indicate the object class that applies, and PROUST should be able to apply its knowledge about the object in order to predict how the students will manipulate, or mis-manipulate, the data. The problem statements that I have looked at rarely dwell on describing data. They simply indicate what kind of data is being manipulated, and assume that the programmer will understand how the data should be handled by the program. This is in part because the data being manipulated are scalars, and thus require little in the way of description. On the other hand, there is nothing which prevents data from being explicitly described in problem statements. Should this happen, PROUST's object descriptions will become inadequate, because it will then be necessary to list the properties of data explicitly in the problem description. There is no problem with extending the range of properties which can be attributed to data, however.

5.5.1.2 Novices understand the concept of data

Assigning names to objects makes an important assumption. We are assuming that students understand that programs manipulate discrete quantities of data, and that each piece of data has a unique realization in the computer. If this were not the case then novices would reason about data in a very different way from what PROUST expects. I occasionally run into programs which show evidence that the concept of data is blurred, but not very often. Some solutions to the Rainfall Problem have two variables, `NewRainfall` and `OldRainfall`, which together denote the input variable. The student uses the name `NewRainfall` when he/she is reading in a new value, and uses `OldRainfall` when he/she is performing computations using that value. Examples such as this cannot be predicted by PROUST, but they could be without changing the problem description language. We must simply allow for the possibility that a single datum is implemented via two separate variables. Other students "mush" variables, using the same variable to mean two different things. For example, the variable `Rainfall` can be taken to mean both the daily rainfall and the total rainfall, causing novices to write assignment statements such as `Rainfall := Rainfall + Rainfall` when they mean to compute a running total. Such cases could cast into doubt the assumption that novices understand what data is. However, I have encountered only one such example in several hundred programs, so I will assume for the time being that it is not significant.

5.5.1.3 Object values need not be inferred from the English

The description of the Bank Problem in Figure 5-8 differs from the problem statement in one major respect. The problem description indicates that the transaction commands are 'd', 'w', and 'e'; this is stated nowhere in the original problem statement. Instead the problem statement refers to the transactions by name: DEPOSIT, WITHDRAWAL, and END-TRANSACTION. An assumption is being made here that the first letters of the transaction names will be used in the program. A significant number of students do not follow this convention, and consequently PROUST has trouble understanding their programs.

In order for PROUST to know what the transaction codes are, it would have to know that they are described via the English words DEPOSIT, WITHDRAWAL, and

148

END-TRANSACTION. This would make the values dependent upon the wording of the problem statement. In order for PROUST's problem description language to remain independent of wording of the problem statement, such oblique references to data must be avoided. The Bank Problem statement should state explicitly what the transaction codes are. I do not think that this is a serious restriction.

5.6 Summary

This chapter has shown that it is possible to devise a problem description language which provides the information which is necessary to allow for variability in novice solutions. This problem description language makes explicit the goals and data described in the problem statement, without introducing extraneous information. As a consequence, problem descriptions can retain aspects of informality which correlate with variability in novice solutions.

Designing such a language requires investigation of the relationships between problem statements and novice solutions. There are differences between the way that novices interpret goal descriptions and the way that experts interpret goal descriptions; these differences can lead to unexpected variability in novice programs. PROUST's problem description language is based upon assumptions about novice behavior which may not always be valid. So far, however, the cases which call these assumptions into question are very few in number, and in most of these cases careful wording of the problem statements should be able to eliminate the difficulties.

The work presented in this chapter is very preliminary. I have so far only represented a few programming problems with PROUST's notation. It is not yet known how many different goals and object classes are needed in order to provide an adequate vocabulary for problem descriptions. It also is not yet known what range of properties must be attributed to objects in order to model their implementation by novices in a general way. However, I am confident that the basic approach, to define problems in terms of goals and object classes, is appropriate for a wide range of programming problems.

6 Constructing Goal Decompositions

This chapter describes PROUST's mechanism for constructing goal decompositions for programs. PROUST uses its knowledge of goals and plans to construct a range of different goal decompositions for the student's program. The plans in the goal decompositions are then matched against the student's code, as was described in Chapter 4. In this manner an interpretation of the student's code is constructed.

The discussion will proceed as follows. I will first describe the model of program design and implementation which underlies PROUST. This model relates problem descriptions to possible goal decompositions; implementations; from it we can see what PROUST must do in order to predict possible goal decompositions, given a problem description. Then I will describe in general terms the approach which PROUST uses to predict novice goal decompositions, and outline the kinds of knowledge PROUST must have, given this approach. Afterwards the specific knowledge about goals and objects that PROUST uses to construct goal decompositions will be described.

6.1 A view of the program synthesis process

In the previous chapter I attempted to show that PROUST's problem descriptions provide the basis for predicting novice solutions, and the variability in those solutions. I mean the following by this. Problem descriptions are assumed to capture the essential information that novices extract from problem statements when solving programming problems. Problem statements describe goals and properties of data, and the novices try to write programs which reflects these. Novices perform a series of steps in going from problem statement to solution. If we can determine what the alternative steps are that novices make at each point on the path from problem to solution, then it should be possible to predict the variety of novice solutions to any given problem.

In order to see where novices make choices during the programming process, and where programming knowledge plays a role, I will adopt the following idealized view of the programming process. I assume that programmers perform the following sorts of steps in solving a programming problem:

1. refine informal goals and data descriptions, filling in information which was not made explicit in the problem;

2. reformulate the stated goals as goals which can be implemented using plans;

3. select plans for implementing the goals.

The first two steps result in constructing a goal decomposition for a solution, and the third step implements the solution. During the problem-solving process, these steps are interleaved, as the programmer focuses on different aspects of the problem. Thus at any one time parts of the problem will already be realized as plans, and others may not even have been considered by the programmer yet.

The steps that programmers go through in solving a programming problem can be viewed as a state space. Each state is the problem at various stages of completion. The initial state is the initial problem description, and the final states are solutions to the problem. At intermediate states, some goals and objects have been implemented, and others have not. Transitions from one state to the next involve performing one of the three operations listed above, i.e., refining informal goals and objects, reformulating goals, and selecting plans. Some of these transitions are correct, i.e., they lead to correct solutions; others are incorrect, and result in bugs. I will call this space the *problem space* for the programming problem. The variability in problem solutions can be accounted for in terms of the variety of transitions which can be made at each point in the problem space.

Note that this model of programming glosses over many details of how programming is done. I am treating goal refinement, goal reformulation, and plan selection as primitive steps; however, performing these individual steps can involve a substantial amount of processing. Some goals, such as the goal "write a program which finds a minimum-cost spanning tree", cannot be easily reformulated into implementable goals by average programmers. The programmer must study the goal extensively, and explore various possible ways of satisfying it, before reformulations

152

can be done. Such reasoning may not be inferrable from the resulting program; all that are observable are the plans that the programmer chose, and their organization. In addition, the order in which the programmer works on different problem goals is not inferrable from the form of the final program. At most we can infer what the programmer's underlying goals were, and how these goals were decomposed into subgoals and plans. For these reasons, in order to predict variability in novice programs, I focus on goals and their realizations, and not on the reasoning process which relates goals to realizations.

In order to predict variability in novice programs, we must identify transitions which novices as a group are likely to make in proceeding from a problem to a solution. It is not feasible to enumerate all possible transitions; there are liable to be many minor variations of transitions, if one considers all of the bugs which might arise. I will address the question of accounting for such minor variations in Chapter 7. What we need here is a means for generating the major alternatives, so that when PROUST analyzes programs by synthesis, it can make general predictions about what the novices are trying to do at each point in their programs.

6.2 PROUST's approach to predicting solutions

In analyzing a student's program, PROUST traverses a state space similar to the problem space that I have described programmers as traversing. I call this space the *interpretation space*. Each state consists of the following:

- an agenda of goals whose implementation in the program has yet to be determined;

- plans which have been matched against the program, and the code that they match; and

- a description of each object and whether or not its realization in the program has been determined.

A state in the interpretation space is thus a partial goal decomposition for the problem, together with a mapping between the goal decomposition and the student's code. The following types of transitions are performed between states:

- goal selection -- a goal is selected from the goal agenda for analysis;

- elaboration -- implied goals are added to the agenda, and/or informal requirements are elaborated upon;

- goal reformulation -- the selected goal is reformulated as a different set of goals;

- plan selection and matching -- the selected goal is implemented using a plan, and the plan is matched against the program. Any subgoals in the plan are added to the goal agenda.

Note the symmetries between the problem space and the interpretation space. States in the problem space are partial solutions of the problem; states in the interpretation space are partial analyses of the program. Of the various types of transitions in the interpretation space, three types, elaborations, goal reformulations and plan selections, have counterparts in the problem space. In performing these transitions, PROUST analyzes programs by synthesis: the steps that it goes through in constructing interpretations for programs are similar to the steps that novices go through in constructing programs.

At the initial state, the goal agenda and the object descriptions are the same as those which are specified in the problem description. In each possible final state, the goal agenda is empty, meaning that all goals in the problem description, as well as all implied goals, have been accounted for. Accounting for a goal involves either determining how the goal is realized in the program, or else concluding that the novice failed to implement code to satisfy the goal. Each path from the initial state to a final state constitutes an interpretation of the program, as follows. We can tell from the transitions that are made between the initial state and the final state how each goal was realized, what goal decomposition was used, what plans were used to implement the goals, and where each plan appears in the program. Thus we can tell what intentions underlie each line of code, and how each requirement is implemented in the program.

PROUST explores the interpretation space, trying to find a suitable path from the initial state to a final state. As it does, it creates a tree of partial interpretations, called the *interpretation tree*. The interpretation tree is implemented literally in PROUST as a tree of nodes, each representing a different state in the interpretation space. Figure 6-1 shows schematically what such a tree typically looks like. The

154

nodes in the diagram are states, and the arcs are transitions. Arcs are labeled E for elaboration, G for goal selection, R for goal reformulation, and P for plan selection. [16] At each state, PROUST considers the possible state transitions that the student might have performed at that point. For each possible transition, PROUST creates a new state, and makes it a child of the current state. PROUST then explores the new paths. P transitions are the only transitions which can be tested directly against the program, by matching the predicted plan against the program. PROUST therefore expands alternative branches until P transitions are reached. By comparing the results of matching different plans, PROUST can usually determine which path is the correct one to pursue further. Eventually PROUST reaches a final state, and hence has constructed a complete interpretation of the program.

6.2.1 The knowledge-based approach

As was indicated in Section 6.1, a substantial amount of reasoning on the part of the programmer may be required to perform transitions in the problem space. Likewise, similar reasoning may be required to perform transitions in the interpretation space. However, I assume in PROUST that little reasoning is necessary in order to predict solutions to novice programming problems. Rather, I assume that if enough knowledge is built into PROUST about how novices write programs, then PROUST will be able to perform transitions in the interpretation space with a minimum of deduction. Furthermore, this knowledge need not be problem-specific; it should be possible to derive predictions about solutions to a new programming problem merely by changing the problem description.

To understand the limitations that this knowledge-based approach places on PROUST, let us examine the limitations of the knowledge-based approach for a similar problem, automatic programming. Barstow [7] has claimed that knowledge-based methods can be used for automatic program synthesis only if the problem

---

[16]In PROUST's actual interpretation trees, a single arc may represent more than one transition simultaneously. For example, plan selection and requirements elaboration are done at the same time, if the plan has a PosteriorGoals slot containing goals which must be added to the goal agenda. (PosteriorGoals slots were discussed in Section 4.4.) In order to keep the diagram simple, however, I have drawn it as if the transitions were performed one at a time. The actual structure of PROUST's interpretation trees is shown in Section 6.7.

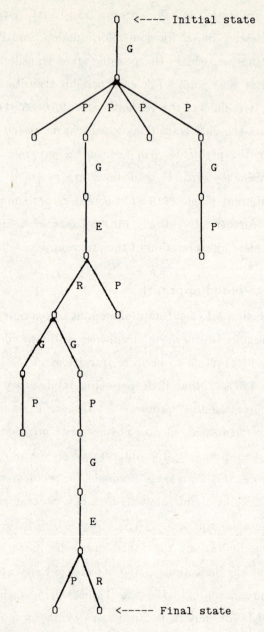

0   <---- Initial state

E = requirements elaboration
G = goal selection
R = goal reformulation
P = plan selection

Figure 6-1: A schematic diagram of an interpretation tree

156

specification is fairly algorithmic. Knowledge-based approaches are inadequate for algorithm design problems. Barstow has since built the ΦNIX system [8], a system which has a combination of programming knowledge and domain knowledge. This system is able to synthesize programs from non-algorithmic specifications phrased in terms of domain concepts. Algorithm creation is still beyond the reach of this system. Kant and Newell [43] have built a computational model of the algorithm creation process, and have demonstrated the complexity of reasoning which is required for automatic algorithm creation.

We would expect that the limitations that the knowledge-based approach imposes on program analysis to be similar to what are imposed on automatic program synthesis. This is because PROUST's analysis process is so closely related to the program synthesis process. In fact, the limitations might be even more severe, since PROUST must be able to analyze a variety of different solutions, not just one. Nevertheless, Barstow's experience with knowledge-based program synthesis suggests that the knowledge-based approach to intention-based program analysis is likely to succeed. PROUST's problem descriptions are not algorithmic, but they are reasonably detailed and straightforward, provided that the original problem statement is detailed and straightforward. Algorithm creation is not necessary for solving novice programming problems. Since PROUST's object descriptions refer to domain concepts, domain knowledge is required. Barstow's success with ΦNIX has demonstrated that domain knowledge can be effectively incorporated into a knowledge-based programming system. Thus to the extent that the experience of past automatic programming research is a guide, PROUST's approach is a valid one.

Experience with PROUST has shown so far that the knowledge-based approach to intention-based program analysis works reasonably well in the novice programming domain. There are, however, cases where PROUST is unable to predict the full variety of novice programs. Once I have described PROUST's knowledge, and how it is used, I will discuss some of these cases.

6.2.2 The structure of PROUST's knowledge base

Before delving into the details of PROUST's programming knowledge, I will give an overview of the structure of the programming knowledge base. PROUST's knowledge is encoded principally as an associative network of frames. There are five different kinds of frames involved: goals, plans, goal reformulations, object classes, and object class implementations. The knowledge base is divided into two parts. One part contains the knowledge relating to goals, i.e., goals, plans, and goal reformulations, and another knowledge base contains knowledge relating to objects, i.e., object classes and object class implementations.

Figure 6-2 shows the structure of the goal knowledge base. Goals are linked to plans, to indicate what plans can be used to implement each goal. Goals are also linked to goal reformulation nodes. Goal reformulation nodes describe sets of goals which a novice may view as equivalent to the goal that the node is linked to. Goal reformulation nodes are thus similar to plans, except that whereas plans always include a plan template, goal reformulations never do. There are two kinds of links from plans to goals, as described in Chapter 4. First, plan templates frequently contain subgoals as plan components. Second, plans can contain in their `PriorGoals` and `PosteriorGoals` slots goals which must be satisfied when the plan is used.

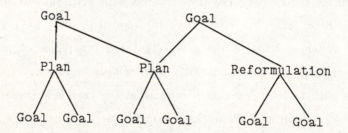

Figure 6-2: The structure of the goal and plan database

The object class database contains just two kinds of knowledge structures: object classes, and object-class implementations. Those properties which apply to all instances of an object class are stored in the object class frame. Properties specific to a particular implementation of the object class, such as the Pascal datatype which is used, are stored in the individual implementation frames.

Possible transitions in the interpretation space are usually determined by following links in the knowledge base. In order to determine what plans can be selected to implement a goal, PROUST follows links from the goal to the plans which implement it. Determining possible goal reformulations involves following links from goals to goal reformulations. Elaborations are achieved by adding to the goal agenda the goals that are attached to each plan, and by selecting implementations of object classes.

6.3 Goal knowledge and its use

Like plans, goals in PROUST are represented as frames containing a collection of slots. These slots contain the following kinds of information:

- ways in which the goals can be implemented,

- the location of the goals in an abstraction hierarchy, and

- assertions about the goals and their arguments.

The characteristics of each type of information, and their realization in PROUST, are discussed below.

The goals currently in PROUST's goal knowledge base are only those which are required for the Bank Problem and the Rainfall Problem. The total number of goals is 30. I do not foresee any major problems with extending the knowledge base, but until this is done it is not possible to determine whether the types of knowledge currently associated with goals are adequate in general.

6.3.1 Links from goals to plans and goal reformulations

The methods for implementing each goal are stored in the `Implementations` slot of the goal. I will use the term "implementation method" to refer collectively to plans and goal reformulations. Both correct and buggy implementations are grouped together in the `Implementations` slot. The most common implementations are first, and the least common are last, to make recognition of common implementations more efficient.

Figure 6-3 shows PROUST's realization of the goal *Sentinel-Controlled Input*

Sequence. Its `Implementations` slot contains a list of six items. The first four are the common plans for implementing *Sentinel Controlled Input Sequence*: SENTINEL PROCESS-READ WHILE, SENTINEL READ-PROCESS WHILE, SENTINEL READ-PROCESS REPEAT, and SENTINEL PROCESS-READ REPEAT. The remaining implementations are buggy implementations of the goal, reflecting common novice misinterpretations of the requirement that a loop be sentinel-controlled. BOGUS YESNO PLAN is a plan in which the program determines whether or not the end of input has been reached by requesting that the user type 'y' or 'n' to indicate whether or not to continue. The sentinel is not checked for in this plan. BOGUS COUNTER-CONTROLLED LOOP reformulates the sentinel-controlled loop as a counter-controlled loop, asking the user to indicate the number of values to typed in. The sentinel is not checked for in this plan either. Figure 4-5 showed a program with a counter-controlled loop in place of a sentinel-controlled loop.

Sentinel-Controlled Input Sequence

Instance of:
  Read & Process
Form: *Sentinel-Controlled Input Sequence*(`?New, ?Stop`)
Main segment:
  `MainLoop`:
Main variable:
  `?New`
Name phrase:
  "sentinel-controlled loop"
Outer Control Plan:
  T
Implementations:
  SENTINEL PROCESS-READ WHILE
  SENTINEL READ-PROCESS WHILE
  SENTINEL READ-PROCESS REPEAT
  SENTINEL PROCESS-READ REPEAT
  BOGUS YESNO PLAN
  BOGUS COUNTER-CONTROLLED LOOP

Figure 6-3: A goal

6.3.2 The goal abstraction hierarchy

PROUST's goals are organized into an abstraction hierarchy. Goals can have
`InstanceOf` slots, which indicate the goal class to which they belong. The goal
Sentinel-Controlled Input Sequence, shown in Figure 6-3, is an instance of the goal
class *Read & Process*, which is the class of goals involving iterative processing of input
data. This goal class is the only goal class which has so far been defined in PROUST.

The main purpose of PROUST's goal abstraction hierarchy is to make it easier to
write plans. Plans frequently make generic references to parts of other plans.
Consider, for example, the RUNNING TOTAL PLAN, shown in Figure 6-4. This plan
consists of two components: an initialization, which sets the running total to zero,
and an update which adds successive values into the running total. The update must
go into the loop which processes the data; the initialization must precede the loop.
There needs to be a way of phrasing a generic reference such as "the loop which
processes the data" in PROUST's plan representation. This is done by placing the
following note in the plan template for RUNNING TOTAL PLAN: *in the* `Process:`
component of goal Read & Process. If a goal has been analyzed which is in the class
Read & Process, PROUST examines the plan which implements this goal, looking for a
`Process:` component. This component is taken to be the one that the RUNNING
TOTAL PLAN refers to.

RUNNING TOTAL PLAN

Variables:

        `?Total, ?New`

Template:

`Init:`   `?Total := 0`

             (in the `Process:` *component of goal Read & Process)*

`Update:`   `?Total := ?Total+?New`

Figure 6-4:   The RUNNING TOTAL PLAN

6.3.3 Assertions about goals

As was indicated in Section 4.3.5, plans have assertions attached to them. These assertions describe preconditions and postconditions which must be valid when the plan is used. One could imagine such precondition and postcondition assertions being attached to goals as well. If an assertion holds for every plan which implements a particular goal, then the assertion is really a fact about the goal, not the plans. Nevertheless, there has not yet been sufficient need to build an assertion-handling mechanism for both plans and goals. At this time precondition and postcondition assertions about goals are attached to the plans that implement the goals, even though this results in a somewhat redundant knowledge base.

There are, however, other facts about goals, aside from preconditions and postconditions, which are attached to goals. The following slots describe goals and their arguments.

- `Form` -- a template showing what arguments a goal requires. The `Form` slot of *Sentinel-Controlled Input Sequence*, for example, is

  Sentinel-Controlled Input Sequence`(?New, ?Stop).`

  The same pattern variable names appear in the `Form` slot of the goal as appear in plans which implement the goal. When plans are instantiated, the `Form` slots of the goals which the plans implement are checked. Suppose, for example, that PROUST were attempting to instantiate plans for implementing the goal *Sentinel-Controlled Input Sequence*(`?Rainfall:DailyRain, 99999)`, which appears in the description of the Rainfall Problem. When PROUST compares this form with the contents of the `Form` slot of *Sentinel-Controlled Input Sequence*, it determines that `?New` should be bound to `?Rainfall:DailyRain` and `?Stop` should be bound to 99999.

- `MainComponent` -- this indicates which component of the plans which are used to implement this goal is the principal component. The `MainComponent` slot of the *Sum* goal, for example, is `Update:`.

- `MainVariable` -- the variable which is bound to the principal quantity which this goal manipulates. In the *Sentinel-Controlled Input Sequence* goal the main variable is `?New`, the input variable.

- `ResultVariable` -- the variable which holds the value which is generated by the goal. An example of a goal with a `ResultVariable` slot is *Average*. When an implicit reference to the value generated by a goal is

162

made,   such   as   in   the   goal   expression
Output(*Average*(`?Rainfall:DailyRain`)),   PROUST   examines   the
`ResultVariable` slot.   This slot determines what variable in the plan
implementing the goal is being referred to.

- `Compounds` -- this slot lists goals that can be subsumed by a goal, and the
  new goals that result from such a subsumption.   Goal subsumption,
  described in Section 6.4.3.2, is a process through which goals are combined
  to produce new goals.

There is another kind of assertion which is attached to goals: an indication of the
relative size and scope of plans implementing the goals. This is needed in order for
PROUST to determine in what order to analyze goals, as described in Chapter 8. A
problem description for a non-trivial programming problem usually has a number of
different goals. Some goals deal with local details; others, such as *Sentinel-Controlled
Input Sequence* in the Rainfall Problem, determine the overall structure of the
resulting program. PROUST tries to select the major plans for analysis first, so that it
can quickly derive a model for the overall structure of the program. Information
about the relative importance of goals is indicated using the `OuterControlPlan`
slot, whose value is either `T` or `NIL`. If `T`, this means that plans satisfying this goal
determine the overall control structure of the program.

There is one more slot which appears in goals, called the `NamePhrase` slot. This
slot contains a description of the goal in English. The descriptions are used in order
to generate English-language descriptions of bugs to present to the student.

6.4 Goal reformulations

There are two ways in which goals are reformulated in PROUST. In one case, PROUST
selects a goal reformulation node from the knowledge base, and instantiates it. In the
other case, PROUST applies a rule for reformulating goals. I will talk about goal
reformulation nodes first.

6.4.1 Goal reformulation nodes

Goal reformulation nodes are collections of goals which are given a name and listed along with plans in the `Instances` slots of the goals. Such goal reformulations are really a kind of plan schema; the difference is that instead of having code patterns as part of the schemata, goal reformulations consist entirely of lists of goals.

An example of a goal which is implemented using reformulations is the *Constant Sum* goal. The *Constant Sum* goal computes the sum of a series of numbers, all of which are the same constant value. This goal appears in the description of the Bank Problem, which stipulates that the total amount of service charges deducted from the customer's account should be printed. The service charge is the same for each transaction: 20 cents. There are (at least) three ways of implementing *Constant Sum:*

- keep a running total of the values;

- count the number of values, and then multiply by the amount of each value; and

- keep a running count of the number of values so far, and each time the count is updated, multiply it by the constant in order to derive the current sum.

The first of these three methods uses a single plan, the RUNNING TOTAL PLAN. The other two methods involve solving two different goals: counting the values and multiplying the count by the amount, i.e., 20 cents. The original goal, *Constant Sum*, is thus reformulated into two other goals. The differences between the two methods result from differences in the way the multiplication goal is implemented; in one case the multiplication is performed during the computation of the count, and in the other case it is performed afterwards.

Figure 6-5 shows the organization of the knowledge used by PROUST to predict possible implementations of *Constant Sum*. *Constant Sum* has two implementations: FACTOR MULTIPLE and FACTOR RUNNING TOTAL. FACTOR RUNNING TOTAL is a variant of the RUNNING TOTAL PLAN, where the value being summed is a constant rather than a variable.[17] FACTOR MULTIPLE is a goal reformulation: it specifies that *Constant Sum* should be reformulated as a combination of a *Count* goal and a *Multiply* goal. The *Multiply* goal is implemented in two ways, using the MULTIPLY PLAN or the FINAL MULTIPLY PLAN.

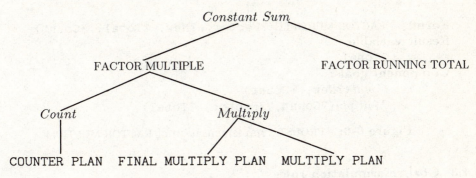

Figure 6-5: Implementations of *Constant Sum*

6.4.2 The contents of PROUST's goal reformulation nodes

Goal reformulation nodes are similar in content to goal nodes. Like goal nodes, they have `ResultVariable` slots and `Form` slots. The one slot which goal reformulation nodes have but which goal nodes do not have is a `ComponentGoals` slot, which lists the goals which result after the goal reformulation has been performed.

Figure 6-6 shows PROUST's implementation of FACTOR MULTIPLE. The `Form` slot of this reformulation is FACTOR MULTIPLE(`?Factor, ?New, ?Total, ?Count`). `Form` slots are required in order to determine the relationship between the pattern variables in the goal reformulation and the arguments of the goal which is being reformulated. If there are more pattern variables in the form than there were in the original goal expression, the extra pattern variables are left unbound. The extra variables are usually temporary variables which are needed to pass data between component goals in the reformulation. `?Count` is such a temporary variable; it is the

---

[17]The RUNNING TOTAL PLAN itself cannot be used here, because PROUST requires that each plan should indicate which of the pattern variables that it uses are constant-valued and which are variable-valued. This reduces the possibility that a plan component will match the wrong statement in the program. However, it would be better for information about the properties of pattern variables to be inherited from the goal description, rather than explicitly marked in the plans.

count of values being summed. One component goal, *Count*(`?New, ?Count`), defines the value of `?Count`; the other component goal, *Multiply*(`?Count, ?Factor, ?Total`), then uses this value.

FACTOR MULTIPLE

Form: FACTOR MULTIPLE(`?Factor, ?New, ?Total, ?Count`)
Result variable:
    `?Total`
Component goals:
    Count(`?New, ?Count`)
    Multiply(`?Count, ?Factor, ?Total`)

Figure 6-6: PROUST's implementation of FACTOR MULTIPLE

6.4.3 Goal reformulation rules

Some goal reformulations in PROUST are performed by applying rules. To the extent that these rules are applied, goal analysis involves reasoning rather than application of pre-stored knowledge. The use of goal reformulation rules is currently quite limited, however. There are three such rules: the Unification Rule, the Subsumption Rule, and the Contingent Realization Rule. These rules are not represented in any special rule formalism; rather, they are implemented as LISP procedures.

6.4.3.1 The Unification Rule

The Unification Rule has the following effect: when PROUST selects a goal for analysis, and another equivalent goal has already been implemented, the new goal is unified with the previous goal. Whatever plans implement the previous goal are also taken to implement the new goal. We see the effect of the Unification Rule in solutions of the Rainfall Problem. The problem statement for the Rainfall Problem says that the number of valid days should be output, implying that a count of the number of valid days should be kept. The average, as it is customarily implemented, also requires that a count of the values to be average should be computed. These two *Count* goals are unified by PROUST, reflecting the fact that programmers generally only compute the count once in such cases.[18]

Goal unification, when combined with other forms of goal reformulation, makes it possible to reformulate sets of goals at once. As a result, goal unification is much more powerful than might first appear. To see how unification and reformulation interact, consider the following goal reformulation problem. In Section 3.5.3, I described various ways in which novices count the number of valid inputs and the number of positive inputs when solving the Rainfall Problem. One method uses separate counter variables for the positive values and for the valid values. Another method uses one counter for the positive values, and another for the zero values; the two counters are added together in order to compute the total number of valid values. I will describe here what is required in order to make PROUST predict these goal decompositions.

The requirements that the valid inputs and the positive inputs be counted are represented as follows in the problem description for the Rainfall Problem:

DefGoal *Count*(?Rainfall:DailyRain);
DefGoal *Guarded Count*(?Rainfall:Rain, ?Rainfall:Rain>0).

The object name `?Rainfall:DailyRain` is abbreviated to `?Rainfall:Rain` here and in the subsequent discussion.

In the more straightforward goal decomposition, each of these goals is implemented using a separate plan. The plan for implementing the *Count* goal is a counter variable. The plan for implementing the *Guarded Count* goal is a counter variable plus a test to ensure that `?Rainfall:Rain` is positive before the counter variable is updated, i.e., something like the following:

if New>0 then Pos := Pos+1.

In the alternative goal decomposition for the *Count* and *Guarded Count* goal, the *Count* goal must be reformulated. One of the implementations of *Count* in PROUST's knowledge base is a goal reformulation node containing the following three goals:

Guarded Count(?New, ?New>0, ?Count1);

---

[18]Actually, some novices fail to unify goals like these when they write their programs, resulting in solutions to the Rainfall Problem with two counters for the number of valid days. PROUST currently applies the Unification Rule unconditionally; in order to model these programs it should also consider the option of not applying the rule.

```
Guarded Count(?New, ?New=0, ?Count2);
Combine Partial Sums(?Count1, ?Count2).
```

Combine Partial Sums simply takes two values and adds them together. Note that the *Guarded Count* goals in this list contain an extra argument. When an extra argument is added to the argument list of a goal, it is bound to the result generated by the goal, in this case the counter variable. This enables the *Combine Partial Sums* goal to refer to the results of the *Guarded Count* goals. An equivalent notation is the following:

```
Combine Partial Sums(Guarded Count( ?New, ?New > 0),
                     Guarded Count(?New, ?New = 0)).
```

When PROUST attempts the above goal reformulation, it substitutes `?Rainfall:Rain` for `?New`, and adds the new goals into the goal agenda. The goal agenda then includes the following goals:

```
Guarded Count(?Rainfall:Rain, ?Rainfall:Rain > 0, ?Count1);
Guarded Count(?Rainfall:Rain, ?Rainfall:Rain = 0, ?Count2);
Combine Partial Sums(?Count1, ?Count2);
Guarded Count(?Rainfall:Rain, ?Rainfall:Rain > 0).
```

The first and last *Guarded Count* goal can now be unified, because the bound arguments in each goal, `?Rainfall:Rain` and `?Rainfall:Rain>0`, are the same. Thus the following goals result after the unification:

```
Guarded Count(?Rainfall:Rain, ?Rainfall:Rain > 0, ?Count1);
Guarded Count(?Rainfall:Rain, ?Rainfall:Rain = 0, ?Count2);
Combine Partial Sums(?Count1, ?Count2).
```

At the present time the reformulation of *Count* states explicitly that one *Guarded Count* subgoal should count positive values and the other should count zero values. Problem-specific knowledge has thus intruded into the goal reformulation knowledge base; it is only in the Rainfall Problem that *Count* is reformulated into a count of positive values and a count of zero values. Such problem-specific knowledge could be eliminated by making the goal reformulation more general, as follows:

```
Guarded Count(?New, ?Pred, ?Count1);
Guarded Count(?New, *NOT* ?Pred, ?Count2);
Combine Partial Sums(?Count1, Count2),
```

`?Pred` is an arbitrary predicate, which must be bound when the goals are added to the goal agenda. The Goal Unification Rule could be used to determine what the binding for ?Pred should be. PROUST should unify

Guarded Count(?New, ?Pred, ?Count1)

with

Guarded Count(?Rainfall:Rain, ?Rainfall:Rain > 0),

and determine that ?Rainfall:Rain > 0 is an appropriate binding for ?Pred.

6.4.3.2 The Goal Subsumption Rule

Another goal reformulation rule which is similar to the Goal Unification Rule is the Goal Subsumption Rule. This rule is used to combine two goals which can be implemented simultaneously using a single plan.

Figure 6-7 shows an excerpt of a solution to the Rainfall Problem where the *Loop Input Validation* goal has been subsumed by the plans implementing the *Input* goals. The program has a process-read loop, with an initial **read** statement above the loop and another **read** statement at the bottom of the loop. However, in addition to the two **Read** statements there are also two loops which test the input for validity and re-read it. One appears above the loop immediately after the initial **read** statement, and the other appears at the bottom of the loop, immediately after the other **Read** statement. I regard each **read** statement and input validation loop as being a component of a larger plan, a VALIDATED PROCESS-READ WHILE INPUT PLAN. This plan implements *Input*, so it appears just where we would expect plans implementing the *Input* subgoals of the SENTINEL PROCESS-READ WHILE PLAN to appear. However, it also subsumes the *Input Validation* goal, meaning that no additional plan is required to validate the input before it is processed in the loop.

The Goal Subsumption Rule works by examining the goal being processed to see if it has a **Compounds** slot. This slot lists the goals that can be combined with the goal, and the new goals that result from this combination process. The slot is filled by a list of pairs, where the **car** of each pair is a goal that can be subsumed, and the **cdr** of each pair is the new goal that results from the subsumption. Figure 6-8 shows PROUST's description of the goal *Input*. Its **Compounds** slot contains the expression

((LoopInputValidation . ValidatedInput)).

```
...
writeln('Enter value');
read(New);
while New < 0 do
  begin
    writeln('Not valid, reenter');
    read(New);
  end;
while New<>99999 do
  begin
    Sum := Sum+New;
    Count := Count+1;
    ...
    writeln('Enter value');
    Read(New);
    while New < 0 do
      begin
        writeln('Not valid, reenter');
        read(New);
      end
  end;
...
```

Figure 6-7: A program in which *Input* and *Loop Input Validation* are combined

The slot lists one goal, *Loop Input Validation*, which can be subsumed by *Input*; the result of this subsumption is a new goal, *Validated Input*, which performs both input and validation. The VALIDATED PROCESS-READ WHILE INPUT PLAN, whose instantiations we see in Figure 6-7, is an implementation of *Validated Input*.

Before PROUST constructs its list of possible implementations of *Input*, it tries to apply the Goal Subsumption Rule. The rule in turn examines the goal agenda looking for goals which could be subsumed by *Input*. The Rainfall Problem description contains a *Loop Input Validation* goal, and *Loop Input Validation* is listed in the Compounds slot of *Input* as subsumable with *Input*. Therefore when PROUST goes to retrieve implementation methods of the current goal, it retrieves implementation methods both of *Input* and *Validated Input*. Therefore VALIDATED PROCESS-READ WHILE INPUT PLAN is included in the list of implementation methods.

170

```
Form:      Input( ?X )
Main segment:
    Input:
Name phrase:
    "input"
Result variable:
    ?X
Instances:
    READ PLAN
    READLN PLAN
Compounds:
    ((LoopInputValidation . ValidatedInput))
```

Figure 6-8:   An example of a goal with a compound link

PROUST matches the plan against the program, finds that it matches successfully, and selects it as the correct implementation for *Input*.

6.4.3.3 The Contingent Realization Rule

In the goal realizations that we have examined so far, the mapping from goals to plans has been direct. The goals may be reformulated before they are implemented, but once an appropriate formulation of each goal is found, the goal is mapped directly into some plan. By realizing the goals explicitly, we are saying that the program must perform some specific action in order to satisfy the goal, and the plan effects that action. I call such realizations *imperative realizations* of goals.

Goals can also be satisfied in a non-imperative fashion. One method which arises in the novice programs is the following. Instead of inserting a plan into a program which satisfies a goal, the programmer adopts a policy of trying to satisfy the goal only in those circumstances where failing to satisfy the goal leads to some invalid computation. Adoption of such a policy is called *contingent goal realization*; the goal is realized contingently in the sense that it is realized in code only when circumstances require it. A goal reformulation rule, called the Contingent Realization Rule, is used by PROUST to recognize when goals have been realized contingently. This rule is actually implemented as a plan-difference rule; however, its action is that of goal reformulation, so I will discuss it in this section. The task of modeling contingent goal realization may much more involved in general than PROUST's model suggests However, the mechanism provided in PROUST seems to be a reasonable first pass at a solution, and is adequate for the instances of contingent goal realization that have been encountered so far.

Figure 2-16 in Chapter 2 shows an example of a program in which a *Loop Input Validation* goal has been realized contingently. The example is repeated in Figure 6-9. This example is a solution of the Rainfall Problem. As I argued in Section 2.3.3.1, the novice who wrote this program appears to have decided to compensate for the effects of invalid input only when it is necessary. The count of valid inputs can be affected by invalid input; if an invalid input is processed, one will be added erroneously to the count of valid inputs. The running total can also be affected by invalid input; invalid inputs will erroneously be added into the running total. However, invalid input does not affect the computation of the maximum or the count of positive inputs; each of these computations uses an `if` statement which coincidentally excludes invalid input. These `if` statements appear at line 16 and 18, respectively. Thus some means is required for compensating for the effect of invalid input on the valid input counter and the running total. The method chosen for compensating for the effect is to undo the computations using invalid input. Thus the novice added a line to fix the valid input counter, `Number := Number - 1`. However, the novice failed to take care of the case of the running total, with the effect that negative data is added into the sum and the effect of this addition is never compensated for.

The contingent realization of the *Loop Input Validation* goal is modeled as follows in PROUST. The goal appears in the problem description of the Rainfall Problem as follows:

Loop Input Validation `(?Rainfall:Rain, ?Rainfall:Rain < 0)`.

After PROUST has attempted to match the plans that it knows about for implementing *Loop Input Validation*, it attempts to apply the Contingent Realization Rule. This rule applies to any goal such as *Loop Input Validation* which guards against some boundary condition. It activates a demon which examines every plan which has been matched so far, as well as all subsequent plans which are matched.

172

```
1 program Rainfall (input , output);
2 var
3    Total, Rainfall, Highest, Average : real;
4    Number, Days : integer;
5 begin
6   writeln ('Enter your rainfall data, one at a time');
7   readln;
8   read(Rainfall);
9   Number := 0;
10  Highest := 0;
11  Days := 0;
12  Total := 0;
13  while Rainfall <> 99999 do
14    begin
15      Number := Number + 1;
16      if Rainfall > 0 then
17        Days := Days + 1;
18      if Rainfall > Highest then
19        Highest := Rainfall;
20      Total := Total + Rainfall;
21      if Rainfall < 0    then
22        begin
23          writeln ('Impossible, try again');
24          Number := Number - 1;
25        end;
26      readln;
27      read ( Rainfall)
28    end;
29  Average := Total / Number;
30  writeln ( Number:3,  ' valid rainfalls were entered.');
31  writeln ('The average rainfall was', Average:3:2);
32  writeln ('The highest rainfall was', Highest:3:2);
33  writeln ('There were', Days:3, ' rainy days')
34 end.
```

Figure 6-9: an example solution to the Rainfall Rroblem

The demon checks in each case to see whether or not the function of the plan will be affected by the boundary condition being violated. In the current case, it checks whether or not negative data will be processed by the plan. Whenever this is the case, a goal is added to compensate for the effect of the boundary condition violation. The specific goal that is added depends upon what sort of compensation is required by the affected code. Goals such as the following are therefore added to the goal agenda:

173

Individual Fix-Up(?Code, (Rainfall:Rain < 0), ?Var, ?Offset),

where ?Code is bound to one of the updates, ?Var is bound to the variable whose value is being computed, and ?Offset is an amount which can be subtracted from ?Var to undo the effects of invalid input. PROUST then attempts to identify the realization of each of these goals in the program. These fix-up goals can either be implemented using a guard plan or an update to undo improper computations, such as decrementing a counter variable.

A demon must be used to generate the *Individual Fix-Up* goals because the fix-up method depends on the computation being guarded, and PROUST's plan data base provides no mechanism for making plan selection context-dependent in this fashion. If we were to add annotations to plans in the plan database to indicate the range of input data that the plans operate on, and to indicate how the effect of a plan can be undone, then it would not be necessary to resort to a special demon to perform the plan selection.

6.5 Implementing objects

Now that we have discussed goal realizations, let us turn to the issue of object realizations. Predicting realizations of objects involves retrieving properties of the objects from the knowledge base, selecting data structures for implementing objects, and incorporating them into the evolving implementation.

6.5.1 Representation and use of object properties

The representation and use of object properties in PROUST was illustrated in Chapter 2. The following discussion is an amplification of what was presented there.

When PROUST selects a goal for implementation, it first examines the arguments of the goals to see what object classes they belong to. For example, one of the goals specified in the Bank Problem is *Input*(?Bank:Deposit), which requires that the amount to be deposited be input. The argument of this goal, ?Bank:Deposit, is a member of the object class TransactionAmount. Before proceeding to select implementations for the goal, PROUST first retrieves relevant information about the object class, and selects a possible implementation for the object.

Object classes currently can have the following three properties:

- `Implementations` -- a list of possible implementations of the object class, i.e., Pascal data structures which can be used to implement the object class,

- `ExceptionCondition` -- a predicate indicating the ranges of values which are illegal for this object, and

- `BugRules` -- plan-difference rules for recognizing bugs commonly associated with this object class.

In the general case, object class implementations would have a richness of representation comparable to goal implementations. The implementations of object classes would be defined as data plans, each plan defining a data structure which can be used to implement the object class. The plans would have plan templates indicating how to declare the objects, and how to use them. However, the object implementations which are used in the programs that I have examined so far have only been scalar variables, and they do not encode data in any special way. These object class definitions do not yet motivate the implementation of a full data-plan instantiation scheme.

Figure 6-10 shows the representation for the `TransactionAmount` object class. This object class only has a single implementation, `RealBankTransaction`. This implementation simply specifies that the datatype to be used is `Real`. The object class also has a `BugRules` property and an `ExceptionCondition` property. The `ExceptionCondition` predicate, `?? <= 0`, specifies that whenever a value is less than or equal to zero it is not a legal transaction amount.

Whenever objects are defined which have exception conditions associated with them, *Guard Exception* goals are added to check for the exception conditions. One goal is added for each goal that refers to the object. In the case of `?Bank:Deposit`, there is one goal which refers to this object: *Accumulate*(`?Bank:Balance, ?Bank:Deposit`). Therefore the following goal is added to the goal agenda: *Guard*

Object Class

TRANSACTION AMOUNT

```
Implementations: RealTransactionAmount
Exception Condition: ??<=0
Bug Rules: SloppyTransactionGuard
```

Object Class Implementation

REAL TRANSACTION AMOUNT

Type: real

Figure 6-10: PROUST's representation for transaction amounts

Exception((Update: component of *Accumulate*), ?Bank:Deposit <= 0).[19]

6.6 The interpretation process

Now that most of the knowledge that PROUST uses in constructing program interpretations has been described, I will describe in more detail the process of constructing interpretations in PROUST. First the algorithm for constructing interpretations will be outlined, and its important features highlighted. Then some of the problems with PROUST's interpretation algorithm will be illustrated.

6.6.1 The interpretation algorithm

At any given time a tree of states in the interpretation space has been explored, and one of these states is active. PROUST's interpretation process goes through a cycle, operating on the currently active state. At the beginning of each cycle, a goal is

---

[19] The task of determining what goal to add is actually more complex than I have indicated here. A general solution would take into account the way in which the value of the object is generated. If the object's value is input from the terminal, then it is possible to have the user retype the value if it is out of range. If the value is generated by some other computation, however, then it is not possible to correct the value. Thus the goal generated by the object exception condition should be different in each case; in one case an *InputValidation* goal should be generated, and in the other case a *GuardException* goal should be generated.

selected from PROUST's goal agenda of the currently active state. Then a series of elaboration, reformulation, plan selection and matching, and bug analysis steps are performed on the selected goal. At the end of this processing PROUST moves to a new state, with a new goal agenda. The cycle then repeats.

Each interpretation cycle can be divided into the following phases.

1. Goal selection -- a goal is chosen from the agenda.

2. Reformulation -- the Unification Rule and the Subsumption Rule are applied to the selected goal, and the goal agenda is adjusted accordingly.

3. Elaboration -- the selected goal is elaborated by identifying implied goals, and by elaborating properties of the objects that the goal manipulates. Any new goals which are created in this process are added to the goal agenda.

4. Retrieval -- implementation methods for the selected goal are retrieved from the knowledge base.

5. Analysis -- any plans among the implementation methods are matched. Matching continues until none of the plans can be matched any further. If matching of a plan cannot continue because of match errors, these errors are analyzed for bugs. The Contingent Realization Rule is also attempted at this point. If matching stops because a plan contains a subgoal, PROUST moves to a new interpretation state, whose goal agenda includes the new subgoal. The interpretation cycle then repeats in the new state. If no implementation method fits the program, then the interpretation state is rejected, and PROUST tries another interpretation state. The interpretation cycle then resumes in the new state.

6. Implementation selection -- if one or more plans matches successfully, or if there are goal reformulations among the implementation methods, then PROUST selects one from among these methods. If the current goal is a subgoal of some previous plan, then the state in which the superplan was selected becomes active, and analysis resumes on the superplan. Otherwise PROUST moves to a new interpretation state, with an updated goal agenda. The interpretation cycle then repeats in the new state.

Note that there are two selection steps in this process. First, a goal must be selected. Second, an implementation step must be selected. PROUST's selection heuristics, and the analysis strategies that underlie them, will be described in Chapter 8.

A principal feature of PROUST's implementation algorithm is that it is depth-first.

PROUST selects a goal, analyzes it, and then selects an implementation. At this point PROUST is ready to select another goal, and the process can begin anew. If plans match successfully along the way, then PROUST will select one goal after another until the goal agenda is exhausted. Backtracking occurs in only two cases: when the current goal is a subgoal of a previous plan, and when none of the current implementation methods match the program.

The depth-first approach is essential, if the interpretation process is to complete in a reasonable amount of time. Interpretation trees are potentially very bushy; whenever a goal is to be chosen, there are frequently many goals to choose from. Likewise, there may be several different ways of implementing each goal, when all possible plans and goal reformulations are considered. Thus exhaustive search of the interpretation space is impractical. However, the effectiveness of the depth-first approach depends upon the ability to make good selections of plans and goals, and the ability to detect when an incorrect selection was made.

6.7 Constructing interpretation trees

The actual data structure which PROUST uses for keeping track of interpretations has the following structure. Interpretation trees are stored explicitly in PROUST as a set of nodes and arcs. Each node describes an interpretation state, and each arc represents a transition from one state to another.

There are three kinds of nodes in interpretation trees: goal nodes, plan nodes, and reformulation nodes. Goal nodes are created when goals are selected for analysis. Plan nodes are created when plans are selected for implementing a goal. Reformulation nodes are created when a selected goal is reformulated. There are no separate elaboration nodes: elaborations are performed by modifying the contents of the goal, plan, and reformulation nodes as needed. Since PROUST goes through a cycle of selecting goals and suggesting realizations for them, the children of goal nodes are always either plan nodes or reformulation nodes, and the children of plan nodes and reformulation nodes are always goal nodes.

Figure 6-11 shows a fragment of an interpretation tree for a solution to the Rainfall Problem such as the one in Figure 6-9. The first step is to choose the goal

Sentinel-Controlled Input Sequence to analyze. Therefore there appears a goal node for the *Sentinel-Controlled Input Sequence* goal immediately below the root of the tree. A number of plans are suggested as possible plans for implementing this goal; the two which are listed in the figure are SENTINEL PROCESS-READ WHILE and SENTINEL PROCESS-READ REPEAT. These appear immediately below the *Sentinel-Controlled Input Sequence* node. Each of the plans for *Sentinel-Controlled Input Sequence* has subgoals. These subgoals are selected for analysis by PROUST, in order to determine which plan for *Sentinel-Controlled Input Sequence* is the correct one to match against the program. An *Input* goal was selected in the case of SENTINEL PROCESS-READ WHILE; a *Sentinel Guard* goal was selected in the case of SENTINEL PROCESS-READ REPEAT.

A SENTINEL SKIP GUARD plan, at level 5 in the tree, is selected to implement the *Sentinel Guard* goal; however, this plan cannot be matched successfully against the program, so further exploration of this branch of the tree is suspended. A READLN PLAN is selected to implement the *Input* subgoal of the SENTINEL PROCESS-READ WHILE PLAN. This plan matches successfully, so the *Input* goal is satisfied. The SENTINEL PROCESS-READ WHILE PLAN has two *Input* subgoals, one for the initial input and the other for the input inside the loop. This second *Input* subgoal appears at level 6 in the figure. As this goal can also be satisfied using a READLN PLAN, all of the plan components of the SENTINEL PROCESS-READ WHILE PLAN are matched successfully. Further expansion of the tree then proceeds from the last subplan matched, at level 8; here an *Input Validation* goal is chosen for analysis.

At each node of the tree is stored all information which was gathered during the process of matching the corresponding derivation step against the program. As the analysis proceeds, assertions about the program are stored on the node where the assertion was made. These assertions are then inherited to the descendent nodes. Thus at any node in the tree the facts which are retrievable at that point include everything on the interpretation path from the root down to the node. A broader discussion of the kinds of assertions that are attached to nodes in the interpretation tree appears in Chapter 7.

The interpretation tree behaves functionally much like a database retrieval system

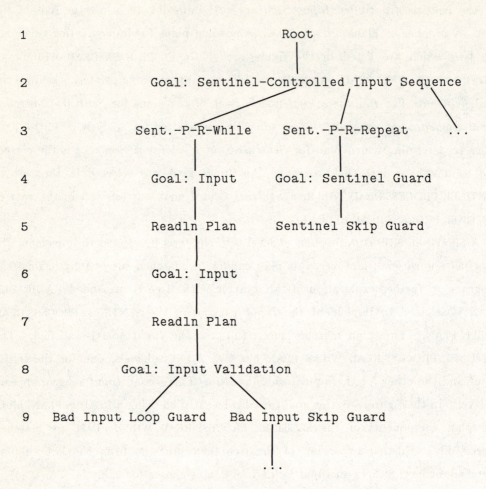

Figure 6-11: The interpretation tree

with multiple contexts or data pools [47]. However, the variety of queries that are made is rather limited. In particular, inference rules are not stored in the interpretation tree, and conjunctive queries are never performed. Therefore retrieval is fast.

6.8 Limitations of PROUST's knowledge-based approach

PROUST's knowledge base of goals, objects, and their implementations is rich enough
to model a wide range of novice goal decompositions. However, we continue to
encounter goal decompositions which PROUST cannot predict. Perhaps as PROUST's
knowledge base is enhanced the incidence of such outlying cases could be reduced. In
the mean time, however, these cases are beyond PROUST's ability to analyze;
fortunately they do not arise more than 10% of the time.

For example, I thought that I had enumerated the different ways that
Sentinel-Controlled Input Sequence can be implemented by students. When I tested
PROUST in the classroom, I found that I had missed some. One such case is shown in
Figure 6-12. This program treats the sentinel value as invalid input in certain cases.
Apparently the programmer felt that if the first value that the user types is the
sentinel, it must be invalid, because the user surely intended that at least one data
point be input. Therefore an additional loop was added above the main loop to
ensure that the first entry is not a sentinel value. When PROUST analyzes this
program it rejects the initial loop as spurious.

```
read(New);
while New = 99999 do
  begin
    writeln('Invalid entry, try again');
    read(New);
  end;
while New <> 99999 do
  begin
    while New < 0 do
      begin
        writeln('Invalid entry, try again');
        read(New);
      end;
    ...
    read(New);
  end;
```

Figure 6-12:   A program which requires that at least one valid datum be input

One can always add additional implementation methods for goals to PROUST, as novel interpretations of goals are encountered. However, some of these novel interpretations have only arisen once in the hundreds of sentinel-controlled loop programs that I have examined. Therefore it is not yet known how many more implementation methods need to be codified, or which ones are worth codifying.

7 Interpreting Unplan-Like Programs

The mechanisms described in Chapters 4 through 6 enable PROUST to predict plans that novices use in writing programs. If the novices' code fits these plans, then matching the plans against the programs allows PROUST to identify the intentions underlying the code. If, however, the code does not fit any plan exactly, then plan prediction is insufficient. Such programs are called *unplan-like* programs. This chapter discusses how PROUST deals with such unplan-like programs. The common causes of plan prediction failure will be described. A mechanism for dealing with such failures, called *plan-difference rules*, will be presented. The means by which PROUST uses plan-difference rules to understand the novices' intentions and explain their bugs will then be described.

The discussion will proceed as follows. First, an example of an unplan-like program will be presented. I will show why a plan knowledge base cannot be used to analyze such programs, and why plan-difference rules must be used to supplement plan analysis. Then the various components of plan-difference rules will be discussed in detail, along with the mechanism which PROUST uses for applying plan-difference rules. Finally, I will talk about the bug descriptions which PROUST's plan-difference rules generate, and discuss how they are used.

7.1 Explaining unplan-like programs using plan-difference rules

If a plan fails to match a program, it may simply be because the plan is an inappropriate match for the program. If a programmer constructs a loop using a process-read plan, for example, then read-process plans do not, and should not, match the programmer's code. The more interesting case is where a plan fails to match, but where the differences between the plan and the code, i.e., the *plan differences*, can suggest ways to improve the match, or to explain the match failure. This can happen in the following ways:

- the plan differences suggest how to modify the plan to make it match the programmer's intentions more closely;

- the plan differences are the result of bugs in the implementation of the plan.

I will discuss each of these types of plan differences in this section. I will show that the variability of novice implementations makes plan differences inevitable; one cannot eliminate plan differences simply by adding more plans. Instead, plan-difference rules, which explain plan differences, will be introduced,

7.1.1 Why plan templates alone are inadequate

Figure 7-1 shows an excerpt from a solution to the Rainfall Problem. The figure shows a fragment of code which was intended to compute the maximum value and the running total. The code which computes the running total is unusual because instead of there being a single statement for updating the running total in the loop, such as `Amount := Amount + Rainfall`, there are two. The updates are embedded in complementary parts of an `if-then-else` statement. One updates the running total when a new maximum value is read in, and the other updates the running total in all other cases.

```
Temp := 0;
Amount := 0.0;
...
while Rainfall <> 99999 do
  begin
    ...
    if Rainfall > Temp
      then begin
        Temp := Rainfall;
        Amount := Amount + Rainfall;
      end
    else Amount := Amount + Rainfall;
    ...
  end;
```

Figure 7-1: An unusual implementation of *Sum*

The code in Figure 7-1 is an example of an unplan-like implementation of the *Sum* goal. There is only one plan in PROUST's knowledge base which implements

Sum, namely the RUNNING TOTAL PLAN. Figure 7-2 shows what happens when this plan is matched against the code. The plan predicts that the `Update:` component of the plan will be in the `Process:` part of the loop. Instead, there are two statements which match the `Update:` component, and they are each embedded inside of an `if` statement. There are thus differences between the plan and the code.

```
Temp := 0.0;
Amount := 0.0;  ◄────────────┐       RUNNING TOTAL PLAN
...                          │
while Rainfall <> 99999 do    \      Variables: ?Total, ?New
  begin                        \
    ...                         \    Template:
    if Rainfall > Temp           \   Init: ?Total := 0
      then begin                        (in segment Process: of goal Read & process)
        Temp := Rainfall;         Update:  ?Total := (?Total + ?New)
        Amount := Amount + Rainfall;╱
      end                          ╱
    else Amount := Amount + Rainfall;╱
    ...
  end;
```

Plan differences:

1) duplicate matches for `Update:` component of the plan
2) each match embedded in an `if` statement

Figure 7-2:   Matching a plan against unplan-like code

The conclusion that we might draw from this example is that we need more plans in PROUST's knowledge base. If novices write programs with two running total updates, then perhaps we should add a variant of the RUNNING TOTAL PLAN with two updates. The problem with this solution is that update duplication is not confined to the RUNNING TOTAL PLAN. We can take any variable update and create a variant plan with two updates both embedded inside of an `if` statement. Thus for every plan in PROUST's database that has an update component, there would have to be an extra plan added to the database. Furthermore, the problem does not stop there. If a loop has three `if` statements, we might find goals implemented using *three* updates! Instances of twice-duplicated updates sometimes arise in novice solutions of the Rainfall Problem. There is no reason not to expect updates to be duplicated four or more times, given enough `if` statements.

As was described in Chapter 4, such unusual implementations can be viewed as resulting from plan transformations. The programmer presumably took the RUNNING TOTAL PLAN or something equivalent and modified it in order to integrate it into the program. The loop which the student was constructing has an `if` statement in it; for whatever reason, the student decided to transform the `if` statement by adding an `else` clause, and then add copies of the running total update to both clauses in the `if` statement. The resulting code is unplan-like, because the transformations obscure the structure of the plans that went into constructing the program.

Bugs are another cause of unplan-like code. Figure 7-3 shows an excerpt of a buggy solution to the Rainfall Problem where the running total update is below the main loop instead of inside it. Thus only the final sentinel value is added into the total. From the standpoint of plan matching, buggy code such as this is no different from transformed code. In both cases PROUST expects to find a plan component at one place in the program, and instead finds it in another place. It just happens that in the first example the misplaced code is correct, and in the second example the misplaced code is incorrect.

```
writeln('Enter value:');
read(Rainfall);
while Rainfall <> 99999 do
  begin
    ...
    Count := Count + 1;
    writeln('Enter value:');
    Read(Rainfall);
  end;
Amount := Amount + Rainfall;
```

Figure 7-3:   Unplan-like code caused by a bug

To a certain extent, the frequency of occurrence of plan differences due to bugs can be reduced by adding buggy plans to the plan knowledge base, as was described Chapter 4. Unfortunately, this can lead to an even worse explosion of the plan knowledge base than transformations do. There are many more ways of writing buggy unplan-like code than there are of writing correct unplan-like code. Thus there is no way of avoiding the problem of plan match failures.

186

7.1.2 Plan-difference rules

PROUST uses plan-difference rules to explain plan differences. Some plan-difference rules identify bugs which account for the plan differences. Others suggest plan transformations which generate the observed plan differences. Plan-difference rules are a type of production rule; they consist of a test part and an action part. The test part is a pattern which is compared against the plan differences. If the test part matches the plan differences, the action part is executed. The action part attempts to eliminate the plan differences, or to explain why they occurred.

The plan-difference rule which applies to the plan differences in Figure 7-2 is called the Distribution Transformation Rule. The function of this rule is illustrated in Figure 7-4. The Distribution Transformation Rule applies whenever plan differences arise because a plan component matches one or more lines of code which are unexpectedly embedded inside of `if` statements. The rule examines the test part of each `if` statement surrounding the matched code, in order to make sure that exactly one of the matched lines of code will execute, no matter what. Such is the case here, since one running total update is executed when `Rainfall > Temp`, and the other is executed when `Rainfall <= Temp`. The rule therefore fires. It marks each running total update, indicating where they would appear if the code were not transformed, i.e., below the `if` statement. The marking of the updates is necessary so that the MAXIMUM PLAN can match the code properly. When PROUST tries to match the MAXIMUM PLAN, it knows that the running-total updates are not involved in computing the maximum, even though they are part of the code which computes the maximum. In addition to marking the proper position of the running-total updates, the Distribution Transformation Rule declares that the novice's running-total updates are not buggy. PROUST requires that each plan-difference rule indicate whether or not the unplan-like code that it applies to is buggy, so that PROUST can decide what bugs must be reported to the student.[20]

The rule which applies to the plan differences in Figure 7-3 is called the Loop

---

[20]We could, if we chose, make the Distribution Transformation Rule declare this transformed code to be stylistically poor. Bug descriptions in PROUST are not confined to descriptions of actual faulty code; stylistic comments are sometimes included as well.

```
if Rainfall > Temp                      if Rainfall > Temp
  then begin                              then begin
    Temp := Rainfall;                       Temp := Rainfall;
    Amount := Amount + Rainfall;          end
  end                                     else;
else Amount := Amount + Rainfall;         Amount := Amount + Rainfall;
```

BUGS: None

Figure 7-4:   The effect of the Distribution Transformation Rule

Straggler Bug Rule. The effect of this rule is illustrated in Figure 7-5. When PROUST attempts to match the RUNNING TOTAL PLAN against this example, the match fails because there is no running total update inside the main loop. The Loop Straggler Bug Rule is then tried. This rule checks whether there are any updates below the loop. If so, it invokes the plan matcher on these updates, to see whether any of them fit the plan component, aside from being misplaced.[21] The update below the loop fits the RUNNING TOTAL PLAN, so the Loop Straggler Bug Rule fires, and marks the running total update as belonging inside the loop. The rule also declares that the running total update is buggy, that it appears below the loop instead of inside it. At the end of the program analysis, PROUST will describe this bug to the student, and will suggest a misconception which caused it, namely that the student thinks that the entire program will iterate instead of just the `while` loop.

We can see from these examples that rules which identify bugs and rules which identify transformations differ very little in their function. The main difference between bug rules and transformation rules is that bug rules mark the code to which they apply as buggy, and transformation rules do not. Even that difference is blurred in cases where PROUST comments on the novice's coding style. In such cases PROUST's transformation rules make notes of stylistically poor code, just as its bug rules make notes of buggy code. These notes then go into the bug report that PROUST generates for the students, just as do the bugs which the bug rules identify. Thus no distinction is made in PROUST between bug rules and transformation rules;

---

[21]If none of the updates below the loop fit the plan component exactly, the plan-difference rule application mechanism would be applied recursively on the new plan differences. This is unnecessary here, since the update below the loop fits the RUNNING TOTAL PLAN exactly.

188

```
read(Rainfall);              read( Rainfall );
while Rainfall <> 99999 do   while Rainfall <> 99999 do
   begin                        begin
      . . .                        . . .
      Count := Count+1             Count := Count+1;
      read(Rainfall);             Amount := Amount + Rainfall;
   end;                          Read(Rainfall);
Amount := Amount + Rainfall;   end;
```

BUG: Update misplaced below loop

Figure 7-5:   The effect of the Loop Straggler Bug Rule

PROUST's plan-difference rule representations and application mechanisms apply equally to bug rules and to transformation rules.

7.1.3 Uses of plan-difference rules

Many different kinds of plan differences can be recognized and interpreted using plan-difference rules. Plan-difference rules are most effective, however, when the plan differences have predictable characteristics, so that it is easy to determine which rules are appropriate to apply. The plan differences in the two examples earlier in this section are predictable: the Distribution Transformation always results in copies of code inside of `if` statements, and the Loop Straggler Bug always results in updates that are below the loop and above any subsequent processing of the data. In addition to predictability, another important characteristic of plan differences is whether they are localized in a single plan component or are spread over several plan components. If a number of different plan components have related plan differences, then a plan difference rule for interpreting them all will be complex, consisting of a number of different subtests. Furthermore, rule application would interact with plan matching, to ensure that all of the relevant plan components have been matched before the rule is applied. In such cases it is easier to add a new plan to the knowledge base, rather than try to interpret the plan differences. The following discussion is concerned with when plan differences are predictable and localized, and hence when plan difference rules are most useful for interpreting unplan-like code.

189

7.1.3.1 Cases where plan-difference rules are best suited

Transformations generally have fairly predictable effects on code. Transformations which move code, such as the Distribution Transformation, can be recognized because they move code to specific places in the program. Transformations which manipulate arithmetic and logical expressions, such as the transformation which changes the expression X <> 'a' into (X = 'b') or (X = 'c'), when X's value is known to be either 'a', 'b', or 'c', can be recognized by applying the transformation to the expression in the plan and seeing whether or not it fits the expression in the code. Plan-difference rules therefore are effective in analyzing transformed code.

When bugs result from misconceptions, they usually can be recognized by plan-difference rules. If novices have misunderstandings about programming, their programs will reflect those misunderstandings by having characteristic bugs. The Loop Straggler Bug is such a predictable bug. Other bugs characteristic of misconceptions are `while` statements in place of `if` statements, and counter overgeneralizations. As long as the effect of a misconception is predictable, a plan-difference rule can be written to recognize the effect.

7.1.3.2 Cases where plan-difference rules are less well suited

Plan-difference rules are less effective on bugs which result from random implementation errors, such as typographical errors and editing errors, than they are on systematic bugs. Such errors can take a variety of different forms, and one cannot predict where they might occur. Furthermore, such errors can be mistaken for other bugs or transformations. Suppose, for example, a programmer types X < 0 instead of X > 0. < and > are adjacent on most keyboards, so the error might be a typographical error. On the other hand, it might be that the programmer really intended to test whether X was negative. It is therefore not clear whether the test is buggy or not.

Although recognition of random errors is more difficult than recognition of systematic errors, it is nevertheless feasible. First, it is necessary to characterize regularities of distribution in random errors. There already exist various error correctors, such as the DWIM package in INTERLISP [67], which make use of regularities in the distribution of typographical errors. Second, one must rely heavily

190

upon the analysis of the intentions underlying the program, to determine what is likely to be an error and what is unlikely to be an error. PROUST has plan-difference rules which recognize various types of random errors. However, it has no rules for many types of typographical errors, because the potential for misinterpretation of the student's code is too great.

Other types of random errors which can cause trouble for plan-difference rules are errors resulting from random attempts at solving goals. If a novice has no idea of how to implement a particular goal, such as the maximum, he or she may be inclined to try something at random and see what happens. This can result in wildly unusual implementations. Fortunately the number of cases where a novice does not have a clue about what is going on is quite small, so this limitation on plan-difference rules is tolerable.

Another problem for plan-difference rules occurs when a plan has multiple buggy components. If a student's code differs in too many respects from the expected plan, it is extremely difficult to write a plan-difference rule which can account for the differences properly. Figure 7-6 contains an example which illustrates this difficulty. The program shown is an excerpt from a solution to the Rainfall Problem whose looping plan is substantially different from any sentinel-controlled loop plan. Instead of reading values and stopping when the stop value is read, this program prompts the user first for the number of values to be read, and then executes the body of the loop that number of times. In other words, instead of implementing a sentinel-controlled loop, this programmer has implemented a counter-controlled loop.

To interpret a buggy program such as the one in Figure 7-6 with a plan-difference rule would require a very complex rule, consisting of several components. One part of the rule would have to look for the erroneous `while` loop test, i.e., it would fire when seeing `while Counter < Limit do ...` instead of `while InchRain <> 99999 do ...` Further tests would then have to be performed to ensure that `Counter` is in fact a counter, and that `Limit` is read before the loop is executed. That would require further plan matching to determine the roles of `Counter` and `Limit`. Because of the complexities of such a rule, it is simpler to include the COUNTER-CONTROLLED WHILE PLAN as a buggy implementation of

```
writeln('How many days to you wish to have computed?');
readln(Limit);
Counter := 0;
...
while Counter <  Limit do
  begin
    writeln('How many inches of rain fell for this day?');
    readln(Inchrain);
    ...
    Counter := Counter + 1;
    ...
  end;
```

Figure 7-6: A program with a wildly different loop structure

Sentinel-Controlled Input Sequence, rather than to recognize the presence of the counter-controlled loop plan using a plan-difference rule.

7.2 Test parts of plan-difference rules

The previous section gave an overview of what plan-difference rules do. The following sections discuss the content of plan-difference rules in detail. They explain the issues which are involved in the design of a plan-difference rule system, in order to motivate PROUST's plan-difference rule formalism and plan-difference rule application mechanism. This section describes the test parts of plan-difference rules. The next section describes the action parts of plan-difference rules.

The structure of this section is as follows. First, the different types of information which plan-difference rules must examine is described. The issues involved in designing a rule test notation which describes such information are then discussed. Finally, PROUST's particular plan-difference test notation is presented.

7.2.1 Key issue: a wide variety of information to test

The primary triggers of plan-difference rules are naturally the plan differences which result from matching plans against a program. However, there is a wide variety of contextual information which plan-difference rule tests must examine, in addition to the plan differences themselves. All told, the following types of information are examined in test parts of plan-difference rules in PROUST:

- plan differences,

- the plan component being matched,

- the plan and goal currently being analyzed, as well as those which have been analyzed previously,

- the structure of the code being matched, or its intended structure, and

- bugs and misconceptions which have so far been identified.

This is not a complete list of the possible kinds of information of relevance to plan-difference rules. PROUST's plan-difference rules could in principle examine other information about the program, such as the program's indentation or the wording of its variable names. Anything which sheds light on the programmer's intentions is potentially relevant. Plan-difference rules thus must be able to perform an open-ended variety of tests.

In order to see how these different kinds of knowledge are used, let us consider some example plan-difference rules. Figure 7-7 is an English paraphrase of the Distribution Transformation Rule. The test part of this rule contains five parts. The first two parts examine the plan differences; the first makes sure that there is at least one partial match, and the second checks that they are each embedded inside of unexpected code. The next two parts examine the code around the match candidates, making sure that the match candidates are contained in `if` statements, and that data flows properly to each match candidate. The final test makes sure that no matter what the input is, exactly one of the match candidates will be executed. Thus this rule examines the context in which the plan differences occur as well as the plan differences themselves.

The Distribution Transformation Rule does not examine the plan component which is being matched; it can apply to most any plan component. The Missing Initialization Bug Rule shown in Figure 7-8 is an example of a rule which examines the current plan component as well as plan components of other plans. This rule fires when an initialization plan component is being matched, and no appropriate match can be found in the program. It also checks whether or not other `Init:`

IF one or more lines of code match the plan component partially
    AND these matches are embedded inside of some other unexpected code
    AND the match candidates are embedded inside `if` statements
    AND nothing interferes with the flow of data to the match candidates
    AND exactly one of the match candidates will be executed during each
        pass through the code
THEN
    combine the match candidates into a single statement and place it
    either above or below the `if` statements, depending upon whether
    the match candidates are at the top or the bottom of their corresponding
    IF statements.

Figure 7-7: A paraphrase of the Distribution Transformation Bug Rule

components have been found in the program.[22]

IF there are no match candidates
    AND the plan component is `Init:`
    AND some `Init:` components are present in previously-matched plans
THEN
    mark the `Init:` component as being accidentally omitted.

Figure 7-8: A missing initialization bug rule

A good example of a rule which examines the current goal and its context is the Sloppy Transaction Guard Bug Rule. This rule was introduced in Section 2.2.2; it is repeated in Figure 7-9. This rule examines the current goal to see if it is *Guard Exception*. It also checks to see whether or not the goal results from an object exception condition violation, and whether the object class in question is `TransactionAmount`.

---

[22]The Missing Initialization Bug Rule in PROUST currently lacks this sophistication. Such sophistication is necessary, however, because if the novice consistently leaves out initializations then the programmer probably has a misconception about variable initialization. Systematicity checks do currently appear in other plan-difference rules in PROUST.

194

IF   the goal is *GuardException*,
 AND the statement is a `while` statement or an `if` statement,
 AND the test is `>=` instead of `>`,
  OR `<=` instead of `<`,
  OR `>` instead of `>=`,
  OR `<` instead of `<=`,
 AND the *GuardException* goal arises from an object exception
 condition,
 AND the object class is `TransactionAmount`,
THEN
 the mismatch is due to a Sloppy Transaction Guard bug.

Figure 7-9: The Sloppy Transaction Guard Bug Rule

7.2.2 Representations for plan-difference rule tests

In many production systems, such as OPS5 [28], the test parts of the rules are strictly declarative. The tests are patterns which are matched against working memory. However, it is impractical to make plan-difference rule tests fully declarative. This is because the vocabulary which is required would be too large. Even though there are 74 different plan-difference rules in PROUST, a fair number have tests which are specific to the rule in which they appear. As new plan-difference rules are added, new generalizations about plan-difference rule tests are discovered, so the requirements of the bug test representation change. This is a direct reflection of the variability in novice programs. Until the vocabulary of plan-difference rule tests has been more fully enumerated, and the characteristics of these tests are better understood, a fully declarative plan-difference rule test representation cannot be achieved.

The necessity of procedural tests is illustrated by one of the tests in the Distribution Transformation Bug Rule, the test to ensure that exactly one match candidate is executed on each pass through the code. This test is currently performed by a Lisp function which does a special-purpose analysis of the program in order to determine whether or not this data-flow condition is met. No other rule examines a variety of data-flow paths like this, although other rules do examine program data flow. It is therefore not yet clear how one would describe this test declaratively.

Because there is so much variety in plan-difference rule tests, it would be desirable to simplify them, preferably without reducing their functionality. One method for achieving this is to introduce high-level abstractions for referring to plans and programs. As we saw in Chapter 4, when plans are represented in an abstract form, there is less variability in them. Because there is less variability, the plan differences which result from matching abstract plans are simpler to describe. It should therefore be easier to come up with a more concise declarative language for plan differences which can be used in plan-difference rule tests.

Suppose for example that plans and programs were described in an abstract data-flow representation, in which all programs with the same data flow are considered equivalent. Then rules such as the Distribution Transformation Rule would become greatly simplified. The Distribution Transformation does not affect the data flow of the code; there may be more copies of the same plan component in the program, but the flow of data among plans is the same. If a plan component does not match because the match candidates are embedded inside of `if` statements, the simplest way of determining whether the Distribution Transformation Bug Rule is applicable is to retry matching the plan component, using a data-flow representation the second time. If the plan now matches, then the plan component must be distributed. Special-purpose analyses of program data-flow are thus eliminated.

If plans and programs are represented in an abstract fashion, then bugs are harder to find, as I indicated in Section 4.3.3. That discussion assumed that there was a single level of representation for plans; here we are considering multiple representations for plans. We do not wish to discard the lower-level representation for plans; we wish to *add* high-level abstractions in order to make the plan-difference rules easier to state. The idea is to perform flow analysis on programs as they are read in, but use this flow analysis only when needed. When the abstract plan representation is used, plan differences become simpler and easier to describe; in the case of the Distribution Transformation Bug Rule, they disappear entirely.

Adding an additional level of program representation has its price, however. We would have to provide both high-level and low-level representations for plans, thus adding to the complexity of the plan knowledge base. The data-flow analysis imposes a fixed computational cost whenever a program is analyzed. Furthermore, PROUST would have to re-analyze the data-flow as its view of the intended function of the

196

program changes, or else keep track of dependencies between the syntactic structure and the data-flow structure.

The loop in Figure 7-10 is an example where re-analysis of data flow would be required. This loop has a bug; a `begin-end` pair is needed from the `else` statement down to the second `read(Rainfall)` statement. The Distribution Transformation appears to be at work here, because the loop has two `read(Rainfall)` statements. However, because the `begin-end` pair is missing, the data flow in the loop is differs from what the programmer intended. As a result, the Distribution Transformation Bug Rule cannot apply, either in a concrete form or an abstract form.

```
while Rainfall <> 99999 do
if Rainfall < 0 then
   begin
      writeln('impossible, try again');
      readln;
      read(Rainfall)
   end
else
   if Rainfall > 0 then
      Days := Days + 1;
if Rainfall > Highest then
   Highest := Rainfall;
if Rainfall >= 0 then
   begin
      Total := Total + Rainfall;
      Number := Number + 1;
      readln;
      read(Rainfall)
   end;
```

Figure 7-10: A program with a control-flow bug

Suppose that there was a bug rule which identifies missing `begin-end` pairs after else statements.[23] Since missing `begin-end` bugs obscure the intended structure of the program, bug rules for recognizing missing `begin-end` bugs must add the missing `begin` and `end` statements back into the program. As soon as we do this, however, we have to re-analyze the data flow of the loop, since it has changed.

At this time, the drawbacks of using data-flow abstractions to simplify plan-difference rule tests outweigh the advantages. I have not found any other trick for reducing the variety of information that bug rules must test for. As a result, it appears inevitable that bug rule tests in PROUST be only partly declarative, with some tests being performed by special-purpose procedures.

7.2.3 Plan-difference rule tests in PROUST

The declarative part of PROUST's plan-difference rules is called the *test pattern*, and the procedural part is called the *test procedure*. The test patterns consist of those tests which are common to a wide variety of rules, and which are cheap to perform. The test procedures contain tests which are special-purpose, or which would require excessive machinery to support in a declarative form.

Like goals and plans, plan-difference rules in PROUST are frames containing a collection of slots. Some slots define the test parts of the rules, and some define the action parts. The slots comprising the test part of each rule define properties which must hold in order for the rule to fire. The test procedure of each rule is usually held in the `TestCode` slot, although parts of the test procedure sometimes are incorporated into the action part of the rule, as will be described in Section 7.2.5. All other test slots are part of the test pattern. The Sum-Is-Counter Bug Rule in Figure 7-11 illustrates how bug tests are constructed. This rule is used to recognize bugs where counter updates have been used instead of running total updates, e.g., the student writes `Sum := Sum + 1` instead of `Sum := Sum + New`. The test pattern in this rule consists of two components, an `ErrorPatterns` slot and a `Goal` slot. The `ErrorPatterns` slot is a description of the plan differences which the rule applies to. In this rule the `ErrorPatterns` slot has the value `((*Ident* .   1))`;

---

[23]There is currently no such rule in PROUST. However, examples such as this motivated PROUST's representation of bug rules and the knowledge that they require.

this means that the plan difference should consist of finding a 1 where an identifier was expected. The `Goal` slot has the value `Sum`; this indicates that the goal which is being analyzed should be a *Sum* goal.

```
(DefineRule SumIsCounter
    ErrorPatterns
    ((*Ident* . 1))
    Goal
    Sum
    TestCode
    (let ((ExprNode
           (nth (PNode-Children (MRet-Node (BuggyMRet))) 1)))
         (any? (lambda (X)
               (symbol? (PNode-Name X)))
               (PNode-Children ExprNode)))
    Bug
    (WrongComponentForPlan
        (HistInst . ,*HistoryNode*)
        (PlanName . Counter)
        (FoundStmt . ,(MRet-Node (BuggyMRet))))))
```

Figure 7-11: A simple plan-difference rule

The remaining slot of this rule, the `Bug` slot, is part of the action part of the rule. Plan-difference rule actions will be discussed in Section 7.3.

7.2.4 Components of PROUST's test patterns

Plan-component rule test patterns are currently built up out of the following components:

- plan-difference categories,

- error patterns,

- goal patterns, and

- plan component patterns.

These tests all share the properties that they are fairly easy to state declaratively, and are also computationally inexpensive.

7.2.4.1 Plan-difference categories

A categorization for plan differences has been described in Bug Collection I [42]; this categorization was used in order to classify different kinds of novice bugs. This categorization scheme is also used in PROUST's plan-difference rule tests in order to describe the kind of plan difference that a plan-difference rule applies to.

Plan differences were categorized along two dimensions in Bug Collection I. One dimension classifies the plan component as being either missing, malformed, misplaced, or spurious. PROUST classifies plan components in the same fashion, although there are no plan-difference rules which look for spurious components. This is because spurious code is analyzed in a separate post-analysis step, which is described in Chapter 8.

The other dimension of classification in Bug Collection I was the type of plan component in which the error occurred. This is denoted in PROUST by the label of the buggy plan component, e.g., `MainLoop:`, `Update:`, etc. The different plan component types PROUST's plans are listed in Section 4.4. The categorization in Bug Collection I also had a Complex Plan category, which was used in cases where an entire plan was buggy, not just one plan component. This is realized in PROUST with the category `Plan`, which is used in cases where an entire plan is buggy, as opposed to just a single plan component.

Plan difference categories appear in the `PlanDifference` slot of plan-difference rules. The Missing Input Initialization Bug Rule, shown in Figure 7-12, is an example of a rule which has a `PlanDifference` slot. This rule says that if the `InitInput:` step of a *Read&Process* loop is missing, and the `Next:` step is present, then it is acceptable to presume that the student omitted the `InitInput:` step. (If the `Next:` step is missing too, then this is not simply a case of an omitted initialization; rather, the student has some basic misconception about how to read a sequence of data.) The `PlanDifference` slot of this rule has the value `(Missing InitInput:)`.

```
(DefineRule MissingInputInitialization
     PlanDifference
     (Missing InitInput:)
     Goal
     Read&Process
     TestCode
     (LocalLabelBinding 'Next: *HistoryNode*)
     Bug
     (Missing (SegmentType . InitInput:)
              (HistInst . ,*HistoryNode*)))
```

Figure 7-12:   A rule using plan-difference descriptions

7.2.4.2 Further characterizations of plan differences

Of the various categories of plan differences, the malformed plan component category covers the widest range of errors. Plan-difference rules must therefore specify exactly what kind of malformed plan component they apply to. This is done using an ErrorPatterns slot.

ErrorPatterns slots contain a list of dotted pairs. Each dotted pair serves as a pattern for the error to be matched. As was indicated in Section 4.6.3, when a statement fails to match the plan pattern exactly a list of dotted pairs is generated describing the errors. The error pattern describes the type of error pair which the rule expects to find among the plan differences. For example, the Update: component of the RUNNING TOTAL PLAN is of the form ?Total := ?Total + ?New, or in PROUST's list notation (:= ?TOTAL (+ ?TOTAL ?NEW)). When this is matched against a counter update, such as Sum := Sum+1, the error (?NEW .   1) is generated. The Sum-is-Counter Bug Rule has an error pattern (*Ident* .   1), which is matched against this error pair. *Ident*, which matches any identifier, matches ?NEW; this is because ?NEW will have been bound to the new-value variable before the plan is matched. 1, of course, matches 1. Thus the error pattern fits the plan difference. Error patterns can have constant symbols in them, such as 1 or +, or special symbols which match certain types of expressions: *Ident*, *Const*, *Expr*, or *Code*.

7.2.4.3 Other components of test patterns

There are currently two additional slots in bug rules which are part of the test pattern: `Goal`, and `StmtType`. Each of these will be described in turn.

The `Goal` slot indicates the goal or type of goal which is being matched. We saw examples of this in Figures 7-11 and 7-12. The goal description can either be the name of a goal, or the name of a goal class, such as *Read & Process*.

The `StmtType` slot indicates the type of statement which the plan pattern matches. For example, if the `StmtType` slot of a bug rule is `if` then the rule will only apply when the plan pattern is an `if` statement. The `StmtType` slot can also be filled with the name of a more general class of statements, such as `*TestingStmt*`, which is the class of all statements which perform tests, i.e., `while`, `repeat`, and `if`.

7.2.5 Tests embedded in rule actions

The procedural part of bug tests usually appears in the `TestCode` part of bug rules. Such test procedures can be fairly arbitrary Lisp code. Sometimes, however, some of the procedural part of a bug rule test is placed in the action part of the rule. Tests which appear in the action part of a rule are thus performed only after the rule has been activated.

Suppose that two rules have a number of tests in common, and some of these tests are computationally expensive. In such a case it is desirable to collapse the two rules into a single rule, and place the tests which differentiate the two rules in the action part of the rule. For example, a variant of the Distribution Transformation Rule deals with plan components which are duplicated, but where not every path through the code has a copy of the duplicated plan component. This usually indicates that the programmer left out one of the plan component copies by mistake. Rather than have a separate rule to deal with such cases, the Distribution Transformation Rule and its variant have been combined into a single rule. The test to ensure that every path has a plan component copy has been placed in the action part of PROUST's implementation of the Distribution Transformation Rule, rather than in the test procedure.

Bug rule tests can appear in the action parts of rules in order to delay the execution of the test, because the information necessary to perform the test is lacking. Such delayed tests are called *verification demons*. An example of a verification demon was discussed in connection with the Contingent Realization Rule in Section 2.3.3.3. There a demon was described which tested whether any *Compensate* goal which corrects the effects of invalid input is explicitly realized in the program. This test cannot be performed until after the *Compensate* goals have been examined, so a verification demon is necessary.

7.3 Action parts of bug rules

Action clauses in plan-difference rules in PROUST perform up to three different kinds of actions:

- plan modification,

- declaring the presence of bugs, and

- modification of the current view of the intended structure of the program.

Plan modification is performed when the nature of the plan differences indicate that a transformed version of the plan is more likely to fit the code. An example of a rule in PROUST which modifies the plan pattern is the `OR` Expression Insertion Rule. This is a transformation which manipulates statements which test for membership in a finite fixed set. For example, if the variable `Cmd` takes values in the set {`'d'`, `'e'`, `'w'`}, then the `or` Expression Insertion Rule will change `while Cmdn<> 'e' do` ... into `while (Cmd='d') or (Cmd='w') do` ... The rule works by noting the `or` in the test in the program, examining the definition of the object being tested, and generating a new plan pattern based upon the set of values which the object can take. The new plan pattern must then be matched against the code, and if necessary more bug rules are applied until all plan differences are accounted for.

Declaring the presence of bugs involves adding a description of the bug to the current node in the interpretation tree. After the analysis is complete, PROUST traverses the path from the final leaf of the interpretation tree back to the root, reading off the bugs that it finds attached to the nodes along this path. This set of bugs is then reported to the student. PROUST's representation of bugs is discussed in Section 7.6.

Modification of the view of the intended structure of the program is performed when it is necessary to make the underlying structure of the program more explicit. Several examples of rules which perform program structure modification have been presented in this chapter; the Distribution Transformation Bug Rule is one such example. Such modifications are performed when the intended location of a statement has to be changed, when missing statements must be added, or when duplicated statements must be merged. Modification of program structure is particularly important in rules which identify bugs resulting from misconceptions, because the novice's misconception can both obscure the intent of the code and affect the function of the code.

Modification of the view of the intended structure of the program is performed by adding assertions to the current node of the interpretation tree. PROUST's internal program representation is can be viewed as a set of nodes, each denoting a statement or expression in the program, and a set of parent-child relations between plans. PROUST changes its view of the structure of the program by asserting new parent-child relations, and adding them to the current interpretation tree node. These new assertions take precedence over any previous relations. As long as the current interpretation is believed, the new program structure will be in force. If for some reason PROUST is forced to abandon this interpretation path and try another one, the changes to the program structure are no longer visible, and hence are no longer in force.

Rule actions in the PROUST are built up out of the following two components:

- a *bug description*, a declarative template for describing the bug which the rule identifies; and

- an *action procedure*, which performs all the other actions of the rule.

Bug descriptions are listed in the `Bug` slots of the rules. Action procedures appear in the `Action` slots of the rules. When PROUST activates a bug rule it first creates an instance of the bug description, stores it on the interpretation tree, and then executes the action procedure.

7.4 Comparison with other rule-based approaches

PROUST is not the only system which uses diagnostic rules for recognizing bugs. However, as Chapter 3 described, it is the only system which uses diagnostic rules within an intention-based framework. Now that we have examined PROUST's plan-difference rules, I will compare them against the rules in the two systems which most closely resemble PROUST, Dan Shapiro's SNIFFER [54] and Anderson *et al.*'s LISP Tutor [27]. This comparison is specifically intended to compare the different systems of diagnostic rules; a more general comparison of diagnostic approaches can be found in Chapter 3.

The structure of SNIFFER's rules is somewhat similar to that of PROUST's rules. The test part of each of SNIFFER's rules consists of two parts. The first part, called the trigger, is a computationally inexpensive test for determining whether or not the rule is likely to be relevant. The second part, called the body of the rule, performs more in-depth analysis of the program. This separation between rule triggers and rule bodies is similar to the distinction between test patterns and test procedures in PROUST. However, there does not appear to be a declarative language for describing such triggers. This is no doubt because Shapiro's system has very few bug rules, so there was no opportunity to characterize the content of Sniffer's rule triggers.

After the body of each rule is executed, a template report generator is executed. This generates a description of the bug, in English, which is presented to the programmer. This serves a similar role to the bug descriptions in the action parts of PROUST's rules. Yet while PROUST's rules generate a bug description representation which in turn can be manipulated by PROUST (see Section 7.6), there is no intermediate representation in SNIFFER. The template report generators are simply output routines.

SNIFFER's rule tests do not examine as wide a range of information as PROUST's rules. In fact, they cannot, because SNIFFER does not have as wide a range of information available about the program as PROUST does. PROUST builds an interpretation of the program, and SNIFFER does not. SNIFFER's rules are restricted to examining the program and its execution trace. This restricts the range of bugs that SNIFFER can find. Since no internal representation of bugs is used, SNIFFER cannot look for co-occurrences of bugs, and hence is less able to identify misconceptions.

Bug rules of a sort appear in Anderson *et al.*'s Lisp Tutor. The Lisp Tutor contains a set of production rules which analyze the students' programming behavior. Some of these production rules are used to interpret buggy implementations. The test parts of these rules tend to be very simple. They usually only look at the current set of active goals. Occasionally they look at working memory, which can contain arbitrary information deposited by other rules. However, no program analysis, correlations of bugs, or other analysis of the program interpretation is performed. This is probably largely due to smaller size of the problems which the Lisp Tutor usually handles. However, because the Lisp Tutor's rules analyze the program as it is being constructed, they do not have to perform as wide a range of analysis as PROUST's rules. The Lisp Tutor can presume that one of the current active goals corresponds to the code which the student is currently writing. As the Lisp Tutor is made to analyze programs of the size that PROUST analyzes, the relation between goals and code will become more involved, with greater possibility of goal reformulation. One would then expect that more effort would be devoted to analyzing the program and constructing an interpretation, and bug rules would become more complex as they perform more detailed examinations of this model.

7.5 Application of plan-difference rules

This section discusses PROUST's mechanism for applying plan-difference rules. Given that a plan has been matched against code, and plan differences have been found, this section describes how rules are applied to explain the differences. I will not address here the issue of how PROUST decides whether or not to try to explain the plan differences, or whether or not an explanation is adequate. These issues will be addressed in the following chapter, in connection with the discussion of PROUST's methods of evaluating and choosing between different program interpretations.

7.5.1 The approach and its motivations

The key requirements of a plan-difference rule application mechanism are that it apply rules which help explain plan differences, and avoid rules which do not contribute to an explanation. It must be able to chain rules and consider alternative rules to apply, but it must avoid blind application of rules.

The example in Figure 7-13 will be used to illustrate the kinds of rule application that must be permitted and the kinds that should be avoided. The loop in this example is the main loop of a solution to the Rainfall Problem. The exit test of the loop is incorrect; it should be `New <> 99999`, but instead it is `(New < 9999) and (New <= 0)`. PROUST's plan-difference rules must establish that this loop really is the sentinel-controlled loop of the program, and explain why its exit test is different from what was expected.

```
while (New < 9999) and (New <= 0) do
  begin
    Count := Count + 1;
    Sum := Sum + New;
    if 0 < New then
      Rainy := Rainy + 1;
    if New > Max then
      Max := New;
    writeln('Next value please:');
    read(New);
  end;
```

Figure 7-13: Buggy code subject to various possible rule applications

In order to explain the bugs in the loop in Figure 7-13, PROUST must permit plan-difference rules to chain. The following three rules apply together. First, a rule called the Conjoined Loop Bug Rule applies, which suggests that the exit test of the loop is performing two tests at once, which are combined using an **and** operator. The actual sentinel-control test should be one of the two clauses of the **and** expression. Second, a Sloppy Sentinel Guard Bug Rule suggests that the student may not be testing specifically for the sentinel value but instead for any value greater than or equal to the sentinel value. Thus the student would be expected to write `New <`

99999 instead of New <> 99999. Finally, the Typo Rule suggests that 9999 is a typographical error, and really should be 99999.

The need for rule chaining means that when PROUST applies a plan-difference rule, it cannot be certain whether or not the rule really accounts for the plan differences. When the Conjoined Loop Bug Rule applies, it can suggest that one of the conjuncts of the **and** clause is the sentinel test, but it cannot determine with certainty which one is the sentinel test. Neither conjunct matches the expected sentinel test exactly. PROUST must therefore try to apply more rules before it can determine whether or not the Conjoined Loop Rule is an appropriate rule to apply. Unfortunately if there is no way of determining at rule application time whether or not a rule is applicable, then all sorts of irrelevant rules might be attempted. PROUST might try commuting the sentinel test, to see if 99999 <> New fits the code better than New <> 99999. Such blind application of rules must be avoided.

Another situation which should be avoided is to apply rules involving unusual explanations of plan differences when more commonplace explanations are available. Consider for example the computation of the rainy day counter in Figure 7-13, if 0 < New then Rainy := Rainy + 1. The plan which PROUST tries to match in this case has a test of the form New > 0 instead of 0 < New; therefore the plan does not match. When the plan fails to match, PROUST could try to apply the Loop Straggler Bug Rule, looking for a counter update below the main loop. Alternatively, it could try to apply the while-for-if Bug Rule, looking for a while loop which the student intended to function as an if statement. However, neither of these rules is appropriate to apply as long as there are if statements in the loop which are partial matches for the GUARDED COUNTER PLAN. In this case all that is needed is to apply a rule to commute the New > 0 expression in the plan, resulting in the expression 0 < New. Once this is done, the plan matches the statement if 0 < New then Rainy := Rainy + 1 exactly.

In order to restrict unnecessary rule application of the types shown above, PROUST's rule application mechanism implements the following policies. First, a constraint-relaxation approach is used. Each rule is given a ranking when it is incorporated into the knowledge base. This ranking takes into account whether or not the rule identifies bugs, and the severity of the misconceptions that cause the bugs. It also takes into account whether the rule attempts to explain the plan differences in a statement which has already been matched, or whether it causes the plan matcher to search elsewhere in the program for possible matches. Those rules which do not presume bugs and which apply to existing partial matches are attempted first; then if necessary rules involving progressively more serious bugs and which involve greater amounts of search of the program are considered. Thus the constraints on rule application are progressively lifted until a suitable explanation is found. Similar constraint relaxation schemes have been employed in other debugging systems such as Davis's [22].

The other policy which PROUST's plan-difference rule application mechanism follows is to apply only those rules which appear to help explain the plan differences. In other words, PROUST has metrics of how good a match is, and tries to apply a rule only if it results in an improved match. I will describe these metrics later in this section, when I describe the details of the rule application mechanism. Note that improvement in the match does not ensure that a rule is appropriate to apply. The new plan differences may be unexplainable, in which case the rule application mechanism must backtrack and try a different rule. Insisting on improvement of the match metric is nevertheless a sufficient restriction to eliminate most unnecessary rule applications.

It should be said at the outset that constraining rule application in the manner described above has a price, in terms of missed diagnoses. The correct diagnosis is not always the most constrained one, and the correct rule to apply does not always produce an immediate improvement in the plan differences. PROUST may ultimately be forced to apply a wider range of rules in order to achieve greater diagnostic accuracy. Alternative rule selection schemes are possible which apply a range of relevant rules without applying too many more irrelevant rules; some of these will be considered below. Another problem with constraining rule application is that it causes PROUST to overlook alternative explanations for plan differences. PROUST currently adopts the first plausible explanation of plan differences that it comes across.

7.5.2 Organizing rules into pools

A ranking of plan-difference rules is achieved in PROUST by organizing rules into pools. PROUST has the following rule pools, in order of decreasing ranking.

- Exact-match rules -- these are rules which apply when an exact match of the plan component has been found, but in an unexpected place. These rules attempt to account for the plan-differences via transformations. The Distribution Transformation Rule is contained in this pool.

- Local rules -- these are rules which attempt to explain plan differences in a given partial match. They are called local rules because their effects are local to the plan component and the partial match. They do not attempt to transform the structure of the plan, or cause the plan matcher to look for partial matches elsewhere in the program.

- Misplacement rules -- rules which look for possible matches in places where the plan matcher does not ordinarily look. The Loop Straggler Bug Rule is an example of such a rule.

- Missing-component rules -- rules which identify missing plan components. The Missing Initialization Rule is such a rule.

- Rules which indicate that a goal has not been implemented. Ordinarily PROUST will not assume that a plan is missing unless there is a rule which indicates that the goal is likely to be omitted. Otherwise PROUST will terminate analysis of the goal and choose a different goal form analysis, and then try the first goal again later on.

Partially-matched plans have rankings, just as plan-difference rules do. These rankings are initially assigned by the plan matcher when the plan match fails. The pool of rules which is applied to a plan depends upon the current ranking of the plan. The possible match rankings are as follows:

- OK -- no rule need be applied.

- ExactChoice -- there exist match candidates which match exactly, but their position is slightly perturbed. The exact-match rule pool is applied here.

- PartialChoice -- no match candidates match exactly, but some match candidates match partially, in the region of the program where an exact match was expected. The local bug and transformation pool is activated.

- NoPartialChoice -- there are no exact or partial match candidates close to the target region. The misplacement-rule pool is activated.

210

- **NoMisplaced** -- there are no possible match candidates of any sort. The missing plan component pool is used.

- **NoMissingSegment** -- no-missing-plan-component rule was able to fire. The missing-plan pool is activated.

- **Rejected** -- all possibilities for explanation are exhausted. The plan which the plan component is part of is rejected.

If plan-difference rules succeed in accounting for the plan differences, the ranking of the plan is set to OK, and plan matching resumes. If no rule from a particular pool applies, the ranking of the plan is reduced one level. Rule application is then suspended. PROUST then typically looks for some other plan with a higher ranking to which plan-difference rules can be applied, or else resumes rule application on the current plan if no alternative plans are available. If rule application is resumed, then since the new ranking is one step lower, the next lower pool of rules will be activated.

7.5.3 Rule application mechanisms for each rule pool

The rule application mechanism that is used for each pool of rules is different, depending upon the amount of chaining that is involved. Different pools of bug rules must chain in different ways. Missing-goal rules, for example, cannot chain, since a goal is either declared missing or is not. For local bug rules, on the other hand, chaining is very important, because the same plan component may be subject to a number of bugs and transformations at once. The while statement in Figure 7-13, for example, has three different bugs; the rules which identify these bugs are all local rules.

If rules in a particular pool do not chain, then the application mechanism for that pool simply applies one rule after another until a rule fires. The missing-goal pool, the missing-plan component pool and the exact-match pool are all in this category. The other pools have more complex application mechanisms; they will be described below.

7.5.3.1 Local rules

There are two types of local bug rules in PROUST. One type is called *serial local rules*, and the other is called *parallel local rules*. The names derive from the way each type of rule is applied. Recall that match errors are described as a list of error pairs. Parallel local rules account for an individual error pair, and do not examine the other error pairs. Such rules thus can be applied in parallel to the error pairs. Serial local rules, on the other hand, account for a plan difference by generating a new plan pattern which hopefully is closer to the code. Once the new pattern is matched, a whole new set of match errors may result. Thus serial local rules must be applied one after another on each successive set of match errors, until a point is reached where all match errors are accounted for.

Of the three rules which apply to the `while` loop in Figure 7-13, one of them, the Conjoined While Loop Rule, is a serial local rule. The other two rules, the Sloppy Sentinel Guard Rule and the Typo Rule, are parallel local rules. The Conjoined While Loop Rule is a serial rule because it generates new plan patterns to be matched against the program. In the example in 7-13 it operates as follows. The original plan pattern for the `while` loop is `while ?New <> ?Stop do ??`. The Conjoined While Loop Rule generates two new plan patterns,

```
while (?New <> ?Stop) and ?? do ??, and
while ?? and (?New <> ?Stop) do ??.
```

The first pattern corresponds to the possibility that the true exit test is the first conjunct of the **and** expression, and the second pattern matches if the true exit test is the second conjunct. When these new patterns are matched against the `while` statement in the example, new sets of plan differences result. In the first case the new plan differences are `(<> . <) (99999 . 9999)` indicating that a `<` operator was found where a `<>` operator was expected, and `9999` was found where `99999` was expected. In the other case the new errors are `(<> . >=) (99999 . 0)`. PROUST then tries to apply further rules to account for these new errors. In the case of the first set of errors, the Sloppy Sentinel Guard Rule and the Typo Rule together can explain the errors. The Sloppy Sentinel Guard Rule triggers on the error pair `(<> . <)`. The Typo Rule triggers on the error pair `(99999 . 9999)`. Since the two rules apply to different error pairs, they can be applied in parallel.

212

Local rules are applied as follows. The rule application mechanism retrieves all the partial match candidates for the current plan component. Rules are applied on each partial match in turn, until one candidate has all of its errors explained, or until all of the partial matches have been processed. For each partial match, the serial rules are first applied. If these rules are insufficient for accounting for the differences, the parallel local rules are then applied.

7.5.3.2 Serial rule application

Serial rules are applied in the following manner. If the test part of a serial rule succeeds, the action part of the rule is executed. This action part generates one or more new plan patterns. These are then matched against the same line of code that was matched previously. The number of match errors which result from matching the new plan patterns is counted. If this number is less than the original number, then another rule is applied to resolve the new errors. If the number of new match errors is greater than or equal to the number of old match errors, then the new plan pattern is thrown out. If all of the new plan patterns are thrown out, the rule fails, and the rule application mechanism goes on to try the next rule.

The number of match errors is thus used as a metric of how close the plan pattern matches the code. This metric is not ideal; sometimes a rule will produce a plan pattern which generates the same number of errors, but the new errors are explainable, whereas the old ones were not. If the constraint were relaxed, so that rules would be applied as long as the number of errors does not increase, then it is possible to go into an infinite loop. The rule application mechanism could apply the same sequence of rules repeatedly, without ever converging on a complete explanation of the match errors. One way of preventing this would be to keep track of the rules which apply, and not allow the same rule to apply to the same set of match errors. Experiments using this approach indicate that it is more effective at finding explanations for match errors, and the cost in terms of extra rule applications does not appear to be excessive.

7.5.3.3 Parallel rule application

Application of parallel rules is done as follows. For each match error, PROUST checks whether or not there is a rule which can explain that error. As soon as a rule fires and explains the error, PROUST goes on to the next match error. If a match error cannot be explained, then the process ends in failure.

Since the parallel rule application mechanism stops as soon as each match error is explained, it does not consider the possibility that there are multiple explanations for the match errors. This means, for example, that the Typo Bug Rule must be severely restricted in its application. It applies in only a few cases, for example when a student types 9999 instead of 99999, and in hardly any other case. If it applied too frequently it would prevent alternative rules from being considered. Even though < might be written in place of <> due to a typographical error, the Typo Bug Rule cannot be permitted to apply in this case because there are other rules, such as the Sloppy Sentinel Guard Rule, which also trigger on this match error. It would be preferable to look for all possible rules which could apply, and then decide among the resulting explanations of the match errors, rather than arbitrarily restrict the applicability of individual rules.

7.5.3.4 Application of misplacement rules

Misplacement rules are tried one after another on a plan, until one of them applies. Currently two misplacement rules cannot apply at the same time; chaining is not allowed. However, chaining from misplacement rules to rules in higher-level pools is supported. For example, imagine that an update which should appear inside of a loop appears instead below the loop, and furthermore has a typo in it. The Loop Straggler Bug Rule would apply, but it would not succeed in accounting for all of the plan differences, because of the typographical error. The local rule pool is therefore activated to account for the remaining differences. The Typo Bug rule is then applied, explaining the typographical error.

214

7.6 Bug descriptions and their use

As PROUST applies plan-difference rules, the rules generate descriptions of bugs and misconceptions. These descriptions are frames characterizing the bug and the context in which it was found. There are two types of representations which PROUST uses for describing bugs. Superficial representations are used when PROUST is able to locate and characterize the plan difference, but cannot identify the cause. Deeper representations are used when PROUST can describe the bug as an error in the student's goal decomposition, or as a misconception.

7.6.1 Superficial bug descriptions

Superficial bug descriptions in PROUST use the notations in Bug Collection I [42] for describing bugs. In this system, the bugs are classified as being either missing plan components, spurious plan components, misplaced plan components, or malformed plan components. The plan components themselves are characterized according to the function that they perform, i.e., initialization, input, output, update, guard, or non-executable statement. The function of the plan component comes from the label assigned to that component in the plan, e.g., `Init:`, `MainLoop:`, etc.

7.6.2 Deeper bug descriptions

If a likely explanation for a bug can be found, PROUST describes the bug in terms of that explanation. The following explanatory descriptions of bugs are used:

- `Implements Wrong Goal` -- some goal was implemented in the program other than the one required by the problem statement. For example, if a student writes a counter-controlled loop instead of a sentinel-controlled loop, this is classified as an `Implements Wrong Goal` bug.

- `Wrong Plan for Goal` -- the student's plan for implementing a goal does not achieve the goal. This happens if the plan is a buggy plan, for example. `Wrong Plan for Goal` is also the category of cases where the student's plan achieves the goal, but also has an unwanted side-effect, such as clobbering a variable which is used later on in the program.

- `Misconception` -- the student's code indicates the presence of a specific misconception. There has to be evidence of a misconception in more than one place in the program for PROUST to classify it as a misconception. This category is further subcategorized according to type of misconception involved. The following misconceptions can be positively identified by PROUST:

- ○ `Data Flow Misconception` -- the novice does not understand how data flows through complex control structures such as loops. The novice does not realize that the statements are executed in strict sequence, so that if one statement modifies a variable subsequent statements will refer to the modified value.

- ○ `Lower Loop Scope Misconception` -- the novice does not understand how the lower boundary of a loop is signaled, i.e., by the end of the `begin-end` block of the loop body.

- ○ `Systematic Missing Guard Exception Misconception` -- the novice systematically fails to introduce *Guard Exception* goals for boundary conditions. This may be because the novice does not know to look for boundary conditions when writing programs.

- ○ `Systematic Missing Initialization Misconception` -- the novice systematically omits initializations. This may be because the novice thinks that the variables will be initialized automatically, or does not properly understand the concept of initialization.

- • `Implements Wrong Goal Argument` -- a goal is implemented in the student's code, but one of the arguments of the goal is incorrect. For example, a *Guard Exception* goal might test for the wrong boundary condition.

- • `Improper Contingent Goal` -- a goal was implemented contingently, and this resulted in a bug, because one or more cases was overlooked where the goal needed to be implemented.

- • `Wrong Component for Plan` -- the student's plan for implementing a goal contains a component which is appropriate to a different plan. For example, the student might write a counter update instead of a running total update.

- • `Mistransformed Code` -- the student attempted to transform a plan, and did not do so successfully, resulting in a bug.

- • `Typo` -- the student made a typographical error.

216

7.6.3 Characterizations of PROUST's analysis

PROUST also uses bug descriptions to characterize the state of completion of the student's program, and the degree of completeness of the rest of the bug analysis itself. Although not bugs per se, they are nevertheless treated as bugs, in that they are passed on to the bug-report generator for presentation to the student. The two types of characterizations are:

- `Incomplete Analysis` -- there are major sections of the program which PROUST is unable to interpret.

- `Incomplete Program` -- some goals were not implemented in the student's program, which the problem statement explicitly required.

7.6.4 The form of bug descriptions

Each bug description which PROUST generates consists of a bug category, together with a set of parameters describing the specific circumstances of the bug. Like everything else in PROUST, these bug descriptions are stored as frames; the bug category and the parameters are all slot fillers. The fillers required for each bug description depends upon the category of bug. The various slots, and the bug categories that use them, are listed below.

- `Name` -- the bug category. This slot appears in all bug descriptions.

- `GoalNames` -- names of goals, e.g., goals which were not implemented. Used in `Incomplete Analysis`, `Incomplete Program`, `Missing`, and `Implements Wrong Goal`.

- `GoalInst` -- an instantiation of a goal, other than the current one. Used in those bug descriptions which make reference to more than one goal. For example, if an output is missing from the program, the bug description must refer both to the missing *Output* goal and to the goal which generated the value to be output.

- `HistInst` -- a node from the interpretation tree, where the bug was found. Virtually all bug descriptions have this slot, to provide a pointer to the appropriate point in the interpretation tree.

- `Statements` -- code where the bug occurs. All bug descriptions except for `Missing` bugs and `Incomplete Program` include this slot.

- **RefStmts** -- statements which provide context for describing a bug, but which are not where the bug actually occurs. For example, if a bug description indicates that a statement is in the wrong place, the `Statements` slot indicates which statement is in the wrong place, and the `RefStmts` slot indicates where the misplaced statement should be located.

- **StmtNames** -- statement which should have been found in the program but were not. `Missing` bugs frequently use this slot.

- **ComponentType** -- the type of plan component in which the bug was found, i.e., `Input:`, `Update:`, etc. Used in `Spurious`, `Missing`, and `Malformed` bugs.

- **ExpectedExpr** -- an expression which the plan pattern indicated should have been in the program. Used in `Typo` bugs and some `Mistransformed Code` bugs.

- **FoundExpr** -- the expression which in fact was found in the program. Always occurs together with `ExpectedExpr` slots.

- **Keyword** -- a symbol indicating the subclass of the bug. This is required in `Misconception` bugs, `Mistransformed Code` bugs, and `Malformed` bugs.

- **Uncertain?** -- indicates the degree of certainty of PROUST's attribution of the cause of the bugs. This is used in `Misconception` bugs.

7.6.5 Reporting bug descriptions

After the analysis of a program is complete, the bug descriptions which were created during analysis are collected and reported to the student. First, the bug descriptions are sorted according to the severity of the bug, and the part of the program in which the bug occurs. Then for each bug, an English description is generated. The English is generated using an ordinary phrasal generator, which selects a phrase to generate based upon the type of the bug and the slot fillers of the bug. Blank fields in the phrase are filled in with the names of goals, the line numbers at which statements occur, the names of variables, and other information which might supply context for the bug.

We are also experimenting with other, non-textual methods for describing bugs. In particular, we have built a mechanism for generating example test data which will cause the bug to manifest itself as invalid input/output behavior. These examples are used to supplement the textual description of the bug. These data are currently generated from templates, indexed by type of bug and by programming problem; each template is entered by hand. Concrete examples appear help students understand their bugs; however, entering the data templates by hand is too cumbersome. It would be worthwhile to build a mechanism which can generate test data automatically from the student's goal decomposition.

7.7. Factors influencing the form of PROUST's interpretations

We have now examined each component of the interpretations that PROUST constructs for programs. These interpretations contain a variety of information; altogether, they may include the following:

- a goal decomposition,

- matches of the plans in the goal decomposition against the code,

- bugs,

- differences between the intended function of individual statements and the actual function of these statements, and

- possible misconceptions.

This information fits into the following general categories:

- what the programmer did in solving the problem,

- what the programmer was trying to do,

- flaws in his/her knowledge which resulted in problem-solving errors.

These same types of information are found in the student models that many ICAI systems generate. All ICAI systems to varying degrees attempt to characterize the student's program-solving process, and the knowledge that underlies this process. ICAI systems tend to differ, however, in how they describe student's knowledge and problem-solving process. The following will point out some of the differences between PROUST's program interpretations and student models in other systems, and will show how these differences result from characteristics of PROUST's domain.

7.7.1 Limited reproducibility of errors

One major difference between PROUST's diagnostic task and that of other ICAI systems is that PROUST must derive its model of the student from a single program. Systems in the subtraction domain, such as DEBUGGY [15], and in the algebra domain, such as PIXIE [58], tend to work off of a series of student solutions. When multiple problems are analyzed in succession, bug hypotheses derived from one problem can be tested by assigning the student another related problem. The system can then check whether the student solves the new problem as the bug hypothesis would predict. In PROUST's domain, however, it is not practical to assign multiple problems to students and then analyze the bugs afterwards. Each programming problem requires substantial effort on the part of the programmer, and programmers want immediate feedback concerning their program before starting a new one. Thus it is incumbent upon PROUST to analyze the student's errors and give feedback as soon as possible, even if the underlying causes of the bugs are not yet clear to PROUST.

One consequence of the fact that PROUST models the intentions underlying a single program is that it often cannot distinguish what the programmer does in the specific case from what the programmer does in general. If a program has a bug, it may result from an accidental error such as a typographical error, or it may result from a deep-seated misconception. Distinguishing the two explanations requires looking for repeated occurrences of the same bug. If a bug occurs just once, it likely to be an accidental error; if it occurs consistently, a misconception may be implicated.

PROUST does have one means for checking whether bugs occur systematically; it can check whether the same bug occurs more than once in the same program. The programming problems that we assign students tend to have multiple goals; PROUST can compare the implementation of similar goals to look for systematic errors. If, for example, all initializations are missing from a program, then there is strong evidence that the programmer has a misconception about initializing variables. In simpler domains such as subtraction or algebra there is less opportunity for the same bug to occur more than once within the same problem solution. Thus systematicity of errors within a single program can compensate in part for the lack of a suite of problems to analyze.

7.7.2 Variability in student problem-solving knowledge and procedure

The models of student behavior underlying many ICAI systems make an important simplifying assumption: they presume that student errors can be traced back to some factual misconception about the domain, rather than to some incorrect method for solving the problem. The students and the experts are all assumed to be following the same problem-solving procedure. Examples of systems that make this simplifying assumption are Genesereth's MACSYMA Advisor [30] and Clancey's proposed GUIDON-2 system [18]. In the MACSYMA Advisor, there is an explicit model of a student problem solver, called MUSER; this same problem solver is used both to solve problems and to model the student solving problems. In GUIDON-2, there will be an explicit model of the diagnostic procedure, namely the NEOMYCIN diagnostic model. It will be assumed that the students are all familiar with the NEOMYCIN model, and that their own problem-solving is in accordance with it. The MACSYMA Advisor assumes that if a student uses MACSYMA incorrectly, it can only be because the student's factual knowledge about how individual MACSYMA commands work is incorrect. GUIDON-2 assumes that if a medical student performs a diagnosis incorrectly, it can only be because the student's knowledge about diseases and pathological states is faulty. The appropriateness of these assumptions cannot be assessed without empirical analyses of how novice MACSYMA users and medical students actually behave. Both systems appear to be based upon observations of only a handful of students.

In contrast to these other systems, PROUST makes fewer assumptions about the students' problem-solving procedure. PROUST assumes that the student's program can be analyzed in terms of goals, but there is no requirement that the goals be decomposed as an expert would. A student might not realize that programmers have to worry about boundary conditions, for example, and still produce a program with a recognizable goal decomposition. Such a student cannot be said to have the same problem-solving procedure as expert programmers, since part of what an expert does is to check systematically for boundary conditions.

This weakening of the assumptions about the student's problem-solving behavior has serious repercussions for error diagnosis. It means that it is not always possible to trace bugs back to the student's factual knowledge. Any given bug may be caused by

221

a factual misconception, a flaw in the student's problem-solving procedure, a failure to follow the problem requirements strictly, or an accidental error. For this reason, bugs must often be described superficially, without reference to the cause of the bugs.

8 Finding the Best Interpretation

The previous chapters have described how PROUST generates interpretations for programs, and how it relates these interpretations to the code. This chapter describes PROUST's techniques for controlling the search for interpretations, so that it arrives at the interpretation which fits the program best. This involves two things. First, PROUST follows analysis strategies which are likely to lead to the best interpretation. These strategies determine the order in which goals are analyzed, and the order in which the components of each plan are matched. Second, PROUST evaluates interpretations as they are generated, choosing between competing interpretations and looking for inconsistencies in the interpretations. Without good strategies for analyzing programs, PROUST would make frequent mistakes. However, no strategy for program analysis eliminates analysis errors completely, or obviates choosing among alternative seemingly valid interpretations. Therefore analysis evaluation is also important.

The discussion in this chapter will proceed as follows. First I will present some program examples illustrating PROUST's analysis strategies and analysis evaluation techniques. Then PROUST's analysis strategies will be described in detail. Finally, PROUST's analysis evaluation techniques will be described.

8.1 Motivation of analysis strategies and analysis evaluation

When PROUST analyzes a program it selects goals for analysis, predicts realizations of them, and compares the proposed realizations against the program. Since PROUST uses an analysis-by-synthesis approach, we might expect goals to be selected in much the same order that programmers implement them. In this section I will show first that if PROUST selected goals in such an order it would frequently have insufficient information about the programmer's intentions to perform the analysis properly. Instead it must adopt an analysis strategy which will help it find the right interpretation. Then I will show why any particular analysis strategy is likely to lead to cases where PROUST cannot tell what the right interpretation is, or mistakenly selects the wrong interpretation. Therefore it must evaluate interpretations as they are constructed, so that it can choose between competing interpretations, and detect when a wrong choice has been made.

8.1.1 Simplistic analysis strategies will not work

Suppose that PROUST were to try to analyze a solution to the Bank Problem, say the program shown in Figure 2-8. A condensed version of this program is shown in Figure 8-1. Figure 8-2 shows the goals in the problem description for the Bank Problem. Suppose that PROUST were to try to analyze goals in this problem in the same order that a programmer might implement them. It might start by examining the first goal in the list of requirements, `DefGoal Input1 = Input(?Bank:AcctID)`. Since this goal is first in the list, and since it does not refer to any objects that are defined by other goals, it may be chosen by programmers as the first goal to implement. Implementations of *Input* goals are usually either `read` statements or `readln` statements, so one of the `read` and `readln` statements in the program is likely to be an implementation of *Input*(`?Bank:AcctID`). Unfortunately, there are five `readln` statements in Figure 8-1, each of which inputs a different variable. Since PROUST is at the beginning of the program analysis, it does not yet know which objects these variables implement. Therefore PROUST cannot tell which `readln` statement implements *Input*(`?Bank:AcctID`). It has no way of anchoring the *Input* goal to the proper statement in the program. PROUST would therefore have to choose a `readln` statement arbitrarily, or else explore multiple interpretations of the program, each of which has `?Bank:InData` bound to a different program variable.[24]

In order to avoid trying to interpret a goal when insufficient information is available, PROUST must select goals whose realizations are likely to be identifiable. The following strategy determines PROUST's choice of goal at this point:
> select goals which will correspond to major control structures in the program.

---

[24]An alternative solution might be to try to read the variable names, and infer the roles of the variables from their names. This is an unreliable technique, particularly in novice programs.

```
...
writeln('Enter account number, please');
readln(Acct);
writeln('Enter initial balance');
readln(Balance);
writeln('Enter type of transaction, w for withdrawal');
writeln('d for deposit and e for end-processing');
readln(Transtype);
while (Transtype <> 'e') do begin
  if Transtype = 'w' then
    begin
      writeln('Enter amount of withdrawal:');
      readln(Withdrawal);
      ...
    end
  else if Transtype = 'd' then
    begin
      writeln('Enter amount of deposit:');
      readln(Deposit);
      ...
    end
  else
    writeln('sorry, type must be w, d or e');
end;
...
```

Figure 8-1: A condensed version of the program in Figure 2-8

Goals which are likely to become major control structures are so marked in the goal database. The only goal in the problem description which is likely to correspond to a major control structure is the goal *Sentinel-Controlled Input Sequence*(?Bank:InData, ?Bank:ETrans). This goal will be realized as the main loop of the program. It should be easy for PROUST to identify the main loop by inspecting the program; there will be only one main loop.

The considerations that go into organizing PROUST's analysis of a program are similar to those that guide speech understanding systems. Speech understanding systems must deal both with ambiguous input and with errorful input. Buggy

225

```
DefGoal Input1 = Input(?Bank:AcctID);
DefGoal Input2 = Input(?Bank:Balance);
DefGoal Loop1 = Sentinel-Controlled Input Sequence (?Bank:InData,
                                                    ?Bank:ETrans);

Input1 Precedes Loop1;
Input2 Precedes Loop1;
DefGoal When(?Bank:InData=?Bank:DTrans,
             GoalBlock(Input(?Bank:Deposit);
                       Accumulate(?Bank:Balance, ?Bank:Deposit);
                       Bind ?Bank:DepositCount = Count(?Bank:InData)));
DefGoal When(?Bank:InData=?Bank:WTrans, GoalBlock(
             Input( ?Bank:Withdrawal);
             CompoundDeduct(?Bank:Withdrawal, ?Bank:Charge, ?Bank:Balance);
             GuardException(Update: component of CompoundDeduct,
                       ?Bank:Withdrawal >= ?Bank:Balance - ?Bank:Charge);
             Bind ?Bank:TotalCharge = ConstantSum(?Bank:Charge);
             Bind ?Bank:WithdrawalCount = Count(?Bank:InData));
Bind ?Bank:TotalCount = Count(?Bank:InData);
DefGoal Output(?Bank:TotalCharge);
DefGoal Output(?Bank:TotalCount);
DefGoal Output(?Bank:DepositCount);
DefGoal Output(?Bank:WithdrawalCount);
```

Figure 8-2: Goals in the description of the Bank Problem

programs are also a kind of errorful input. Speech understanding programs
frequently look for "islands of reliability", i.e., parts of the utterance whose
interpretation is most straightforward [70]. The islands of reliability then provide
context for understanding the less clear portions of the utterance. Likewise, PROUST
looks for parts of the problem description whose interpretation is likely to be
straightforward, and uses them to help understand the more difficult parts of the
program.

8.1.2 Analyses must be evaluated as they are performed

The following happens when PROUST looks for the realization of *Sentinel-Controlled
Input Sequence* in the program in Figure 8-1. PROUST looks up possible
implementations of the goal. The first plan that it selects for matching is the
SENTINEL PROCESS-READ WHILE PLAN, shown in Figure 8-3. The `while` statement in
this plan is `while ?New <> ?Stop do ...`; this matches the loop `while
(Transtype <> 'e') do ...` in the program. This means that `?Bank:InData`
must be implemented using the variable `Transtype`. Next, the plan has two
subgoals *Input*(`?New`); these must be mapped onto the program. Since `?New` is

226

known to be `Transtype`, PROUST looks for input statements of the form `readln(Transtype)`. It expects to find two; however, instead there is just one. One of the following conclusions might be drawn here.

- A `readln` statement is missing.

- The desired `readln` statement is reading in the wrong variable; *e.g,* when the student wrote `readln(Deposit)` he/she really meant `readln(Transtype)`.

- The student really had a different plan in mind, such as SENTINEL READ-PROCESS WHILE, which has only one *Input* subgoal.

Constants:
    ?Stop
Variables:
    ?New
Template:
InitInput: *subgoal Input* (?New)
MainLoop: while ?New <> ?Stop do
              begin
Process: ?*
Next: *subgoal Input* (?New)
              end

Figure 8-3:   The SENTINEL PROCESS-READ WHILE PLAN

How is PROUST to deal with the above choice of interpretations of the match failure? One approach is to punt on the issue, and go try to analyze another goal. In other words, PROUST could adopt a policy of avoiding cases where the choice of analysis is not clear-cut. PROUST does organize its analysis so as to analyze first those parts of the program which it predicts will be easy to analyze, such as the main loop. However, it cannot always predict which parts of the program will be difficult to analyze. Whenever a program has bugs, the buggy parts of the program are likely to be subject to various interpretations. If a program has multiple bugs, there may be no way of analyzing the program which avoids making guesses about bugs.

Another approach which PROUST could take is to keep a number of possible interpretations of the program active at once. A heuristic search of the interpretation space could then be performed. An evaluation heuristic which might be used for deciding between interpretations is to count the number of bugs assumed by each interpretation. Such an approach would work acceptably well, assuming that a good enough evaluation heuristic was chosen. However, at best it would require major portions of the program to be analyzed multiple times. We will encounter examples later on where it is not possible to decide between interpretations until after the entire program is analyzed. Heuristic search could therefore lead PROUST reanalyze the program many times, a time-consuming proposition.

PROUST's approach relies upon careful evaluation of alternative interpretations early on, in order to avoid needless search. In nearly all cases PROUST identifies the right interpretation choices to make. PROUST checks the interpretation for consistency as it is constructed, so that it can be repaired or rejected later on if need be.

In order to decide which interpretation of the main loop is correct, PROUST compares the account of the code based upon the SENTINEL PROCESS-READ WHILE PLAN against the account based on the SENTINEL READ-PROCESS WHILE PLAN, shown in Figure 8-4. In this case the deciding factor is the number of plan components that each plan succeeds in matching onto the program. Both plans predict that there will be an *Input* subgoal inside the loop, so both plans lead to the same conclusion that the `Next:` component of the plan is missing. The difference between the two plans is that the initialization step of the process-read plan can be matched, but the initialization of the read-process plan cannot be matched. The read-process plan requires that the new-value variable be initialized to a constant value, `?Seedval`; instead, it is read from the terminal. The process-read plan, on the other hand, predicts that the initialization will be read from the terminal, so it matches the initialization without error. Therefore more components of the process-read plan match than do components of the read-process plan, so the process-read interpretation is preferred.

The comparison of the process-read plan and the read-process plan in the preceding paragraph assumed that the *Input* subgoal in the loop was missing. The possibility that the wrong variable is used, that the student intended to write `readln(Transtype)` instead of `readln(Deposit)`, was not considered. The

```
Constants:
            ?Stop, ?Seedval
Variables:
            ?New
Template:
Init:       ?New := ?Seedval
MainLoop: ->while (?New <> ?Stop) do
            begin
Next:             subgoal Input(?New)
InternalGuard:    subgoal Sentinel guard(?New, ?Stop, Process: ?*)
            end
```

Figure 8-4: The SENTINEL READ-PROCESS WHILE PLAN

reason for this is that it is extremely dangerous to assume that `Deposit` was meant to be `transtype` when the role of `deposit` in the program is not yet known. If PROUST were to substitute `Transtype` for `Deposit` in the statement `readln(Deposit)`, then when it later tries to analyze the goal *Input*(?Bank:Deposit) it would conclude that the goal is unimplemented. PROUST's interpretation of the program would thus be very confused. It is safer to assume that every variable is written as intended, and retract this assumption later if necessary, after PROUST knows as much as possible about the meaning of each statement and each variable. Therefore PROUST has no plan-difference rule for recognizing wrong variables. Some of PROUST's interpretation evaluation heuristics are thus implicit in the knowledge base.

Now suppose that PROUST's choice heuristics were wrong. Imagine that there really were an additional input statement at the bottom of the loop such as `readln(Deposit)`, where the programmer meant to write `transtype` instead of `Deposit`. We need PROUST to recognize that the wrong-variable bug is the right interpretation. This is achieved by having PROUST look out for inconsistencies in the interpretation of the program. In the case where the programmer writes `readln(Deposit)` instead of `readln(Transtype)`, PROUST first assumes that the `readln(Deposit)` statement is not intended to input the transaction code. Later on PROUST will discover that it understands what each line in the loop is supposed to do except for the `readln(Deposit)` line. The problem description does not indicate that the deposit amount should be read a second time. The program interpretation is

229

therefore inconsistent; every line of code should be accounted for, yet here is a line of code that is left over. If PROUST could repair the inconsistency, then it would recover from having made the wrong interpretation decision.

PROUST's interpretation could be repaired as follows. PROUST would trace the interpretation path so far, looking for a point where the extra `readln` statement might fit it. When it reaches the instantiation of the SENTINEL PROCESS-READ WHILE PLAN, it would note that it had assumed that an input statement was missing at that point. It would then hypothesize that the extra input statement should fit into the process-read plan. The revised interpretation is consistent, in that no goals or code is left dangling. This interpretation is therefore more likely to fit the programmer's intentions.

Note that a heuristic search of the interpretation space might have to analyze the entire program at least twice in this case; one interpretation would not appear clearly superior until all of the goals in the goal agenda had been analyzed. Of course an analysis repair mechanism could be incorporated into a heuristic-search approach. However, at that point the difference between PROUST's approach and heuristic search is nil. PROUST could then be viewed as a heuristic search program whose evaluation heuristics are so good that it hardly ever backtracks.

PROUST currently cannot repair inconsistent interpretations. The reason for this is that PROUST does an accurate enough job of analyzing programs without attempting repairs. However, PROUST is capable of evaluating interpretations and spotting inconsistencies. This enables PROUST to abort or curtail the analysis when inconsistencies arise, thus avoiding the possibility of giving the novice a bug report based upon a flawed interpretation. When the need arises this curtailment of analysis will be replaced by analysis repair. Later on in this chapter I will discuss what is necessary to make PROUST perform the kinds of analysis repairs that have been described here.

8.2 Strategies underlying plan matching

This section and the following one describe PROUST's analysis strategies, and the ways in which they are implemented. This section deals with strategies involved in deciding how to match plans against programs. Section 8.3 discusses the strategies involved in selecting goals. The basic strategies in each case are the same:

- select goals, plans, and plan components which are intrinsically easier to match against programs,

- take advantage of whatever information is available about the programmer's intentions, and

- try to organize the analysis so that further information about the programmer's intentions becomes available when it is needed.

As was mentioned in Section 4.6.2, PROUST's plans are compiled before they are used. PROUST's plan compiler takes plan templates and breaks them up into individual plan component patterns. It then assigns an order to the plan components. The strategies which the plan compiler uses will be described below. I will also discuss some ways in which analysis strategies are implicit in PROUST's plan representation.

8.2.1 Why plan matching strategies are needed

We saw in Section 8.1.1 that simplistic goal selection strategies will not work. For similar reasons, simplistic plan matching strategies will not work. Consider again the SENTINEL PROCESS-READ WHILE PLAN in Figure 8-3. This plan template contains several different components. One might choose any of several different orderings for these components. The most obvious method would be to start at the top of the template and work down, i.e., first resolve the initial *Input* subgoal, then match the `while` loop, then match the contents of the while loop. Such a top-to-bottom approach would never work in programming problems such as the Bank Problem. If PROUST starts with an *Input* subgoal it faces the same problem as before of trying to find an input statement without knowing what variable is being input.

What we want to happen is for PROUST to match the `while` statement in the SENTINEL PROCESS-READ PLAN first. There are likely to be fewer `while` statements in a program than input statements or initializations; even fewer will be testing a variable against a specific stop value. Furthermore, although novices may leave out initializations by mistake, they are less likely to omit a main loop by mistake. Therefore matching the `while` statement first is much more likely to succeed. Even if the `while` statement is buggy there is less likely to be ambiguity as to which `while` statement in the program was intended to be the sentinel-controlled loop. Since the `while` loop tests the new-value variable, matching the `while` statement enables PROUST to determine what variable is serving as the new-value variable. The *Input* subgoals can then be processed, since it is now known what variable should be input.

To summarize, PROUST's plans must be ordered so that the key components of the plans, or the "beacons", as Brooks calls them, [13] are matched first. According to Brooks, beacons are the parts of the code which the reader of a program focuses on first when trying to understand a program. Likewise, the beacons in PROUST's plans help PROUST to focus the process of matching plans.

8.2.2 Compiled plan component orderings

The plan compiler performs two actions on plans. It decides in what order to match plan components, and it determines the expected position of each plan component with respect to the components which have been previously matched. In the case of the SENTINEL PROCESS-READ WHILE PLAN, for example, it decides that the `while` statement should be matched before the initialization step. It indicates that the plan matcher should look above the `while` statement for the initialization. The orderings of plan components serve to guarantee that the plan matcher follows the strategies of making use of whatever contextual information is available, and to focus first on components which are more likely to provide useful information about the plan. Determining the position of each component with respect to previously-matched components also causes the plan matcher to take advantage of available contextual information.

Unless given explicit indications to do otherwise, the plan compiler places plan components into the following order:

232

1. references to components of other plans which already have been matched,

2. Pascal statement patterns, and

3. subgoals.

By resolving all references to previously-matched plans first, all relevant information about the programmer's intentions is acquired as quickly as possible. By matching statement patterns before subgoals, the analysis of the subgoals can take advantage of contextual information gained from matching the statements in the superplan. Furthermore, by matching the statement patterns first, it is often possible to determine whether or not a plan is a likely match before the going through the effort of matching implementations of the subgoals.

8.2.3 Ordering by component type

Because the plan compiler places statement patterns before subgoals, the ordering of plan components depends upon which components are treated as subgoals and which are not. Upon examining PROUST's plan knowledge base, certain patterns emerge as to which types of plan components tend to be subgoals. Furthermore, some plans have components marked with the processing directive ->; these components must be matched first (see Section 4.4.3.2). The ->'s tend to fall only on certain types of plan components. As a result, some types of plan components are matched before others in virtually all plans.

`MainLoop:` components are matched before other plan components in all plans. `Update:` components also take precedence over other components. Next in the hierarchy are `Guard:` components. At the bottom of the hierarchy are the remaining component types, `Init:`, `Input:`, `Output:`, `Next:`, etc.

8.2.4 The dependence on contextual knowledge

The current plan component ordering mechanism assumes that there is a single best method for matching each plan. This assumption turns out to be false. The best ordering for plan components depends upon the available contextual information, such as the pattern variables that are bound before the plan is matched. If different pattern variables are bound, the component ordering may need to change.

Furthermore, the best ordering can depend upon the bugs in the particular program. Eventually these issues will make it necessary for PROUST to order plan components in a more flexible fashion.

Consider the two plans in Figure 8-5, the SENTINEL SKIP GUARD PLAN and the INDIVIDUAL SENTINEL SKIP GUARD PLAN. Both plans are used in the process of constructing sentinel-controlled loops. The SENTINEL SKIP GUARD PLAN is used to keep a region of the main loop from processing sentinel values as data. This is required, for example, when the loop is a read-process loop: when the input statement reads in the sentinel value, the computations that follow must all be skipped. The INDIVIDUAL SENTINEL SKIP GUARD is used to protect a specific computation against sentinel input, instead of protecting an entire section of the loop body. This is invoked when inspection of the computation reveals that it requires a guard. In the case of the SENTINEL SKIP GUARD, the `then` clause of the `if` statement is `?*`, meaning that it can be anything. This component is labeled `GuardedCode:`. In the INDIVIDUAL SENTINEL SKIP GUARD PLAN, on the other hand, the `then` clause of the `if` statement is bound to the code variable `?GuardedCode`, which presumably has been bound before the plan is matched. Otherwise the two plans are identical.

SENTINEL SKIP GUARD

```
Variables: ?New
Constants: ?Stop
Template:
InternalGuard:      if ?New <> ?Stop then
GuardedCode:            ?*
```

INDIVIDUAL SENTINEL SKIP GUARD

```
Variables: ?New
Constants: ?Stop
Labelvars:  ?GuardedCode
Template:
InternalGuard:      if ?New <> ?Stop then
                        contains ?GuardedCode:
```

Figure 8-5: Two plans with the same underlying structure

I originally thought that these were two different plans. In fact, the plans are the same. The differences are in the assumptions about what knowledge of context is available beforehand. In the case of SENTINEL SKIP GUARD, it is not yet known what code is being guarded. Whatever code is being guarded will be labeled `GuardedCode:` in the process of matching the plan. In the case of the INDIVIDUAL SENTINEL SKIP GUARD, on the other hand, it is known beforehand what the guarded code is, and the pattern variable `?GuardedCode` will be bound to the guarded code. The plan compiler takes these assumptions into account, and compiles the two plans differently. In the SENTINEL SKIP GUARD PLAN, the `if` statement pattern is matched first, and the `GuardedCode:` label is assigned to the `then` clause of the `if` statement. In the INDIVIDUAL SENTINEL SKIP GUARD PLAN, the value of `?GuardedCode` is looked up, and then the `if` statement pattern is specified as surrounding the statements in `?GuardedCode`. Thus the `if` statement pattern is matched in different places, depending upon whether or not it is known beforehand what code is being guarded.

We see in this example that processing considerations have made their way into PROUST's plan representation. PROUST's plan representation was intended to be as processing-neutral as possible. It would be desirable to merge SENTINEL SKIP GUARD PLAN and INDIVIDUAL SENTINEL SKIP GUARD PLAN into a single plan, and let component ordering be determined by information about whether or not the location of the guarded code is known beforehand.

Plan component ordering not only makes plans dependent upon surrounding context; it also makes some plan components depend upon other components of the same plan for context. When the SENTINEL PROCESS-READ WHILE PLAN is compiled, for example, the initial *Input* subgoal is ordered after the `while` statement pattern. Furthermore, the part of the program in which to look for the *Input* subgoal is described relative to the position of the `while` statement. If for some reason the `while` statement cannot be found in the program, then the initial *Input* subgoal will not be found either. Thus the plan compilation process tends to make plan matching more brittle than it ought to be.

If bugs obscure the desired plan components, and there is a potential for ambiguity of interpretation, then plan components may not be matchable. Suppose that PROUST is trying to match a `while` loop, and there are two `while` loops in the program. If the `while` loop that PROUST is looking for has a bug in it, then PROUST might match the wrong `while` loop by mistake. In such cases it might be better to try to match a different component of the plan first. As programs become larger, the potential for ambiguity is greater, so the need for flexibility in plan component ordering is greater. There is essentially no need for it in the Rainfall Problem; in the Bank Problem, on the other hand, it could occasionally come in useful.

These examples call into question the present scheme of defining a fixed ordering of plan components ahead of time. One way of remedying this problem is to make the plan compiler generate multiple compilations, where each compilation makes different context assumptions. Then PROUST would be able to choose at analysis time how the plan should be matched, depending upon the contextual information available at the time. If bugs prevent a plan component from matching, PROUST could try a different ordering. This approach would retain the simplicity that linearized plans provide, without sacrificing flexibility and cleanliness of representation.

8.3 Strategies for ordering goal analysis

This section discusses the strategies which govern PROUST's selection of goals for analysis. I will first talk about the ordering heuristics which are currently implemented in PROUST. Then an example will be presented where PROUST's ordering heuristics fall short, and where ordering hints must be added to the problem description. I will discuss what must be done to eliminate the need for such hints.

8.3.1 Goal selection heuristics

Suppose that PROUST is in the midst of analyzing a solution to the Rainfall Problem. Imagine that the *Sentinel-Controlled Input Sequence* goal has already been analyzed. In so doing, the object `?Rainfall:DailyRain` was found to be implemented by the Pascal variable `New`. The status of the goal agenda and the object definitions therefore is as depicted in Figure 8-6. All of the goals in the problem description except for *Sentinel-Controlled Input Sequence* appear on the agenda, just as they appear in the problem description.

Agenda

Loop Input Validation (?Rainfall:Rain, ?Rainfall:Rain < 0);
Output (*Average* (?Rainfall:Rain));
Output (*Count* (?Rainfall:Rain));
Output (*Guarded Count* (?Rainfall:Rain, ?Rainfall:Rain > 0));
Output (*Maximum* (?Rainfall:Rain));

Object Definitions

?Rainfall:Rain = New

Figure 8-6: An intermediate stage in the analysis of the Rainfall Problem

PROUST must select from the agenda a goal which is appropriate to work on next. Goals are appropriate for selection if all necessary contextual information is known. This includes all arguments of the goals. It also includes descriptions of the location in the program that the goal is likely to be found in, should any such descriptions exist. The goals in Figure 8-6 have no descriptions of goal location; we will see examples of such descriptions below. Thus the only thing which can prevent goals in this example from being analyzable is if they refer to objects that have no binding. The arguments to the goal *Loop Input Validation* (?Rainfall:Rain, ?Rainfall:Rain < 0) are all bound, since ?Rainfall:Rain is bound. Therefore this goal can be selected for analysis.

The remaining goals on the agenda are compound goals, where the result of one goal is used as the argument of another goal. PROUST assumes that in such cases the inner goal should be analyzed first, and the outer goal should be analyzed later. In the case of a goal such as *Output* (*Average* (?Rainfall:Rain)) this works as follows. PROUST analyzes *Average* (?Rainfall:Rain). Let us suppose that the average variable in the student's program is called Avg. Any references to the value generated by *Average* (?Rainfall:Rain) are bound to Avg, so the *Output* goal becomes *Output* (Avg). This goal now has its context fully specified, so it is ready for analysis.

As we see in this example, once a certain amount of contextual information is available, it is easy to order goals so that each has the contextual information that it needs. Suppose that such contextual information is not available, as is the case at the beginning of the analysis, before `?Rainfall:Rain` is bound. At that point, every goal refers to at least one unbound object, so by the previous choice criteria no goal is ready for analysis. We have already seen what happens in this case: PROUST selects first those goals which define the larger control structures in the program. Such goals are called major control goals. Each goal in PROUST's goal database is marked as to whether or not it is a major control goal, using the `OuterControlPlan` slot, as described in Section 6.3.3. The *Sentinel-Controlled Input Sequence* goal is so marked, so it is chosen first.

These selection heuristics are all that is necessary for ordering goals in problems of the complexity of the Rainfall Problem. There is one additional heuristic which PROUST uses, however, which should be mentioned. If two goals both have their contextual requirements satisfied, the goal which has the fewest number of possible implementations should be analyzed first. The reason for this is that the goal with the smallest number of possible implementations will be analyzed quickly. This in turn may provide further contextual information which will assist the analysis of the other goals.

8.3.2 Towards smarter selection heuristics

Although adequate for the Rainfall Problem, the current set of goal selection heuristics is not adequate for the Bank Problem. The main difficulty is that there exist dependencies among goals which PROUST cannot resolve. One goal which exhibits such dependencies appears in Figure 8-7. This is the *When* goal which describes what happens in the Bank Problem when the user's command is the DEPOSIT command. The *When* goal contains as one of its arguments a *GoalBlock* goal, which contains a list of other goals to be analyzed. The selection heuristic for compound goals indicates that the inner goals should be analyzed before the outer goals. The problem is that the inner goals refer to unbound objects, so they cannot be analyzed. Thus analysis of this goal expression is deadlocked.

PROUST needs to recognize here that the context dependency between *When* and

```
DefGoal When(?Bank:InData=?Bank:DTrans,
             GoalBlock(Input(?Bank:Deposit);
                       Accumulate(?Bank:Balance, ?Bank:Deposit);
                       Bind ?Bank:DepositCount = Count(?Bank:InData)));
```

Figure 8-7:   An excerpt from the Bank Problem description

GoalBlock is different from the context dependency between *Output* and *Average*. The *When* goal provides context for the *GoalBlock* goal, not the other way around. Assuming that the bindings for `?Bank:InData` and `?Bank:DTrans` are known, PROUST should go ahead and analyze the *When* goal, and then do the *GoalBlock* goal later. PROUST's selection heuristics currently do not do this.

Even if the *GoalBlock* goal is analyzed first, there is still the problem that it contains goals which refer to unbound objects. The goal *Input*(`?Bank:Deposit`), for example, refers to the object `?Bank:Deposit`. As we saw earlier, the *Input* goals are particularly problematic in the Bank Problem, because there are so many different variables which are input.

In order to resolve the *Input* goal, PROUST should be able to recognize that the *Input* goal is the only goal in the goal block, hence it should be uniquely identifiable even if the binding of `?Bank:Deposit` is not known. This is a non-trivial inference. `Input(?Bank:Deposit)` is the only *Input* goal listed in the goal block, but in order to ensure that the *Input* goal is unique PROUST must ensure that none of the other goals has *Input* as a subgoal. PROUST thus needs the ability to predict the possible realizations of more than one goal at once. Instead, PROUST's goal implementation mechanism currently analyzes the realizations of one goal at a time.

Since PROUST's goal selection heuristics do not select an appropriate strategy in this case, I modified the problem description of the Bank Problem in order to get it to work. I broke apart goal expressions which PROUST otherwise would try to resolve in the wrong order. References to unbound objects were removed. Instead, explicit descriptions of the location of various goals were indicated. PROUST's selection heuristics select a goal for analysis only if such location descriptions are resolvable, i.e., if the goals that they refer to have already been analyzed. Thus these new dependency relations ensure that the goals are analyzed in the proper order. The modified goal descriptions are shown in Figure 8-8.

239

```
DefGoal When1
        When( ?Bank:InData = ?Bank:DTrans);
DefGoal GoalBlock1 GoalBlock()
    at (Span (Ref When1) (At (ComponentOf When1 GuardedCode:)));
Bind ?Bank:Deposit = Input()
    at (ContainedBy (Ref GoalBlock1)
                    (In (ComponentOf GoalBlock1 Process:)));
Bind ?Bank:Balance = Accumulate(?Bank:Deposit)
    at (ContainedBy (Ref GoalBlock1)
                    (In (ComponentOf GoalBlock1 Process:)));
Bind ?Bank:DepositCount = Count(?Bank:InData)
    at (ContainedBy (Ref GoalBlock1)
                    (In (ComponentOf GoalBlock1 Process:)));
```

Figure 8-8:   A massaged excerpt from the Bank Problem statement

This hand-coded ordering of goals shown in Figure 8-8 only makes sense if the *When* goal can be resolved before any of the goals which refer to it. The *When* goal can be resolved first only if the bindings of `?Bank:InData` and `?Bank:DTrans` are known. Unfortunately, the Bank Problem statement does not state specifically what the DEPOSIT command should be. It only says that there are three commands, DEPOSIT, WITHDRAWAL, and EXIT. The current problem description for the Bank Problem assumes that these commands will be `'d'`, `'w'`, and `'e'`. Suppose instead that they are `'a'`, `'s'`, and `'x'`. PROUST would then be unable to analyze either *When* goal in the program, because it would not know which command is DEPOSIT and which is WITHDRAWAL.

PROUST currently gives up if the student uses command names that it does not expect. What it should do is to construct an alternative strategy for determining where the deposits and withdrawals are processed; this could be done as follows. The *When* goal in Figure 8-7 contains an *Accumulate* goal. There is no other *Accumulate* goal in the problem description; furthermore, none of the goals in the problem description has *Accumulate* as a subgoal. Therefore an alternative plan for analyzing the program would be to look for the *Accumulate* goal first, and infer from that what the DEPOSIT command must be.

The need to construct alternative goal orderings is strictly analogous to the need for flexible orderings of components of plans. In fact, the two go hand in hand. In order to allow analysis of the *When* goals to proceed both from the inside out and from the outside in, we would need two alternative plan component orderings for plans implementing the *When* goal.
240

8.4 Differential evaluation of analyses

The following two sections discuss PROUST's methods for evaluating program interpretations. This section is concerned with differential evaluation of interpretations, i.e., deciding which of a set of possible interpretations is best. Section 8.5 describes how PROUST evaluates individual analyses, looking for inconsistencies.

8.4.1 Differential diagnosis in program analysis

Differential diagnosis is a diagnostic technique commonly practiced by physicians. In performing differential diagnosis a physician compiles a set of hypotheses of diseases which might cause the patient's symptoms. This set of hypotheses is called a differential. The physician then tries to narrow down the differential by comparing hypotheses against each other, and looking for evidence which confirms one subset of hypotheses and disconfirms the others. Eventually the differential is narrowed down to a single diagnosis. Because the diagnostician decides upon the diagnosis by comparing competing diagnoses, the diagnosis which wins out at the end will be demonstrably superior to the alternatives. If, on the other hand, the diagnostician cannot distinguish between competing hypotheses, the diagnosis must be considered inconclusive.

The intention-based approach to program analysis lends itself naturally to differential diagnosis. When a goal is selected for analysis, different implementations of the goal are suggested. The set of candidate implementations forms a differential. PROUST then decides which among these implementations fits the program best.

Figure 8-9 shows an example of a program which requires differential analysis in order to be interpreted correctly. This program is the example solution to the Rainfall Problem discussed in Chapter 1, the one which had a `while`-for-`if` bug. It has three loops, one of which tests the input to see whether it is negative, and two of which test whether the input is equal to 99999. PROUST must determine which is supposed to be the main loop of the program, and what plan is used to implement the *Sentinel-Controlled Input Sequence* goal. PROUST has four plans in its knowledge base which implement *Sentinel-Controlled Input Sequence*, as was shown in Figure 6-3. Two of these plans contain `repeat` loops which compare the new-value variable against the sentinel; the other two have `while` loops which compare the new-value variable against the sentinel. The program in Figure 8-9 has a `while` loop *and* a `repeat` loop which compare the new-value variable and the sentinel value. Therefore all four plans match partially, and PROUST must choose between them.

Using each of the four plans for implementing *Sentinel-Controlled Input Sequence* as a basis, four interpretations of the code can be derived. These interpretations are listed below. Each interpretation identifies a different set of bugs in the program. I mention only those bugs which relate to the looping plans.

1. The SENTINEL PROCESS-READ WHILE PLAN is the underlying plan. This plan appears at *(5)* in the program. The initial input of the loop is at *(3)*. The loop at *(4)* checks this initial input to see whether or not it is valid. The program's bugs include the following:

   a. there is no input statement inside the loop;

   b. there is a spurious `repeat` loop at *(2)*.

2. The SENTINEL READ-PROCESS WHILE PLAN is the underlying plan. The main loop of this plan is at *(5)*. The initialization of the new-value variable is at *(1)*. The program's bugs include the following:

   a. there is no input statement inside the loop;

   b. the input validation loop is outside the loop, at *(4)*, instead of inside the loop;

   c. there is a spurious `repeat` loop at *(2)*;

   d. there is a spurious `read` statement at *(3)*.

3. The SENTINEL PROCESS-READ REPEAT PLAN is the underlying plan. The main loop of this plan is at *(2)*. The program's bugs include the following:

   a. instead of an initial read at *(1)*, `RAIN` is initialized to zero;

   b. there is no check for the sentinel value before the `repeat` loop is executed;

   c. the `read` statement at *(3)* is at the top of the loop; it should be at the bottom;

   d. the `while` loop at *(5)* is spurious.

```
 1 program Rainfall ( input, output );
 2
 3 var
 4   Rain, Days, Totalrain, Raindays, Highrain, Averain: real;
 5
 6 begin
 7   Rain := 0;                                                    (1)
 8   repeat                                                        (2)
 9     writeln ('Enter rainfall');
10     readln;
11     read (Rain);                                                (3)
12     while Rain < 0 do                                           (4)
13       begin
14         writeln ( Rain:0:2,'is not possible, try again');
15         readln;
16         read ( Rain )
17       end;
18
19     while Rain <> 99999 do                                      (5)
20       begin
21         Days := Days + 1;
22         Totalrain :=  Totalrain + Rain;
23         if Rain > 0 then
24           Raindays := Raindays + 1;
25         if Highrain < Rain then
26           Highrain := Rain
27       end;
28   until Rain = 99999;
29
30   Averain := Totalrain / Days;
31
32   writeln;
33   writeln ( Days,'valid rainfalls were entered');
34   writeln;
35   writeln ('The average rainfall was',Averain,'inches');
36   writeln;
37   writeln ('The the highest rainfall was',Highrain);
38   writeln;
39   writeln ('There were',Raindays,'in this period');
40 end.
```

Figure 8-9: A program requiring differential diagnosis

4. The SENTINEL READ-PROCESS REPEAT PLAN is the underlying plan. The main loop of the plan is at *(2)*. The program's bugs include the following:

    a. the `while` loop at *(5)* should be an `if` statement.

For PROUST, the determining factor in differentiating these interpretations is the number of correctly-placed components in each plan. PROUST starts by considering the SENTINEL PROCESS-READ WHILE PLAN, since that is the most common implementation of *Sentinel-Controlled Input Sequence*. When PROUST discovers that one of the inputs is missing under the SENTINEL PROCESS-READ WHILE PLAN interpretation, it looks for another plan whose components all appear to be present. The SENTINEL READ-PROCESS REPEAT PLAN is the only plan whose components all appear to be present, and are located in the proper place. One of the components is buggy, being a `while` statement instead of an `if` statement; nevertheless it appears exactly where the plan predicts it should be. Therefore the SENTINEL READ-PROCESS REPEAT PLAN is chosen as the preferred interpretation.

8.4.2 Problems with applying differential techniques

The principal difficulty to be faced in applying differential diagnosis to program analysis is that a complete differential of possible program interpretations can be very large. First, a complete differential of interpretations must include a wide range of possible buggy interpretations. I call the range of different interpretations in a differential the *breadth* of the differential. Second, a choice of interpretation at one point in the analysis can affect the interpretation of other parts of the program. For example, the input validation loop at *(4)* in Figure 8-9 is interpreted in different ways, depending upon the choice of plan for implementing *Sentinel-Controlled Input Sequence*. If the loop at *(5)* is assumed to be the main loop, then the input validation loop at *(4)* is buggy, because it is outside of the main loop. If the loop at *(1)* is assumed to be the main loop, then the input validation loop is not buggy. A complete differential would include all of the effects of each interpretation choice on the analysis of the rest of the program. I call the range of effects which are taken into account when making an interpretation choice the *depth* of the differential. The challenge is to make PROUST's differentials broad enough and deep enough that they cover the cases that need to be covered, but are not too costly to evaluate.

244

8.4.2.1 The breadth of differentials

Ideally we would like differentials to include enough alternative interpretations for a goal that PROUST can be certain that it contains the right interpretation. The problem with this is that we do not know beforehand what parts of the program implement the goal. If the differential is too broad, there will be false matches of code which implements other goals. Furthermore, no matter how broad a differential is, we can never be certain that it contains the right interpretation, because there is always some risk that the program has a novel bug which is not included in the differential.

The averaging program in Figure 8-10 illustrates the kinds of recognition confusions that arise if one tries to construct an implementation differential which covers all cases. Suppose that the goals *Sentinel-Controlled Input Sequence* and *Average* have already been analyzed, and we wish now to analyze the *Count* goal. The following possibilities must be considered:

1. the counter update is `Counter := 1;`

2. the counter update is `New := New + 1;`

3. the counter update is `Sum := Sum + New;`

4. the counter update is not implemented.

Taken in isolation, each of these hypotheses is plausible. I have seen novice programs which mix up their variables, which have running total updates instead of counter updates, and which have statements missing. I have never seen a program with `Counter := 1` in place of `Counter := Counter + 1`, but I do not doubt that such a bug is possible. Thus if differential diagnosis is going to work here, the differential would have to include just about any possible update.

If arbitrary updates are considered as possible implementations, then we are virtually certain to get false matches. This averaging program ought to have a running total update, and `Sum := Sum + New` clearly must be this running total update. `New := New + 1` is probably supposed to get the next value of the new-value variable. Yet both of these updates are in the differential for the *Count* goal. If one of them is chosen as the implementation for *Count*, then we have a false match.

245

```
            program Average(input, output);
            var Sum, Count, Counter, New: integer;
                Avg: real;
            begin
                Sum := 0;
                Count := 0;
                read(New);
                while New <> 99999 do
                  begin
                    Sum := Sum + New;
                    Counter := 1;
                    New := New + 1
                  end;
                if Count <> 0 then
                  begin
                    Avg := Sum / Count;
                    Writeln('The average is ', avg);
                  end;
            end;
```

Figure 8-10: A buggy averaging program

8.4.2.2 The depth of differentials

If a differential is broad enough that it covers all, or nearly all, interpretations of a goal, it should also take into account the consequences of each interpretation, in order to handle false matches. If PROUST hypothesizes that a counter is being implemented using a running-total update, and the program should also implement a sum, then PROUST should consider the consequences of the decision about the counter update on the analysis of the sum.

One way to be sure of identifying all consequences resulting from an analysis choice is to analyze the program completely, once for each candidate in the differential. PROUST would then compare the interpretations and note differences. Such an approach is computationally explosive. A typical interpretation tree for the Bank problem has a depth of around 30 nodes. The average branching factor at each point is around 3. If PROUST were to generate complete program interpretations for every choice, the number of interpretations generated would be extremely high.

246

Instead of analyzing the program completely each time there is a choice of interpretations, PROUST could identify the goals whose analysis might be affected by the choice. In other words, we could make PROUST look for dependencies between goal analyses. The depth of the differential could then be made just deep enough to include the dependent goals, and no others. Thus in the Averaging Problem the interpretation of the *Count* goal affects the interpretation of the *Sum* goal. Therefore the effects on the *Sum* goal must be taken into account when comparing different interpretations of the *Count* goal.

Unfortunately, every analysis decision can be viewed as affecting every subsequent analysis decision. Suppose, for example, that PROUST decides that goal X is implemented by line A in the program, and then considers another goal Y. Two situations can arise; either X unifies with Y or it does not. If X unifies with Y, then the interpretation of Y depends upon the interpretation of X, because the two goals have to map onto the same code. If X does not unify with Y then the interpretation of Y is still affected by the interpretation of X, because whatever code implements X cannot also implement Y. Either way the interpretation of X has an impact on the interpretation of Y. According to this view of analysis dependencies, taking dependencies into account when differentiating interpretations is the same as differentiating complete interpretations of the program.

The interpretation of the input validation loop in Figure 8-9 showed how an interpretation choice can have pervasive effects. We saw that the choice of interpretation of the *Sentinel-Controlled Input Sequence* goal affected the interpretation of *Loop Input Validation*. There was nothing special about the *Loop Input Validation* goal; any goal which might be implemented using code which appears inside the main loop could be affected in the same way. That includes most goals in the requirements of the Rainfall Problem.

8.4.3 Approaches to differential diagnosis

Two different approaches to differential diagnosis are taken in PROUST. One approach, called post-analysis differentiation, is used when the consequences of an interpretation decision are known to have little effect on the rest of the analysis. In this approach, PROUST guesses an interpretation, and then when the interpretation of the program is complete it differentiates the alternatives and patches the interpretation if need be. The other approach, called mid-analysis differentiation, presumes that a differential which is deep enough to identify all of the consequences of an analysis decision is too costly to construct. Instead, PROUST does the best it can, given the information available at the time. It is assumed that if a misinterpretation results, then an inconsistency in the analysis will be discovered later on in analyzing the program, which will permit the misinterpretation to be corrected.

8.4.3.1 Post-analysis differentiation

Section 2.3 discussed an example of post-analysis differentiation. The example in question is repeated in Figure 8-11. The issue which required differentiation in this example was how the programmer intended to exclude invalid data from the main loop. The issue being differentiated was whether the programmer wanted to guard against invalid data on a case-by-case basis, or whether he/she thought that printing an error message was sufficient. The decision was made by waiting until the end of the analysis, and then checking whether there were any plans in the program which guarded against invalid data.

The different interpretations of the *Loop Input Validation* goal in the example in Figure 8-11 are ideal for post-analysis differentiation; the effects of the implementation choice on the rest of the program are strictly limited. We may interpret the code that validates the input differently, depending upon which implementation decision is made, but the interpretation of the rest of the program stays the same regardless. Therefore the decision about the *Input Validation* goal does not affect the rest of the analysis, and can safely be postponed to the end.

8.4.3.2 Mid-analysis differentiation

Mid-analysis differentiation is required when the boundaries of the differential are fuzzy or when the effects of the implementation choice on the subsequent course of the analysis are poorly understood. This is the case in the example in Figure 8-9. There are four different implementations of *Sentinel-Controlled Input Sequence* in PROUST's knowledge base; however, there is no guarantee that some student will not invent some other implementation. The effects of the plan choice are widespread; as

248

```
 1 program Rainfall (input , output);
 2 var
 3    Total, Rainfall, Highest, Average : real;
 4    Number, Days : integer;
 5 begin
 6   writeln ('Enter your rainfall data, one at a time');
 7   readln;
 8   read(Rainfall);
 9   Number := 0;
10   Highest := 0;
11   Days := 0;
12   Total := 0;
13   while Rainfall <> 99999 do
14     begin
15       Number := Number + 1;
16       if Rainfall > 0 then
17         Days := Days + 1;
18       if Rainfall > Highest then
19         Highest := Rainfall;
20       Total := Total + Rainfall;
21       if Rainfall < 0    then
22         begin
23           writeln ('Impossible, try again');
24           Number := Number - 1;
25         end;
26       readln;
27       read ( Rainfall)
28     end;
29   Average := Total / Number;
30   writeln ( Number:3,  ' valid rainfalls were entered.');
31   writeln ('The average rainfall was', Average:3:2);
32   writeln ('The highest rainfall was', Highest:3:2);
33   writeln ('There were', Days:3, ' rainy days')
34 end.
```

Figure 8-11: An example solution to the Rainfall Problem

we saw, the interpretation of the *Loop Input Validation* goal depended upon it. Such effects are difficult, if not impossible, to predict. Therefore differentiation cannot wait until the end of the analysis. Some sort of tentative differentiation is required quickly, to avoid pursuing fruitless analyses.

In PROUST differentiation is usually performed as soon as the candidate plans have been matched against the program. If the analysis strategies have done their job, then at this stage there usually is enough information available about the program to perform a correct differentiation.

8.5 Analysis criticism and correction

I will now describe an analysis evaluation method which allows PROUST to analyze the validity of an interpretation overall. This method is called *analysis criticism*. The term is an allusion to Sacerdoti's "critics" [51]. In Sacerdoti's planning scheme, critics examine a plan as it is being generated, looking for specific kinds of planning errors. Similarly, PROUST's critics inspect the analysis of the program both while and after it is being performed, looking for inconsistencies. These inconsistencies indicate when the interpretation is incorrect, either because an improper analysis decision was made or because PROUST is unfamiliar with the plans and bugs in the program. PROUST currently responds to criticism by stopping bug analysis on the parts of the program that it has misunderstood. Ultimately it will be able to respond to criticism by repairing the faulty portion of the interpretation.

8.5.1 Why analysis criticism works

Analysis criticism takes advantage of the interdependence of analysis decisions in interpreting a program. If PROUST makes a wrong choice in analyzing a program, this may force other incorrect choices later on. However, later on PROUST has more knowledge about the programmer's intentions. This additional knowledge makes it possible to recognize when PROUST is being forced into an inconsistent interpretation. PROUST's critics identify such inconsistencies. PROUST then uses the information gained from such criticism to identify the faulty analysis decision.

We have already seen what analysis critics can do in Section 8.1.2, in the example where the student writes `readln(Deposit)` instead of `readln(Transtype)`. There PROUST found that it could not interpret the `readln(Deposit)` line, so the interpretation of the program was inconsistent. The cause of the inconsistency was that PROUST had assumed that the `readln(Deposit)` statement was missing. PROUST uses an analysis critic to spot this inconsistency.

The critic which identifies spurious input statements cannot execute until the end

250

of PROUST's analysis of a program, because it has to wait until all of the *Input* goals have been analyzed. In fact, most critics currently wait until the end of the analysis, whether this is necessary or not. However, it is possible in many cases to spot inconsistencies while the analysis is in progress. To see this, consider the averaging program in Figure 8-12. In this program the numerator and the denominator of the average computation are reversed. Instead of writing `Avg := Sum / Count`, the programmer has written `Avg := Count / Sum`. This will result in an incorrect interpretation of the role of the variables `Sum` and `Count`; PROUST will think that `Sum` is a counter variable and `Count` is a running-total variable. Then when lines 10 and 11, `Sum := Sum + New` and `Count := Count + 1`, are analyzed, it appears that line 10 has a counter-is-sum bug and line 11 has a sum-is-counter bug. In order to keep from being misled by an example such as this, PROUST needs a critic which would notice that two bugs have been identified that are inverses of each other. As soon as the two bugs have been hypothesized, the critic could activate, leading to a correction of the interpretation of the *Sum* and *Count* goals.

8.5.2 Current analysis criticism

There are two classes of critics in PROUST. One class of critics applies in PROUST when the analysis is complete. The anomalies that these critics detect usually involve goals which were never successfully analyzed and/or code which was never interpreted. The other class of critic is applied as the analysis is being performed.

Here are some examples of what post-analysis critics look for:

- spurious initializations of variables which require no initialization,

- spurious updates, at the same time that goals which involve updates are reputed to be unimplemented, and

- loops which appear to be unnecessary.

The most important post-analysis critic is one which looks for evidence that one or more goals have been misinterpreted. This critic functions as follows. It first examines each uninterpreted statement, to determine what kind of plan component it is likely to be. For example, if the statement assigns a value to a variable, prior to any use of that variable, then the statement probably was intended to be an

```
1       program Average(input, output);
2       var Sum, Count, New: integer;
3           Avg: real;
4       begin
5         Sum := 0;
6         Count := 0;
7         read(New);
8         while New <> 99999 do
9           begin
10            Sum := Sum + New;
11            Count := Count + 1;
12            Read(New);
13          end;
14        if Count <> 0 then
15          begin
16            Avg := Count / Sum;
17            writeln('The average is ', avg);
18          end;
19      end;
```

Figure 8-12: A program where a bug throws off PROUST's interpretation

initialization. If the statement is a `while` statement, it probably was intended to be a loop. Next, the critic identifies the main plan component type of each missing goal.[25] Finally, the component type of each left-over plan component is compared against the set of goals for which implementations could not be found. If the types of the left-over plan components overlap with the main plan-component types required by the goals, then the analysis is criticized as being possibly inconsistent. For example, if PROUST cannot find an implementation of the goal *Average* in a Rainfall Problem solution, but it does find an extra update in the program, the analysis of the program will be criticized.

Mid-analysis critics look for the following things:

- two plans attempting to assign different interpretations to the same line of code;

---

[25]This information appears in the `MainComponent` slot of each goal.

- two plans attempting to assign different roles to the same variable.

8.5.3 Responding to criticism

PROUST's current responses to criticism are quite rudimentary. PROUST makes some attempt to identify the cause of an inconsistency, but it cannot yet repair an inconsistent interpretation. The best that it can do at this time is to point out to the student where the inconsistency lies, so that he/she can identify the bug which causes the inconsistency.

The principal response to analysis criticism at this time is to classify the interpretation as complete, partial, or aborted. An analysis is complete if a reasonably complete mapping exists between goals and code. An analysis is partial if there are major criticisms of the interpretation; the analysis is called "partial" because PROUST deletes parts of the analysis which might be invalid due to the analysis inconsistency. An analysis is aborted if it has been criticized so severely that it is deemed totally unreliable.

If an inconsistency was found between missing goals and left-over plan components, then the analysis is declared partial, and the student is shown the left-over goals and left-over code. Output such as the following results:

```
This analysis is incomplete.  There are parts of this program
that I could not understand, so this analysis may not be
totally correct.
This program does not implement the maximum.
I had problems with some of the code.
The statements in question are:
        IF RAINFALL > HIGHESTRAINFALL THEN ...
        RAINFALL := HIGHESTRAIN
```

PROUST requires that a minimum number of goals be interpreted in order for it to be successful. If this minimum number is not reached, then the analysis is aborted.

Mid-analysis criticisms currently handled as follows. If an interpretation is criticized, PROUST throws it out and PROUST considers the alternative interpretations. PROUST does not attempt to identify the source of the inconsistency.

8.5.4 Future responses to criticism

Analysis criticism will come into its own when criticism leads to re-interpretation of code. This response will involve the following two steps:

- identifying the goal interpretations on which the inconsistent code depends, and

- coming up with an alternative interpretation which resolves the inconsistency.

In some cases, searching for dependencies is unnecessary. The example where `readln(Deposit)` is written instead of `readln(Transtype)` is such a case. The critic discovers the `Missing Input` bug and the uninterpreted `readln(Deposit)` statement. The `readln` statement can be made to fit the loop if `Deposit` is changed to `Transtype`; thus inconsistencies in the analysis can be resolved without examining other parts of the analysis.

In the more general case, dependency-directed backtracking is required. For example, when PROUST analyzes the averaging program in Figure 8-12, it interprets the line `Sum := Sum + New`, as a buggy counter update, and the line `Count := Count + 1` as a buggy running-total update. An analysis critic detecting the presence of symmetrical counter-is-sum and sum-is-counter bugs could be used to detect the inconsistency. However, the analysis cannot be repaired simply by reinterpreting the two updates. PROUST must also determine what caused the misinterpretation. The cause of the misinterpretation here is that the average update has the numerator and denominator reversed. When the AVERAGE PLAN is matched, the plan matcher erroneously binds `?Sum`, the pattern variable representing the running-total variable, to `Count`. It binds `?Count`, the counter variable, to `Sum`. These incorrect bindings cause the counter update and the running-total update to be mismatched. By tracing the incorrect bindings back to their source, the match of the AVERAGE PLAN, PROUST could determine that the average update is buggy, not the running-total or counter updates.

The process of coming up with an alternative interpretation usually involves relaxing some set of assumptions which PROUST ordinarily makes when interpreting a program. In the previous example, the assumptions that must be relaxed are the

254

bindings of the pattern variables ?Sum and ?Count. The more assumptions that can be relaxed, the greater the range of analysis inconsistencies that in principle can be resolved.

9 Empirical Evaluation of PROUST

The bottom-line issue in evaluating the work that has gone into PROUST is whether or not it has resulted in effective tool for finding novice bugs. The previous chapters have shown how PROUST analyzes various examples of programming constructs and bugs. PROUST's performance cannot be judged on a few examples, however. It can only be judged by evaluating PROUST in realistic situations, on a wide range of novice programs. This chapter presents the results of such an evaluation.

The discussion in this chapter will proceed as follows. First I will describe how the evaluations were conducted, and what they attempted to test. Then the results of each test will be presented. Afterwards I will summarize, and discuss what these tests indicate about the effectiveness of PROUST.

9.1 Overview of the evaluation

The evaluation of PROUST was intended to answer the following questions.

1. How well can PROUST handle the variability in novice programs?

2. What level of analytic accuracy is PROUST's intention-based approach capable of producing?

3. What range of programming problems can PROUST analyze?

4. Is PROUST effective as an on-line debugging tool?

In order to address the above questions, two kinds of evaluations were performed. First, PROUST was tested off line on sets of novice programs. This provided information about PROUST's analytic capabilities, and the range and limitations of those capabilities. Then PROUST was tested on line in the classroom, and its interactions with students were studied. This made it possible to assess PROUST's effectiveness in helping novices debug their programs.

The off-line tests were performed as follows. As Section 1.1.1 mentioned, we gave introductory programming students a modified Pascal compiler which saved each version of their programs on tape. The collected student programs were then run through PROUST. The same programs were debugged by hand, and the results were compared against PROUST's bug reports.

In order to assess PROUST's ability to cope with variability, PROUST was run on the first syntactically-correct version that each student generated for a given programming problem. The first syntactically-correct versions were chosen because they have the greatest variety of bugs. In order to see whether or not PROUST's performance is dependent upon the particular group of students being studied, we assigned the same programming problems to more than one programming class, so as to collect solutions of the same problems from different classes. PROUST's performance on each set of programs was compared. Dependence upon the programming problem was tested by comparing PROUST's performance on two different programming problems, the Rainfall Problem and the Bank Problem. There were large numbers of programs in each set of Rainfall programs and Bank programs studied, about 100 on the average. This helped to ensure that novice variability was being accurately represented in each set of programs.

Because the tests were performed off line, it was possible to make modifications to student programs, and determine what modifications caused PROUST to succeed or fail in its analysis. This made it possible to assess PROUST's limitations in detail. If PROUST was unable to analyze a particular program correctly, I could determine why this was the case, whether it was due to a minor flaw in PROUST or an essential problem with PROUST's intention-based approach. This made it possible to determine the practical limits of PROUST's approach.

The on-line tests of PROUST were performed as follows. Another modification was made to the Pascal compiler that the students used; the new "compiler" first invoked the real Pascal compiler, then ran PROUST, and saved both the program and PROUST's analysis on tape. Then the programs were analyzed as before: the programs were debugged by hand, and the hand analyses were compared to PROUST's analyses. In addition, the interaction between PROUST and the students were examined, in order to see whether or not PROUST provided the help that the students needed.

9.2 Test 1: off-line test on the Rainfall Problem

The first off-line test of PROUST was on 206 students in one class solving the Rainfall Problem. I will call this set of programs Corpus 1. The Rainfall Problem was assigned fairly early in this particular programming course, so Corpus 1 contains a wide range of programming errors. These same programs had been previously analyzed by Steve Draper, various people in the Cognition and Programming Project at Yale, and myself; the results of these analyses were presented in Bug Collection I [42].

Corpus 1 was used for the initial test of PROUST because the work in building Bug Collection I identified nearly all of the bugs in these programs. Without an accurate accounting of the bugs in each corpus it is not possible to determine how accurate PROUST really is. Hand debugging of code is not particularly reliable: evaluations of code inspections in industry have shown that such inspections overlook substantial numbers of bugs [26, 49]. In fact, when PROUST analyzed Corpus 1 it identified a number of bugs which we had overlooked. These new bugs were subsequently added to the bug collection. I am presuming that the resulting bug catalog is nearly complete, and thus provides a good basis for measuring PROUST's performance.

The results of running PROUST on this sample of data is shown in Figure 9-1. As the chart indicates, there were three types of analyses generated by PROUST: complete, partial, and no analysis. These categories were described in Section 8.5.3. A complete analysis is where the goals have been mapped against the code, and where nearly all of the code has received some interpretation. Partial analyses are where substantial portions of the program have been analyzed, but major sections were unanalyzable. If a program is unanalyzed, it is either because the program is so unusual that PROUST cannot interpret it at all, or because the program uses a construct which PROUST cannot analyze, such as gotos.

9.2.1 Accuracy of bug reports overall

First, I will point out the strong points of these results. When PROUST was able to generate complete analyses of the programs, it correctly identified 94% of the bugs. This level of accuracy is higher than what the team that produced Bug Collection I

```
Total number of programs:                           206
    Number of programs with bugs:                   183    (89%)
    Number of programs without bugs:                 23
    Total number of bugs:                            795

Number of programs receiving full analyses:         155    (75%)
    Total number of bugs:                            532    (67%)
    Bugs recognized correctly:                       501    (94%)
    Bugs not recognized:                             29     (5%)
    False alarms:                                    46

Number of programs receiving partial analyses:      40     (20%)
    Total number of bugs:                            222    (28%)
    Bugs recognized correctly:                       79     (36%)
    Bugs not reported:                               143    (64%)
    False alarms:                                    36

Number of programs Proust  did not analyze:         11     (5%)
    Total number of bugs:                            41     (5%)
```

Figure 9-1: Results of running PROUST on Corpus 1: the Rainfall Problem

was able to achieve. I am able to assess PROUST's accuracy in these cases only because PROUST overlooks different bugs than people do. People miss bugs because they do not analyze programs systematically enough. PROUST usually overlooks bugs because it misinterprets the code or because it has no plan-difference rules for identifying the bugs.

PROUST produced a complete analysis of 75% of the programs. This is a very substantial fraction, but it could be improved. Notice that the 75% of the programs which PROUST analyzed completely contained only 67% of the total bugs in the data set. Thus on the whole the programs which PROUST analyzed completely had fewer bugs. It turns out, for example, that 20 out of 23 bug-free programs were analyzed completely.

Although PROUST identifies a high fraction of bugs when it analyzes programs completely, it also generates a number of false alarms. By "false alarm" I mean any bug description which PROUST generates but which should not be present in a correct bug report. This includes bugs which are misinterpreted by PROUST, as well as code which PROUST thinks is buggy but really is not.[26] In the 155 programs which received complete analyses, there were 46 false alarms. 26 of the 155 programs had one or more false alarms. PROUST tends to err on the side of flagging bugs which do not exist, rather than ignoring bugs which do exist; in only two cases did PROUST give a buggy program a clean bill of health.

20% of the programs got partial analyses. 36% of the bugs in these programs were correctly reported. Of the bugs which were not reported, some were deleted from the analyses by PROUST when it determined that parts of the analysis were unreliable. Others PROUST simply failed to identify. In the programs with partial analyses there were 36 false alarms, a fairly high number. However, PROUST informs the student when its analysis is partial, and indicates that the analysis should be taken with a grain of salt. This is so that the students will be less likely to be misled by the false alarms.

Note that when PROUST cannot analyze a bug, and therefore gives a program a partial analysis, the analysis can still be useful. PROUST attempts to localize the bug by identifying goals and code which might relate to each other. When PROUST cannot fully understand a program, it indicates why. usually the bug is well-enough localized that it should be clear to the student where the problem is. Figure 9-2 shows an example of PROUST attempting to localize a bug. In this example, PROUST has narrowed a bug down to three statements.

```
This analysis is incomplete. There are parts of this program that
I could not understand, so this analysis may not be totally correct.
This program does not implement the maximum.
I had problems with some of the code.
The statements in question are:
        RAINFALLNEW := RAINFALLOLD
        IF RAINFALLOLD > HIGHEST THEN ...
        HIGHEST := RAINFALLOLD
```

Figure 9-2: PROUST attempting to localize a bug

---

[26]Typically, 65% of PROUST's false alarms are misinterpreted bugs, and 35% are correct code which is flagged as buggy.

The remaining 5% of the programs were unanalyzable. It is unfortunate that PROUST cannot analyze some of the novice programs, but as long as the fraction of such programs is this low it is not a major concern.

9.2.2 Frequency of identification of major bugs

Another way of assessing the success of PROUST at identifying bugs is to count the number of programs where PROUST correctly identified the most serious bug in the program. There may of course be disagreement as to which bugs are more important than others. I chose as most significant bugs which reflect some major misconception, and/or which are manifested in the program's behavior in a serious way. I consider these types of bugs to be important because they are most likely to lead to confusion and frustration on the part of the students.

The results of examining PROUST's performance on the most serious bugs is as follows. Of the 183 programs which had bugs, PROUST found the most serious bug in 141 programs. That is, it found the most serious bug 77% of the time. This high percentage indicates that PROUST should provide significant assistance to students, particularly in getting started with debugging their programs.

9.3 Test 2: on-line and off-line test on the Rainfall Problem

PROUST's high performance in analyzing Corpus 1 is in some ways unsurprising. Bug Collection I was used as the basis for building PROUST's bug knowledge base, although not every bug in the collection was incorporated into the knowledge base. A good match between PROUST's knowledge base and Corpus 1 was therefore expected. In order to see whether PROUST's performance was confined to Corpus 1, or whether the same performance can be achieved on any set of solutions of the Rainfall Problem, a second test was performed with the Rainfall Problem. This second test was an on-line test, performed with a different introductory programming class. The purpose of this test was not only to make sure that PROUST can analyze Rainfall programs written by different classes, but also to see how PROUST performs as an on-line debugging aid.

The results of the on-line test are shown in Figure 9-3, in the column labeled "On

Line". Unlike Corpus 1, I hand-debugged Corpus 2 by myself. It therefore may not be as complete as the bug catalogue for Corpus 1, so the number of bugs listed as not being recognized by PROUST are likely to be a bit lower than they should be.

	On Line	Reanalysis
Total number of programs:	76	76
Total number of bugs:	378	378
Number of full analyses:	30 (39%)	53 (70%)
Total number of bugs:	133 (35%)	252 (67%)
Bugs recognized correctly:	131 (98%)	247 (98%)
Bugs not recognized:	2 (2%)	5 (2%)
False alarms:	5	18
Number of partial analyses:	33 (43%)	19 (25%)
Total number of bugs:	179 (47%)	105 (28%)
Bugs recognized correctly:	65 (40%)	42 (40%)
Bugs not recognized:	98 (60%)	63 (60%)
False alarms:	20	17
Number of unanalyzed programs:	13 (17%)	4 (5%)
	66 (17%)	21 (6%)

Figure 9-3: Results of running PROUST on Corpus 2: the Rainfall Problem

The results of the on-line test were surprisingly poor: instead of analyzing 75% of the programs completely, PROUST analyzed only 39% of the programs correctly. Both the number of unanalyzed programs and the number of partially-analyzed programs went up. I ran PROUST on the same data off line in order to determine what the problem was, and discovered that two problems had slipped my attention when I was preparing PROUST for the on-line test. First, there were incompatibilities between the syntax of VMS Pascal, which the students were using, and that of Unix Pascal, which is what I used to test PROUST.[27] PROUST was expecting Unix Pascal, so it rejected as syntactically incorrect a number of programs which had passed through

---

[27]VMS Pascal allows underscores in identifier names, whereas Unix Pascal does not.

the VMS Pascal compiler without error. As a result, the frequency of unanalyzed programs shot up. Second, a bug in one of the analysis critics caused many more interpretations to be rejected than I had intended. I fixed these problems and re-ran PROUST on the programs, and found that PROUST's performance increased dramatically. The fraction of complete analyses went up to 70%, and the fraction of unanalyzed programs went down to 5%. The 70% completion rate is comparable to the 75% completion rate achieved on Corpus 1.

Two conclusions can be drawn from these results. First, PROUST's accuracy stays much the same from one group of students to the next. Second, PROUST had not been tested well enough to make it useable as an on-line tool. Subsequent on-line tests of PROUST must be performed only after adequate testing has been done in the environment in which the students will use PROUST.

Since PROUST analyzed programs completely less than half the time, there were only a few cases where it analyzed completely every syntactically correct version of a student's program. Therefore PROUST could not provide as much assistance to students in most cases as it should, so it was not possible to get an accurate assessment of how helpful PROUST could be to novices. In the cases where PROUST did succeed in analyzing every intermediate version completely, it appeared to be helpful. Appendix I shows the interaction between one student and PROUST. When the students understood PROUST's complaints and were able to figure out what to do about them, they could debug their programs fairly quickly. The program in the appendix required only three syntactically-correct versions before all bugs were removed.

Two problems became apparent from looking at how the students reacted to PROUST. First, students frequently lost faith in PROUST when it analyzed a version of the student's program partially or not at all. Second, even when PROUST analyzed programs completely the students often could not understand PROUST's error messages. The first problem will be alleviated as the fraction of complete analyses increases. The second problem will be solved only when some sort of tutoring component is attached to PROUST which can try to make certain that the students understand the bugs.

264

Another problem was speed. Several students were frequently running PROUST at the same time on the same VAX 11/750. When this happened the PROUSTs were constantly competing for memory, and were being swapped in and out. It sometimes took five minutes for each PROUST to start up. Once PROUST was loaded it took substantially less time to analyze successive versions of the program, but it could still take up to a minute per run. PROUST's resource requirements will have to be reduced before it can be used widely by students.

9.4 Causes of analysis errors in the Rainfall Problem

Let us now look beyond the gross statistics, and analyze in detail under what conditions PROUST fails to analyze Rainfall programs correctly. The programs in Corpus 1 will be used in this analysis. We need to know whether PROUST's errors can be easily corrected, or are a result of fundamental flaws in PROUST's approach. This will make it possible to estimate how much further PROUST's performance can improve on the Rainfall Problem, and what the practical limitations are.

9.4.1 Causes for total analysis failure

I will first discuss the programs which PROUST was unable to analyze at all. Of the 11 programs in Corpus 1 which were not analyzed, six programs were unanalyzed because PROUST cannot yet interpret the constructs that the novices were using. PROUST can interpret only a subset of the constructs in Pascal; when it encounters a construct which it is not equipped to handle, it aborts the analysis. The following three unsupported constructs appeared in these examples: boolean variables, the operator not, and gotos.

One of the eleven analyses was aborted because of an unimplemented feature in PROUST. There was a verification demon in PROUST whose action part had not been written yet. This demon tried to fire on one of the programs in Corpus 1; when this happened PROUST trapped it and aborted the analysis.

Four program analyses failed because PROUST could not interpret a sufficient number of goals in the program description. The specific cause in these cases was that PROUST could not interpret the programs' main loops. As I explained in

Chapter 8, PROUST's program analysis focuses first on the main loop. If the main loop is not constructed in one of the ways that PROUST expects, and no plan-difference rule can account for the plan differences, then PROUST cannot analyze the loop. Since the rest of the analysis depends upon identifying the main loop, the analysis cannot proceed. Of the four programs with unanalyzable loops, one used -99999 as the sentinel value, two terminated whenever any negative number was input, and in one case the sentinel was an uninitialized variable.

Most of analysis failures listed in this section are correctable. Some of the previously unsupported Pascal constructs are supported in the current version of PROUST. The incomplete verification demon has been fixed. However, the number of unanalyzed programs can never be reduced to zero. We might be able to write plan-difference rules to identify the unusual bugs in Corpus 1, but as soon as PROUST analyzes programs which are not in Corpus 1 it will encounter further bugs that it is not prepared to handle. The only real solution is to make PROUST's analysis strategies more flexible, so that the analysis does not fail if the main loop cannot be analyzed.

9.4.2 Causes of partial analyses

I will now give a breakdown of the causes for partial analyses in Corpus 1. In order to identify these causes, the following procedure was followed. 20 programs were selected at random from among the 40 programs which were analyzed partially. In each case PROUST's output was analyzed to determine which parts of the program could not be interpreted correctly, and why. Where feasible the student's program was then modified to eliminate the interpretation problem. For example, if the code could not be understood because of the application of a transformation which was not in PROUST's knowledge base, the code was de-transformed. If PROUST could not understand the code because of the bug, the bug was corrected. The program was then run through PROUST again, and the fault identification process was repeated until the program could be analyzed completely. In this way an estimate was derived of the number of changes which would have to be made to PROUST to get it to analyze each program completely. This estimate is low, because some bugs and transformations hide the presence of other bugs and transformations.

A major cause of partial analyses was where a programmer used a wrong variable. Novices frequently use the wrong variable when there are two variables with similar names, such as `Sum` and `Num`, or `Rainfall` and `Totalrain`. Such programs are partially analyzed when the wrong variable causes PROUST to be unable to interpret a statement in the program, and an analysis critic indicates that this interpretation failure is significant. Of the 20 partially-analyzed programs which were studied, eight had an incorrect variable usage which contributed to completion failure.

Another major cause of partial analysis was inadequate differential diagnosis. Proust's ability to choose between alternative interpretations of the same goal was not well developed; it often selected the wrong plan. Five of the programs in the set of 20 had differential-diagnosis problems. The problems with selecting the wrong plan from among several plans implementing the same goal have since been largely corrected in PROUST. Part of the cause of misdiagnosis has not been corrected, however: there is no way of comparing two plans implementing different goals to see which one matches a given block of code best.

Some partial analyses were caused by a plan-difference rule that failed to fire. Some plan-difference rules were insufficiently refined to deal with peculiar cases, and others were simply missing from PROUST's knowledge base. An example of an inadequately-refined rule is the following. The bug rule which identifies missing `begin-end` pairs after `while` statements does not determine exactly which statements belong within the missing `begin-end` pair. Instead, it simply makes a guess. Incorrect guesses can lead to misinterpretations of part of the code in the `while` loop. Missing and unrefined plan-difference rules affected the interpretation of 6 out of the 20 programs.

Three programs had problems where it was not possible to de-transform or correct the program and retain something similar to the original structure. In such cases further identification of analysis errors was pointless. Additional modifications might have been necessary to handle these cases, but there was no way of knowing at the time.

None of the problems mentioned above are particularly surprising. PROUST's analysis critics were intended to detect interpretation errors, and they do just that;

however, analysis repair is currently not attempted. It is no surprise that plan-difference bug rules need to be modified or added; PROUST's knowledge base is still in the process of development.

9.4.3 Causes for false alarms

In order to identify the causes of the false alarms in Corpus 1, I went through the same procedure that I went though in analyzing the causes for partial analysis. Twenty programs were chosen from among those which PROUST analyzes completely and generates false alarms. The immediate cause of each false alarm was identified, the program was modified to avoid the false alarm, and then PROUST was run again on the program, until all causes of false alarms in the program were identified.

Improper use of variables caused false alarms, just as it caused partial analyses. If an incorrect variable usage is caught by an analysis critic, the result is a partial analysis; otherwise the result is one or more false alarms. In order to prevent these false alarms we must first presume that variable usage errors can be corrected when the analysis critics find them, and then new analysis critics must be added to catch the cases which currently are slipping through and causing the false alarms.

Some false alarms were caused by insufficiently general plan-difference rules, or missing plan-difference rules. Rules for recognizing missing `begin-end` pairs were again a prime culprit. Also plan-difference rules sometimes failed to fire on transformed code. All told seven programs had false alarms because of improper plan-difference rule application.

Improper differential diagnosis resulted in some false alarms, just as it led to some partial analyses. Again the difference in the two cases is that PROUST's analysis critics failed to catch the cases that resulted in false alarms. Two programs had false alarms because of incorrect analysis choice.

Two programs had false alarms due to a bug in PROUST. This bug has since been fixed.

Another source of false alarms was a failure to generate a wide enough set of alternative implementation methods for goals. Currently PROUST's Unification Rule (see Section 6.4.3) applies unconditionally; if two goals can be unified, PROUST unifies them, and does not consider the possibility that the programmer failed to unify them.

268

In the Rainfall Problem two *Count* goals must be satisfied. One is mentioned explicitly in the program description; this is the requirement that the count of valid inputs be output. The other is introduced by the AVERAGE PLAN; the AVERAGE PLAN computes the average by dividing a count into a sum, resulting in the need for a count to be computed. PROUST expects these two *Count* goals to be unified. Thus it expects that the same variable which is used in the average will also be output. However, in one of the 20 programs analyzed, two counter variables were used; evidently the two *Count* goals had not been unified by the student. PROUST therefore complained that the valid input counter was not output, when the real problem was that the valid input counter was a different variable from what PROUST thought it was.

Of the 20 programs, two had false alarms which could not easily be prevented by adding new bug rules, and were not covered by the other changes listed above. They were so far-removed from a well-constructed program that it was not clear how to get PROUST to generate a meaningful interpretation of them.

9.4.4 The practical limits of PROUST's capabilities

If the errors described in this section are a representative sample, then there are few limitations on what Rainfall programs PROUST is able to analyze. The limitations which do exist are as follows. PROUST cannot analyze programs which are extremely far removed from the problem statement, particularly if the main loop is constructed in an unfamiliar fashion. If goals are unified in a peculiar fashion, PROUST may not be able to understand the student's goal decomposition. Misuse of variables currently misleads PROUST, although the analysis critic mechanism provides part of what is needed for correcting such misinterpretations.

An estimate of the practical limitations of PROUST can be achieved as follows. Many of the analysis failures described in this section are the result of bugs in PROUST, or bugs in some of PROUST's plan-difference rules. A well-tuned PROUST would have such problems corrected. A relatively small number of missing rules were responsible for a large number of failures; a reasonably complete rule base would be expected to include the missing rules which are required most frequently. A more complete PROUST would be able to interpret a wider range of Pascal constructs. In addition, a well-tuned PROUST would do a better job of evaluating and differentiating interpretations, and it would be able to recover from certain kinds of analysis mistakes using analysis critics. By counting how many of PROUST's current analysis failures would disappear if PROUST were improved in these ways, we can get a sense of what PROUST's ultimate capabilities are likely to be.

Of the 11 programs in Corpus 1 which were unanalyzable, all but 5 would become at least partially analyzable if the range of Pascal constructs were extended to include booleans and NOT, and bugs in PROUST were fixed. Eleven of the 20 partially-analyzed programs would probably be analyzed completely if PROUST were well-tuned. False alarms would disappear in 9 of the 20 completely-analyzed programs with false alarms. Thus the frequency of each type of analysis failure would drop in half if PROUST were well-tuned.

Subsequent work on PROUST indicates that the above estimate of PROUST's potential capabilities is accurate. As will be shown in Section 9.6, current performance of PROUST already achieves a completion rate of over 80%, and many improvements to PROUST remain to be made. This improvement did not result from special tuning for handling the Rainfall Problem. Thus PROUST is well on its way toward the eventual goal of an 85% completion rate with a reduced incidence of false alarms.

9.5 Test 3: on-line and off-line test on the Bank Problem

At the same time that the on-line test with the Rainfall Problem was performed, an on-line test with the Bank Problem was performed. 67 students ran PROUST on their solutions to the Bank Problem. The PROUST's performance on these programs in shown in Figure 9-4, in the column labeled "On Line". The results were much worse than was the case with the Rainfall Problem. Out of 67 first syntactically-correct versions, only one was analyzed completely. 38 programs, or 56%, were analyzed partially, and 28, or 42%, were unanalyzed.

Altogether, PROUST was able to identify 17 bugs in the students' programs. Nine of these bugs were found in the one program which PROUST analyzed completely. The rest came from the partially analyzed programs. The number of false alarms in

	On Line	Reanalysis
Total number of programs:	68	68
Number of full analyses:	1 (1%)	7 (10%)
Bugs recognized correctly:	9	18
False alarms:	0	2
Number of partial analyses:	38 (56%)	42 (62%)
Bugs recognized correctly:	8	17
False alarms:	28	33
Number of unanalyzed programs:	28 (41%)	19 (28%)

Figure 9-4: PROUST's performance on Corpus 3: the Bank Problem

the partial analyses far exceeded the number of correct bug analyses. Thus PROUST's analysis accuracy was poor indeed.

9.5.1 Causes of the poor performance

Some of the problems which PROUST had on the Bank Problem were the same as those that it had on the Rainfall Problem in Corpus 2, for example regarding incompatibilities in VMS and Unix Pascal syntax. When PROUST was re-run on the Bank Problem solutions, performance improved slightly, as shown in the "Reanalysis" column of Figure 9-4. The number of complete analyses went up to 7 (10%), the number of partial analyses went up to 42 (62%), and the number of unanalyzed programs went down to 19 (28%). Nevertheless, this level of performance is far from sufficient.

There turned out to be two basic reasons why the analysis of the Bank Problem was so poor. First, PROUST's knowledge base had not been expanded enough to handle the variability in Bank programs. Second, the Bank programs are more complex than Rainfall programs; more work is required to interpret them, and more opportunities are available for misinterpretation.

I analyzed the causes of the failures in analyzing Bank programs in much the same way that the analysis failures in the Rainfall Problem were analyzed. 30 programs were chosen at random from among the programs which PROUST did not analyze completely. The immediate cause for each analysis failure was determined, removed from the program, and the program was re-analyzed, the next cause for analysis failure was determined, etc.

Analysis of PROUST's analysis failures uncovered several plan-difference rules which were missing from the knowledge base. An example of a missing plan-difference rule is one for dealing with case conversion on input. Since the problem statement for the Bank Problem does not specify whether the transaction codes should be in upper case or lower case, some students used upper-case transaction codes and others used lower-case transaction codes. Proust's problem description states that the transaction codes should be lower case, so it cannot analyze programs that use upper-case transaction codes. Missing plan-difference rules contributed to analysis failure in at least 19 of the 30 programs.

Another major difficulty came from the fact that PROUST did not predict all possible boundary conditions which might be applied to a program. Some boundary conditions were not listed in PROUST's object class knowledge base. For example, PROUST did not have any boundary condition attached to account numbers, but a number of students tested for invalid account numbers. Unexpected boundary condition tests contributed to analysis failure in 14 of the 30 programs.

As was the case with the Rainfall Problem, PROUST sometimes failed because it was unable to analyze a Pascal construct. Since the students who solved the Bank Problem were further along in the course, they used more constructs which PROUST could not analyze. These constructs contributed to analysis failure in 7 of the 30 programs.

A number of Bank Problem solutions had main loops which differed significantly from what the problem statement required. Some students, for example, wrote loops which stopped when the transaction amount was 99999. The frequency of such improperly-constructed loops was much greater in the case of the Bank Problem than was the case for the Rainfall Problem; 8 programs had improperly-constructed loops.

Unexpected goal unification and non-unification were major problems in the Bank Problem data. 2 analyses failed for these reasons.

272

There were several cases of computations which were performed in such a way that PROUST could not follow the intermediate steps. For example, one student computed the final balance by starting with a zero balance, adding in the deposits and withdrawals, and then adding in the initial balance only after the exit command had been entered. Such unusual methods for performing the computations resulted in analysis failure in 6 programs.

Two programs were analyzed incorrectly because the plan matcher in the version of PROUST used in the test assumed that there was a one-to-one correspondence between PROUST objects and Pascal variables. This restriction has since been relaxed.

To summarize, many of the problems which PROUST had in analyzing solutions to the Bank Problem were similar to problems that it has had in analyzing solutions to the Rainfall Problem. Bug rules were missing, Pascal constructs were not supported, and code is not constructed as PROUST expected. Some of these flaws have since been corrected: a wider range of Pascal constructs is now supported, and some plan-difference rules have been added to the knowledge base. However, even assuming that the knowledge base can be expanded as needed, there remain many more cases where PROUST cannot interpret the students' code because the code differs so much from PROUST's predictions. Improperly constructed loops, unexpected goal unifications and non-unifications, and peculiar methods of performing computations together would cause analysis of fourteen of the 30 programs to fail, even if all other problems are eliminated. Therefore, unless substantial changes are made to PROUST, we can expect an effective limit of 50-55% on complete analyses.

9.6 Latest results with PROUST

Recently, further work has been done to PROUST to improve its performance. This effort has already resulted in some improvements, although further work remains to be done.

Figure 9-5 shows the latest results of running PROUST on the Corpus 1 Rainfall Problem data. The percentage of programs which have been analyzed completely is now 81%. The increase in complete analyses is due to a decrease both of unanalyzable programs (from 5% to 4%) and of partially analyzable programs (from

20% to 15%). The number of false alarms increased with the number of complete analyses, from 46 to 66, but this is partially offset by a decrease in the false alarms among the partially-analyzed programs, from 36 to 20. Still, further improvement in the false alarm rate would be desirable.

```
Total number of programs:              206
     Number of programs with bugs:     183    (89%)
     Number of programs without bugs:   23
     Total number of bugs:             795

Number of full analyses:               167    (81%)
     Total number of bugs:             598    (75%)
     Bugs recognized correctly:        562    (94%)
     Bugs not recognized:               36     (6%)
     False alarms:                      66

Number of partial analyses:             31    (15%)
     Total number of bugs:             167    (21%)
     Bugs recognized correctly:         61    (37%)
     Bugs not reported:                106    (63%)
     False alarms:                      20

Number of unanalyzed programs:           9     (4%)
     Total number of bugs:              32     (4%)
```

Figure 9-5: New results of running PROUST on Corpus 1

Figure 9-6 shows PROUST's current performance on the Bank Problem. The frequency of completed analyses is much higher now; instead of 10%, it is now 50%. PROUST's performance on the completely-analyzed programs is now almost good as it is on completely-analyzed solutions of the Rainfall Problem. 91% of the bugs in the Bank Problem solutions were correctly identified, compared with 94% of the bugs in the Rainfall Problem solutions. The incidence of false alarms, however, is relatively high; there were 41 false alarms in the completely-analyzed Bank Problem solutions, compared with 211 total bugs in the same group of programs.

The percentage of unanalyzed programs has come down substantially, from 28% to 9%. All of the six unanalyzable programs could not be analyzed because their

```
Total number of programs analyzed:        64
    Total numbers of bugs:               420

Number of full analyses:              32 (50%)
    Total number of bugs:            211 (50%)
    Bugs recognized correctly:       191 (91%)
    Bugs not reported:                20  (9%)
    False alarms:                     41

Number of partial analyses:           26 (41%)
    Total number of bugs:            168 (40%)
    Bugs recognized correctly:        56 (33%)
    Bugs not reported:               112 (67%)
    False alarms:                     24

Number of unanalyzed programs:         6  (9%)
    Total number of bugs:             41 (10%)

Number of programs omitted from analysis: 4
```

Figure 9-6:   New results of running PROUST on Corpus 3

main loops were constructed in unusual ways. Four of the six deviated radically from the problem requirements, and PROUST's knowledge base was not adequate for predicting the deviation. The other two cases had unusual goal decompositions, but were correct, except that they dealt with boundary conditions in unexpected ways. The limitations in PROUST's ability to generate possible goal decompositions was responsible for analysis failure in each of these two cases.

The proportion of solutions which are analyzed partially has gone down from 62% to 41%. The accuracy of analysis among these programs is similar to the accuracy of partial analyses of Rainfall Problem solutions.

Four programs were omitted from analysis because they were very far-removed from an expected solution, apparently due to the ambiguities in the problem statement. Ambiguities in the problem statement affected PROUST's performance on many of the other programs, but on these cases the effect was so extreme that they were not considered a fair test of PROUST.

9.7 Concluding remarks

To conclude, let us reconsider the questions which were asked at the beginning of the chapter, to see what answers we have found for them.

The evaluations described in this chapter have shown that PROUST can cope well with novice variability, at least in the Rainfall Problem. It analyzes programs completely in most cases, and when it does so it identifies bugs accurately. Furthermore, this performance does not vary significantly from one group of students to the next.

An investigation of the causes of PROUST's analysis failures indicated that the practical limit in performance has not yet been achieved. Simple enhancements of PROUST were expected to lead to an improvement in analysis completion rate of 5% to 10%, with a concomitant decrease of false alarms. More recent work on PROUST has achieved the expected increase in analysis completion rate, but the decrease in false alarm rate has not yet been realized.

Results of PROUST on the Bank Problem indicate that PROUST's performance degrades as problem complexity and problem ambiguity increase. Increased problem complexity degrades performance because the probability that PROUST will fail to understand some part of a program increases. Increased problem ambiguity degrades performance because it increases the likelihood that PROUST will be unable to predict the students' decompositions of the problem.

Finally, the requirements that PROUST be useable as an on-line debugging tool impose orthogonal constraints beyond the constraints on analytic performance. PROUST has to be made more understandable, so that students can profit from its analyses. It must be made faster and smaller, or else the machines which the students use must be less heavily loaded. And finally it must be thoroughly tested in the environment in which it will be used, to make sure that it does not fail unexpectedly.

10 Concluding Remarks

This book has claimed that accurate debugging of novice programs requires an understanding of the intentions underlying programs. Knowledge of intentions makes it possible to distinguish buggy code from unusual but correct code. There is a wide range of variability in novice programs; each solution to a given programming problem is likely to have a different set of underlying intentions. Therefore the intentions cannot be known beforehand; they must be inferred from the individual program being debugged. This intention identification process must proceed while the program is being debugged. If intentions are identified without knowledge of bugs then the bugs may cause the intentions to be misinterpreted. If bugs are identified without knowledge of intentions then buggy and correct code cannot always be distinguished. Thus identifying bugs and understanding programmer's intentions are intertwined.

A model of programmers' intentions in terms of goals, their decomposition, and their realization in terms of plans was developed. This model was based in part upon the work of Soloway *et al.* with programming plans [10, 60]. An approach to program analysis based upon this framework was developed and implemented in a program called PROUST. The key feature of the approach is analysis by synthesis. Analysis by synthesis makes it possible to construct detailed predictions how a program is likely to be implemented, which can then be tested against the code. These detailed predictions make the debugging process robust, because bug identification is unlikely to be thrown off by buggy code which, when viewed out of context, might be interpreted incorrectly.

10.1 Generality of intention-based diagnosis

Intention-based debugging is a technique whose usefulness is not confined to programming; intention-based debugging is applicable to a wide variety of domains. Whenever a tutor observes a student's behavior in solving a problem and tries to understand what the student is attempting to do, the tutor is engaged in the process of identifying intentions. An example of a domain which is amenable to intention-based diagnosis, yet which is far removed from programming, is case-method instruction in medicine. In medicine, students take turns diagnosing cases, and the instructor observes what questions they ask and what tests they call for, interrupting when the student appears to be going about the diagnosis incorrectly.

The ease of identification of a student's intentions depends upon whether or not information about the intermediate problem-solving steps is available. Case-method tutoring of medicine is a domain where such information is available. The tutor can evaluate each question that the student asks in solving the case, in order to determine what the student is trying to accomplish at each point in the work-up. The range of possible intentions at each point is limited. The tutor can use information about what the student has done so far, to predict what the student is likely to do next.

In domains involving analysis of designed artifacts, in contrast, no information about intermediate problem-solving steps is available. All the tutor has to work from is the completed artifact. Because less information is available, identification of intentions is more difficult. Instead of trying to understand the problem-solving steps one at a time, the tutor must try to understand the various components of the artifact all at once.

Analysis by synthesis in PROUST can be thought of as a way of recreating some of the intermediate problem-solving steps in the programming process. PROUST tries to place itself in the student's position, to see what it would expect the student to do next; it then compares these expectations against the student's program. Thus the analysis-by-synthesis technique of debugging is specifically designed for use on designed artifacts such as programs, where the intermediate problem-solving steps are not known. The technique of understanding the student's behavior by predicting what the student will do next is equally applicable to medicine as to programming, however.

PROUST's analysis methods should be applicable to design domains other than programming, for the following reasons. The plan-goal model underlying PROUST is not specific to programming, but could be applied to any domain in which students construct artifacts out of stereotypic components. The suitability of PROUST's approach depends upon the extent to which stereotypic components are used. As we saw in Chapter 6, PROUST relies heavily on a knowledge base to come up with its predictions. If the problem space is well-structured, where the relationships between goals and plans are clear, then PROUST's approach is well-suited to the domain. If the problem space is ill-structured, where it is hard to tell how to relate requirements to solutions, then PROUST's approach is not appropriate. Thus PROUST could probably help teach digital circuit design; it would be less able to teach architectural design.

10.2 Contributions to the understanding of programming

The exercise of building PROUST has provided insight into how programming is done. In order to be able to predict the variety of programs that students write, it has been necessary to reach a better understanding of the knowledge and types of processing that programmers use in writing programs. Much of this knowledge has been made explicit in PROUST.

Substantial amounts of knowledge relevant to programming have been found to be associated with object classes. Object classes serve an important role in the refinement of informal program requirements. A problem statement may indicate that a datum belongs to an object class, and the programmer must then use his/her knowledge about the object class in order to determine what precise properties the data has.

Programming pragmatics is another type of knowledge which novices must learn. By programming pragmatics I mean knowledge about how programs are expected to interact with their environment. Experienced programmers know what it means to check input for validity, but far too many novices fail to re-read input if it is faulty, or do so only once.

Work with PROUST has led to a better understanding of goals and operations on goals, in particular goal reformulations. Novice programmers reformulate their goals in ways which probably would not occur to an experienced programmer. If one were to codify what sorts of goal reformulations lead to decreased comprehensibility of code, as well as bugs, and include this as part of the curriculum, the quality of novice programs would be greatly improved.

Plans have been discussed in detail in Soloway's work. In PROUST the concept of plan has been put to extensive use. By looking at the plans that PROUST uses, we can get a sense of what range of plans are required to write programs. It would be interesting to try to extend PROUST's knowledge base of plans further to see how many are required for a reasonably complete knowledge base.

Finally, plan transformations are sometimes necessary in order to combine plans in a program. Many of the plan transformations of which PROUST has knowledge serve to obscure the underlying plan structure of programs. It would be interesting to try to characterize what makes these transformations undesirable, and what makes other transformations acceptable to experienced programmers.

10.3 Prospects for the future

Let us now consider what additional research needs to be done, and what sorts of improvements could be made to PROUST. One of the most immediate needs at this time is to test PROUST on a wider range of programming problems. Now that an acceptable level of performance has been achieved on two programming problems, the time has come to try to generalize and extend PROUST's knowledge.

Until PROUST is coupled with a tutoring module, PROUST's ability to diagnose programming errors will remain limited to the information that is extractable from the buggy programs themselves. A tutoring component would be able to ask students questions in order to select between alternative explanations of bugs. It would also be able to construct a model of the individual students' abilities, which would help PROUST to predict the errors that each student is likely to make. Thus adding a tutoring component should make possible dramatic improvements in PROUST's diagnostic ability.

It would be a good idea to build a version of PROUST for a different programming language, such as Ada or Lisp. This would clarify even further the kinds of knowledge that programmers use, and in particular what knowledge is common to all programming tasks. It would also be useful to consider another design domain, such as digital circuits. That would demonstrate the generality of PROUST's problem-solving model, and would further test the effectiveness of the knowledge-based approach to predicting novice solutions. Since programming is such a complex task, it behooves us to try to understand what parts of it are really examples of more general cognitive processing.

Another question to ask is whether or not a tool such as PROUST is really the best thing to build, or whether a better kind of debugging tool could be built. PROUST as currently designed suffers from a major shortcoming. Although it can find a range of bugs in programs of the level of complexity of the Rainfall Problem, we have seen that its performance falls off on more complex programs. One of the reasons for the difficulties with complex programs is that PROUST is forced to use a relatively low-level representation for programs in order to catch the widest range of bugs. The low-level representation is needed in order to make sure that PROUST's plan-difference rules can recognize low-level syntactic bugs, such as spurious semicolons, reversed updates, and misplaced `begin-end` pairs. This low-level representation means that an abundance of transformation rules are required in order to understand code written by more advanced students, who rearrange their code at will. If the syntactic bugs could be ignored, then PROUST could use a more abstract program representation, which would reduce the impact of variability on PROUST's performance.

There is a pedagogical issue which relates to the plan representation issue in PROUST. If students make a wide range of low-level bugs, then their grasp of the programming language, or of the plans that they are trying to use, is poor. If such is the case then it would be better for the student to work on simple problems, before trying to apply this imperfect knowledge to harder problems.

Imagine, then, that one were to reorganize a programming curriculum as follows. When new constructs and programming plans are taught to the class, two sets of programming problems are assigned. The first set consists of small problems utilizing the new concepts. The student solves these problems in order to resolve any glaring misconceptions about the material. Then once a basic grasp of the constructs has been achieved, a second set of harder problems is tackled. These help the student to understand better how to organize groups of plans, and help to identify subtler misconceptions that the programmer might have. One could then construct two PROUSTs: a PROUST1 which specializes in low-level bugs, but is confined to fairly small programs, and a PROUST2 which specializes in high-level bugs, and which works on larger programs.

Low-level errors can never be eliminated entirely; even expert programmers make typographical errors. However, many low-level misconceptions could be eliminated by having novices work on small problems first; this would substantially reduce the variety of low-level errors. PROUST2 would therefore be substantially freed to concentrate on high-level planning bugs. It could use a more abstract plan and program representation, simplifying the diagnostic process. This in turn would free it to explore a wider range of goal decompositions. Thus if a programming curriculum were suitably structured, a combination of a low-level PROUST and a high-level PROUST could easily do the work of the current general-purpose PROUST, and would probably be applicable to a wider range of programs.

Appendix I A Session with PROUST

This appendix presents an example of PROUST giving feedback to a student over a series of program versions, until all the bugs in the program were corrected. The example is a solution of the Rainfall Problem, taken from the second on-line test described in Chapter 9. This test is the most recent on-line test of PROUST on the Rainfall Problem, but it was still performed about a year before the time of this writing. Substantial improvement has been made to PROUST since the test was performed, particularly in terms of PROUST's presentation of bug descriptions to students. The wording and organization of the bug reports which you will see in this example are thus somewhat out of date, but the bug analyses themselves are similar to what PROUST currently generates.

The following is the first syntactically-correct version of the rainfall program which the student generated.

```
 1 Program Rain(INPUT,OUTPUT);
 2
 3 VAR
 4    count, days: Integer;
 5    total, rain, maxrain, avgr: Real;
 6
 7 BEGIN
 8    count:= 0;
 9    total:= 0;
10    rain:= 0;
11    maxrain:= 0;
12    days:= 0;
13    avgr:= 0;
14
15    Writeln('Please input the amount of a days rainfall in inches.');
16    Readln(rain);
17
18    WHILE rain<0 DO
19       BEGIN
20          Writeln('Bad data, Please input a non-negative number');
21          Readln(rain);
22       END;
23
24    WHILE (rain<>99999) and (rain>=0) DO
25       BEGIN
26          total:= total + rain;
```

```
27          count:= count + 1;
28          IF rain>0
29            THEN days:= days + 1;
30          IF rain>maxrain
31            THEN maxrain:= rain;
32          Write('Please input the rainfall for the next day, if you have');
33          Writeln(' reached the end of you data or wish to stop, please ');
34          Writeln('type "99999"');
35          Readln(rain);
36        END;
37
38   Avgr:= total/count;
39   Writeln('The average rainfall per day in New Haven was ', avgr:3:2);
40   Write('There were ', days , ' rainy days.');
41   Writeln('Out of ',count , 'valid inputs.');
42   Write('The maximum amount of rain for one day was ', maxrain:3:2);
43   Writeln(' inches.');
44
45 END.
```

The following is PROUST's output for this program. PROUST's output is essentially correct, except for the following point. PROUST claims that once control has entered the main loop the program does not check for invalid input anymore. The loop does in fact test for invalid input, but this test has been embedded in the exit test of the loop, at line 24. PROUST does, however, point out to the student that line 24 performs two tests instead of one. PROUST's description of the bug ought to be clearer, but it has done most of the work necessary for identifying the bug. All of the other bug descriptions are accurate.

```
Proust output follows...

Hint:

Remember, WHILE-DO is used for loops (repetitive tests), and
IF-THEN is used for single tests.  Be certain your loops
and tests are correctly placed.

Affected bug(s):

1. You have a separate loop for testing input validation at line 18.  Once
you get into the main loop, you don't test the input any more.
The statement in question is:
        WHILE RAIN < 0 DO ...

Other bug(s):

2. You need a test to check that at least one valid data point has been
input before line 39 is executed.  The average is not defined when
there is no input.
```

3. You need a test to check that at least one valid data point has been input before line 38 is executed. The average is not defined when there is no input.

4. You need a test to check that at least one valid data point has been input before line 42 is executed. The maximum is not defined when there is no input.

5. The initialization at line 10 appears to be unnecessary.
The statement in question is:
        RAIN := 0

6. The initialization at line 13 appears to be unnecessary.
The statement in question is:
        AVGR := 0

7. You are trying to perform two tests at once in your WHILE statement.
The WHILE loop test should be the exit test of the loop and nothing else.

After receiving PROUST's bug report, the student modified his program. The resulting program appears below. The programmer made the following changes. First, the spurious initialization of the average variable, AVGR, was deleted. Second, the exit test of the main loop was corrected. Instead of reading (rain<>99999) and (rain>=0), it now reads (rain<>99999). Deleting the (rain>=0) test introduces a new problem with input validation, however. Now the only test for valid input is the WHILE rain<0 DO ... loop at line 17. This loop only serves to validate the first value read in. Once control enters the main loop, no further validation tests are made.

```
 1 Program Rain(INPUT,OUTPUT);
 2
 3 VAR
 4    count, days: Integer;
 5    total, rain, maxrain, avgr: Real;
 6
 7 BEGIN
 8    count:= 0;
 9    total:= 0;
10    rain:= 0;
11    maxrain:= 0;
12    days:= 0;
13
14    Writeln('Please input the amount of a days rainfall in inches.');
15    Readln(rain);
16
17    WHILE rain<0 DO
18      BEGIN
19        Writeln('Bad data, Please input a non-negative number');
20        Readln(rain);
```

```
21      END;
22
23   WHILE (rain<>99999)  DO
24      BEGIN
25         total:= total + rain;
26         count:= count + 1;
27         IF rain>0
28            THEN days:= days + 1;
29         IF rain>maxrain
30            THEN maxrain:= rain;
31         Write('Please input the rainfall for the next day, if you have');
32         Writeln(' reached the end of you data or wish to stop, please ');
33         Writeln('type "99999"');
34         Readln(rain);
35      END;
36
37   Avgr:= total/count;
38   Writeln('The average rainfall per day in New Haven was ', avgr:3:2);
39   Write('There were ', days , ' rainy days.');
40   Writeln('Out of ',count , 'valid inputs.');
41   Write('The maximum amount of rain for one day was ', maxrain:3:2);
42   Writeln(' inches.');
43
44 END.
```

The following is PROUST's output for the second version of the program. The bug report is the same as the previous one, except that the bugs which the student attempted to fix are no longer flagged. This leaves five bugs. Three of the bugs are failures to check for boundary conditions: division by zero when the average is computed, and outputing the average and the maximum when no valid data was entered. The other two bugs are the input validation bug, and a spurious initialization.

```
Proust output follows...

Hint:

Remember, WHILE-DO is used for loops (repetitive tests), and
IF-THEN is used for single tests.  Be certain your loops
and tests are correctly placed.

Affected bug(s):

1. You have a separate loop for testing input validation at line 17.  Once
you get into the main loop, you don't test the input any more.
The statement in question is:
        WHILE RAIN < 0 DO ...

Other bug(s):
```

2. You need a test to check that at least one valid data point has been input before line 38 is executed. The average is not defined when there is no input.

3. You need a test to check that at least one valid data point has been input before line 37 is executed. The average is not defined when there is no input.

4. You need a test to check that at least one valid data point has been input before line 41 is executed. The maximum is not defined when there is no input.

5. The initialization at line 10 appears to be unnecessary. The statement in question is:
       RAIN := 0

The following is the next version of the student's program. The following changes were made. First, the spurious initialization RAIN was removed. Second, the input validation loop was moved inside the main loop. Third, the student added a test to make sure that COUNT is positive before computing the average and outputing the average and maximum. Fourth, the student has made some minor changes to the loop; the running total update has been moved below the counter update, and the indentation of the positive input count, at line 25, has been changed. Thus the student has attempted to correct all of the bugs which PROUST previously pointed out. Unfortunately the input validation plan is still not quite right. The input is now validated by the WHILE rain<0 DO ... loop at line 18, inside the main loop. The side effect of this input validation plan is that if the user enters 99999 while control is inside this input validation loop, control will exit from the input validation loop, and then the 99999 will be processed as if it were a datum rather than the sentinel value. This would occur, for example, if the input sequence were -1 99999.

```
1 Program Rain(INPUT,OUTPUT);
2
3 VAR
4    count, days: Integer;
5    total, rain, maxrain, avgr: Real;
6
7 BEGIN
8    count:= 0;
9    total:= 0;
10   maxrain:= 0;
11   days:= 0;
12
13   Writeln('Please input the amount of a days rainfall in inches.');
14   Readln(rain);
```

```
15
16    WHILE (rain<>99999)  DO
17      BEGIN
18        WHILE rain<0 DO
19          BEGIN
20            Writeln('Bad data, Please input a non-negative number');
21            Readln(rain);
22          END;
23        count:= count + 1;
24        total:= total + rain;
25        IF rain>0 THEN days:= days + 1;
26        IF rain>maxrain
27          THEN maxrain:= rain;
28        Write('Please input the rainfall for the next day, if you have');
29        Writeln(' reached the end of you data or wish to stop, please ');
30        Writeln('type "99999"');
31        Readln(rain);
32      END;
33
34  Writeln('There were  ',count , 'valid inputs.');
35
36  IF count>0 THEN
37    BEGIN
38      Avgr:=total/count;
39      Writeln('The average rainfall per day in New Haven was ', avgr:3:2);
40      Write('There were ', days , ' rainy days.');
41      Write('The maximum amount of rain for one day was ', maxrain:3:2);
42      Writeln(' inches.');
43    END;
44 END.
```

The following is PROUST's bug report for the current version of the program. The only bug now reported is the sentinel-after-invalid-input bug. PROUST reports this bug by supplying both an English description of the bug and an example of data which will cause the program to fail. A concrete example such as this is particularly useful here because the programmer probably did not think of this sort of test case, and may need to be shown a situation where his/her program will fail.

```
Proust output follows...

1. You're missing a sentinel guard.
If a sentinel value is input immediately following a negative value,
your program will process it as if it were data.

See what happens when you enter this data in your program:
    -1 99999

Here's the correct output:
    There were 0 valid rainfalls entered.
```

The next version of the student's program corrects the sentinel-after-invalid-input bug. Now instead of one input validation loop there are two. This solution is somewhat inelegant, but it does work. When PROUST processes this version, it reports that it detects no errors.

```
1 Program Rain(INPUT,OUTPUT);
2
3 VAR
4    count, days: Integer;
5    total, rain, maxrain, avgr: Real;
6
7 BEGIN
8    count:= 0;
9    total:= 0;
10   maxrain:= 0;
11   days:= 0;
12
13   Writeln('Please input the amount of a days rainfall in inches.');
14   Readln(rain);
15   WHILE rain<0 DO
16     BEGIN
17       Writeln('Bad data, Please input a non-negative number');
18       Readln(rain);
19     END;
20
21   WHILE (rain<>99999)  DO
22     BEGIN
23       count:= count + 1;
24       total:= total + rain;
25       IF rain>0 THEN days:= days + 1;
26       IF rain>maxrain
27         THEN maxrain:= rain;
28       Write('Please input the rainfall for the next day, if you have');
29       Writeln(' reached the end of you data or wish to stop, please ');
30       Writeln('type "99999".');
31       Readln(rain);
32       WHILE rain<0 DO
33         BEGIN
34           Writeln('Bad data, Please input a non-negative number');
35           Readln(rain);
36         END;
37     END;
38
39   Writeln('There were  ',count , 'valid inputs.');
40
41   IF count>0 THEN
42     BEGIN
43       Avgr:=total/count;
44       Writeln('The average rainfall per day in New Haven was ',avgr:3:2);
45       Writeln('There were ', days , ' rainy days.');
46       Write('The maximum amount of rain for one day was ', maxrain:3:2);
47       Writeln(' inches.');
```

```
48     END;
49 END.
```

Proust output follows...

No errors detected.

Appendix II PROUST's Goals and Plans

This appendix is shows the goals, plans, and goal reformulations currently in PROUST's knowledge base. The first section shows PROUST's goals and goal reformulations, and the second section shows PROUST's plans.

II.1. The goal and goal-reformulation database

Accumulate is the goal of adding a series of data values, ?New, to a pre-defined value, ?Total.

Accumulate

Form:	*Accumulate(?New, ?Total)*
Result variable:	?Total
Main component:	Update:
Name phrase:	*"accumulation"*
Instances:	RUNNING ACCUMULATION

Average is the goal of computing the average of a series of values. Three implementations of *Average* are included in PROUST's knowledge base:

- AVERAGE PLAN, the ordinary averaging plan which divides the sum of the data by the number of values,

- REPETITIVE AVERAGE, which is similar to AVERAGE PLAN except that the average computation must appear inside of the loop that generates the data values, and

- RUNNING AVERAGE, which keeps a running average and uses each successive datum to update this running average.

Average

Form:	*Average*(?New, ?Avg)
Result variable:	?Avg
Main component:	Update:
Name phrase:	*"average"*
Instances:	AVERAGE PLAN
	REPETITIVE AVERAGE
	RUNNING AVERAGE

BOGUS COUNTER-CONTROLLED LOOP is a buggy reformulation of *Sentinel-Controlled Input Sequence* as a counter-controlled loop. This reformulation is required in order to understand programs where the programmer erroneously used a counter-controlled loop in place of a sentinel-controlled loop.

BOGUS COUNTER-CONTROLLED LOOP

Form:	BOGUS COUNTER-CONTROLLED LOOP(?New, ?Stop)
Component goals:	*Counter-Controlled Loop*(?Cnt, ?New, ?Max)

BOGUS DEDUCT is a buggy reformulation of the goal *Compound Deduct*, where only one value is deducted instead of two.

BOGUS DEDUCT

Form:	BOGUS DEDUCT(?New, ?Const, ?Total)
Component goals:	*Deduct*(?New, ?Total)

Combine Partial Sums is a reformulated version of the goal *Count*. Instead of maintaining a single counter variable, two separate counter variables, ?Sum1 and ?Sum2, are maintained and then added together, yielding ?Count. ?Sum1 and Sum2 each count a subset of the total number of values.

Combine Partial Sums

Form:	*Combine Partial Sums*(?Sum1, ?Sum2, ?Count)
Result variable:	?Count
Main component:	Update:
Name phrase:	*"sum of partial counts"*
Instances:	COMBINE PARTIAL SUMS PLAN

Compensate protects a block of code, ?Code, from being effected by processing data which satisfies a predicate ?Pred. The particular realization of the goal depends upon the plan which the ?Code implements. Currently the realization can be *Individual Fix-Up* or *Individual Variable Fix-Up*. The choice of implementation is currently made by a special-purpose procedure.

Compensate

Form:	*Compensate*(?Code, ?Pred)

Compound Deduct is the goal of subtracting two quantities, ?New and ?Const, from a third quantity, ?Total. There are a four correct methods for performing this operation, and three buggy methods.

Compound Deduct

Form:	*Compound Deduct*(?New, ?Const, ?Total)
Result variable:	?Total
Main component:	Update:
Name phrase:	*"deduction"*
Instances:	COMPOUND DEDUCT PLAN 1
	COMPOUND DEDUCT PLAN 2
	COMPOUND DEDUCT PLAN 3
	COMPOUND DEDUCT PLAN 4
	BUGGY COMPOUND DEDUCT 1
	BUGGY COMPOUND DEDUCT 2
	BOGUS DEDUCT

Constant Sum is the goal of computing the sum of a series of values, where the values in the series are all equal. This goal can be achieved either by counting the number of items and then multiplying by the constant value, as in the FACTOR MULTIPLE and RUNNING MULTIPLE methods, or by maintaining a running total, using the method FACTOR RUNNING TOTAL.

Constant Sum

Form:	*Constant Sum* `(?Factor, ?New, ?Count, ?Total)`
Result variable:	`?Total`
Name phrase:	*"sum of constant factor"*
Main component:	`Update:`
Instances:	FACTOR MULTIPLE
	FACTOR RUNNING TOTAL
	RUNNING MULTIPLE

Count is the goal of counting the number of values in a set, denoted by `?New`. Two methods of *Count* included in PROUST's knowledge base: COUNTER, which is the ordinary counter update plan, and SPLIT COUNTER, which reformulates the count as two counters, each of which counts a subset of the total set of values.

Count

Form:	*Count* `(?New, ?Count)`
Result variable:	`?Count`
Main component:	`Update:`
Name phrase:	*"counter"*
Instances:	COUNTER
	SPLIT COUNTER

Counter-Controlled Loop is the goal of processing a stream of data using a counter-controlled loop. ?Cnt is the counter variable, ?New is the input variable, and ?Max is the number of times to loop.

Counter-Controlled Loop

Form:	*Counter Controlled Loop*(?Cnt, ?New, ?Max)
Instance of:	*Read & Process*
Name phrase:	*"counter-controlled loop"*
Main component:	Mainloop:
Main variable:	?New
Outer control plan:	*T*
Instances:	COUNTER CONTROLLED FOR

Deduct is the goal of subtracting one quantity from another, yielding the result ?Total.

Deduct

Form:	*Deduct*(?New, ?Total)
Result variable:	?Total
Main component:	Update:
Name phrase:	*"deduction"*
Instances:	RUNNING DEDUCTION

EXCEPTION FIX-UP is a reformulation of the goal *Individual Fix-up*, the goal of preventing the value of variable from being corrupted by processing invalid data. *Exception Fix-Up* reformulates this goal as an exception condition guard, guarding some set of computations ?Code from executing when ?Pred is true.

EXCEPTION FIX-UP

Form:	EXCEPTION FIX-UP(?Code, ?Pred)
Component goals:	*Guard Exception*(?Code, ?Pred)

Factor Multiple is a reformulation of the goal *Constant Sum*. It involves counting the number of values being summed and then multiplying by the constant factor.

Factor Multiple

Form:	*Factor Multiple*(`?Factor, ?New, ?Count, ?Total`)
Result variable:	`?Total`
Component goals:	*Count*(`?New, ?Count`)
	Final Multiply(`?Count, ?Factor, ?Total`)

Final Multiply is the goal of multiplying two numbers. It is equivalent to *Multiply*, and will eventually be replaced by *Multiply*.

Final Multiply

Form:	*Final Multiply*(`?Factor1, ?Factor2, ?Product`)
Result variable:	`?Product`
Name phrase:	*"multiplication"*
Instances:	MULTIPLY PLAN
	FINAL MULTIPLY PLAN

Goal Block is used for taking a series of goals and grouping then together to function as one compound goal. This compound goal can then be referred to as group by other goals in a problem description. It is implemented using a `begin-end` block.

Goal Block

Form:	*Goal Block*()
Instances:	CODE BLOCK

Guard Exception is the goal for guarding some block of code, `?Code`, against a boundary condition, `?Pred`. There are three implementations of this goal: GUARD EXCEPTION PLAN and HACKED GUARD EXCEPTION PLAN, which involve wrapping the code to be guarded inside of an `if` statement, and LOOP GUARD EXCEPTION PLAN, which rereads invalid data. This goal should really be split up into goals, one which routes control flow around the guarded code, and one which rereads invalid data.

Guard Exception

Instance of:	*Guard Plan*
Form:	*Guard Exception*(`?Code, ?Pred`)
Instances:	GUARD EXCEPTION PLAN
	HACKED GUARD EXCEPTION PLAN
	LOOP GUARD EXCEPTION PLAN

Guarded Count counts the number of cases in which a predicate `?Pred` is true of a variable `?New`.

Guarded Count

Form:	*Guarded Count*(`?New, ?Pred, ?Filtered`)
Result variable:	`?Count`
Main component:	`Update:`
Instances:	GUARDED COUNTER PLAN
	GUARDED BACKOUT PLAN
	GUARDED REPETITIVE BACKOUT
Name phrase:	*"guarded counter"*

Individual Fix-Up is the goal of preventing the value of a variable `?Var` from being corrupted by processing invalid data. Data is invalid if a predicate `?Pred` is true. It is assumed that if the variable is corrupted, its value can be restored by subtracting some quantity, `?Offset`. Improper computation is preventeed either by guarding the computations against invalid data, using EXCEPTION FIX-UP, or by undoing the effect of the computation, using CONDITIONED CONSTANT BACKOUT.

Individual Fix-Up

Form:	*Individual Fix-Up*(`?Code, ?Pred, ?Var, ?Offset`)
Instance of:	*Fix-Up*
Instances:	EXCEPTION FIX-UP
	CONDITIONED CONSTANT BACKOUT

Individual Sentinel Guard is used to guard a specific computation, `?GuardedCode:`, against the effect of the sentinel value in a loop. This guarding can be achieved either using an *IF* statement, as in the plan INDIVIDUAL SENTINEL SKIP GUARD, or by subtracting out the sentinel, as in the plan VARIABLE BACKOUT ADJUSTMENT.

Individual Sentinel Guard

Form:	*Individual Sentinel Guard*(`?New, ?Stop, ?Var, ?Offset,` `?Guardedcode:`)
Instances:	INDIVIDUAL SENTINEL SKIP GUARD
	VARIABLE BACKOUT ADJUSTMENT

Individual Variable Fix-Up is the goal of repairing the value of a variable which has been corrupted.

Individual Variable Fix-Up

Form:	*Individual Variable Fix-Up*(`?Code, ?Pred, ?Var, ?Offset`)
Instance of:	*Fix-Up*
Instances:	EXCEPTION FIX-UP
	CONDITIONED VARIABLE BACKOUT

Input is the goal of inputing the value of a variable `?X`. There are two basic methods for achieving *Input*. One way is to satisfy the goal directly using either a `Read` statement or a `Readln` statement. The other way is to combine the goal with a *Loop Input Validation* goal, and then perform the inputing and the validation at the same time, i.e., perform a *Validated Input* goal.

Input

Form:	*Input* (`?X`)
Main component:	`Input:`
Name phrase:	*"input"*
Result variable:	`?X`
Instances:	READ PLAN
	READLN PLAN
Compounds:	*((LoopInputValidation . ValidatedInput))*

Loop Input Validation is the goal of validating a variable, `?Val`, which is being input repeatedly in a loop. Validation involves ensuring that a predicate `?Pred` never becomes true.

Loop Input Validation

Form:	*Loop Input Validation* (`?Val, ?Pred`)
Name phrase:	*"input validation"*
Main component:	`Guard:`
Instances:	BAD INPUT SKIP GUARD
	BAD INPUT LOOP GUARD

Maximum is the goal of finding the maximum of a set of values.

Maximum

Form:	*Maximum* (`?New, ?Max`)
Result variable:	`?Max`
Main component:	`Update:`
Name phrase:	*"maximum"*
Instances:	MAXIMUM PLAN

Multiply is the goal of computing the product of two numbers.

Multiply

Form:	*Multiply*(?Factor1, ?Factor2, ?Product)
Result variable:	?Product
Instances:	MULTIPLY PLAN

Output is the goal of printing the value of some variable, ?Val, to the terminal.

Output

Form:	*Output*(?Val)
Main component:	Output:
Name phrase:	"output statement"
Instances:	WRITELN PLAN
	WRITE PLAN

Output Diagnostic is the goal of printing an error message.

Output Diagnostic

Form:	*Output Diagnostic*()
Main component:	Output:
Instances:	ERROR MESSAGE
	WRITE ERROR MESSAGE

RUNNING MULTIPLE is a reformulation of the goal *Constant Sum*. The goal is achieved by counting the number of values being summed, and then multiplying by the constant factor, ?Factor.

RUNNING MULTIPLE

Form:	RUNNING MULTIPLE(?Factor, ?New, ?Count, ?Total)
Result variable:	?Total
Component goals:	*Count*(?New, ?Count)
	Multiply(?Count, ?Factor, ?Total)

Sentinel-Controlled Input Sequence is the goal of reading and processing a series of input values, ?New, stopping when a sentinel value, ?Stop, is input. *Sentinel-Controlled Input Sequence* has six implementation methods in PROUST. The first four are correct plans for implementing the goal, constructed either in read-process or process-read fashion, and using either a while loop or a repeat loop. The remaining two methods are buggy methods. BOGUS YES-NO PLAN asks the user to indicate whether or not to continue by typing 'y' or 'n'. BOGUS COUNTER-CONTROLLED LOOP uses a counter-controlled loop instead of a sentinel-controlled loop.

Sentinel-Controlled Input Sequence

Instance of:	*Read & Process*
Form:	*Sentinel-Controlled Input Sequence*(?New, ?Stop)
Main component:	Mainloop:
Main variable:	?New
Name phrase:	*"sentinel-controlled loop"*
Outer control plan:	*T*
Instances:	SENTINEL PROCESS READ WHILE
	SENTINEL READ PROCESS WHILE
	SENTINEL READ PROCESS REPEAT
	SENTINEL PROCESS READ REPEAT
	BOGUS YES-NO PLAN
	BOGUS COUNTER-CONTROLLED LOOP

Sentinel Guard is the goal of guarding a block of code, ?GuardedCode:, to prevent it from processing the sentinel value, ?Stop.

Sentinel Guard

Form:	*Sentinel Guard*(?New, ?Stop, ?Guardedcode:)
Instances:	SENTINEL SKIP GUARD
	HACKED SENTINEL SKIP GUARD

Simple Input is the goal of inputing a variable, `?X`. Unlike *Input*, *Simple Input* may not be combined with an input validation goal.

Simple Input

Form:	*Input* (`?X`)
Main component:	`Input:`
Instances:	READ PLAN
	READLN PLAN

Single Input Validation is the goal of checking an input variable `?Val` for validity, i.e., ensuring that a predicate `?Pred` never comes true. *Single Input Validation* is used when when the input does not occur inside of a loop, but instead appears within straight-line code.

Single Input Validation

Form:	*Single Input Validation* (`?Val, ?Pred`)
Name phrase:	*"input validation"*
Main component:	`Guard:`
Instances:	SIMPLE VALIDATION LOOP

SPLIT COUNTER is a reformulation of the goal *Count*. The reformulation involves computing two separate counters, `?Plus` and `?Zero`, and then adding them together.

SPLIT COUNTER

Form:	SPLIT COUNTER (`?New, ?Count`)
Result variable:	`?Count`
Component goals:	*Guarded Count* (`?New, (?New > 0), ?Plus`)
	Guarded Count (`?New, (?New <= 0), ?Zero`)
	Combine Partial Sums (`?Plus, ?Zero, ?Count`)

Strict Individual Sentinel Guard is the goal of preventing a section of code, `?GuardedCode:`, from being executed when a sentinel value is read. The only way of realizing this goal is through the use of a guard; it is assumed that `?GuardedCode:` contains computations which cannot be undone if they process the sentinel value.

Strict Individual Sentinel Guard

Form: *Strict Individual Sentinel Guard*`(?New, ?Stop, ?GuardedCode:)`
Instances: INDIVIDUAL SENTINEL SKIP GUARD

Sum is the goal of finding the sum of a series of values, `?New`.

Sum

Form: *Sum*`(?New, ?Total)`
Result variable: `?Total`
Main component: `Update:`
Name phrase: *"sum"*
Instances: RUNNING TOTAL

Supercede Value is the goal of superceding the current value of a variable, `?Var`, with the value of a different variable, `?Val`. Two methods are available for achieving this, one which is correct and one which is stylistically dubious. The correct method, SUPERCEDE PLAN, uses an assignment statement to assign the one variable to the other. The other method, EXCHANGE PLAN, exchanges the values of the two variables, thus changing the value of `?Val` unnecessarily.

Supercede Value

Form: *Supercede Value*`(?Var, ?Val)`
Result variable: `?Var`
Main component: `Update:`
Instances: SUPERCEDE PLAN
                             EXCHANGE PLAN

Validated Input is the goal of inputing a variable, `?X`, and making sure that a predicate `?Pred` does not hold. This goal is generated by combining the goals *Input* and *Loop Input Validation*.

Validated Input

Form:	*Validated Input*(`?X, ?Pred`)
Main component:	`Mainloop:`
Instances:	VALIDATED INPUT PROCESS READ WHILE
	VALIDATED INPUT READ PROCESS REPEAT
	VALIDATED INPUT PROCESS READ REPEAT

When is the goal of achieving some goal, `?Action`, when a predicate `?Pred` is true. `?Var` and `?Val` are components of `?Pred`. Two methods are available for achieving *When*: use an `if` statement, as in CONDITION IF TEST, or use a `case` statement, as in CASE BRANCH.

When

Form:	*When*(`?Pred, ?Var, ?Val, ?Action`)
Main component:	`Guard:`
Name phrase:	*"condition test"*
Instances:	CONDITION IF TEST
	CASE BRANCH

II.2. The plan database

AVERAGE PLAN is the ordinary method for implementing the goal *Average*. The average computation is performed below the main loop.

AVERAGE PLAN

Variables: ?Avg, ?Sum, ?Count, ?New

Posterior goals:

> *Count*(?New, ?Count)
> *Sum*(?New, ?Sum)
> *Guard Exception*(*component* Update: *of goal Average*,
> $\qquad\qquad\qquad\qquad$ ((?Count *from goal Count*) = 0))

Exception condition:

> ((?Count *from goal Count*) = 0)

Template:

> (*component* Mainloop: *of goal Read & Process*)
> *followed by:*

Update: ?Avg := (?Sum / ?Count)

The following plan prints out an error message when input is invalid, i.e., when a predicate ?Pred is true.

BAD INPUT DIAGNOSTIC

Variables: ?Val, ?Pred

Template:

> (*in component* Process: *of goal Read & Process*)
> $\qquad$ *spanned by:*

Guard: if ?Pred then
> $\qquad\qquad$ subgoal Output Diagnostic()

Process: ?*

The following plan appears inside of a read-and-process loop. It loops until input data is valid. A consequence of this goal is that a *Sentinel Guard* goal is added to the goal agenda. A bug demon is used to check whether or not there is an input statement inside the code guarded by the sentinel guard. There should be no input there; once the sentinel is read, input should cease. However, since PROUST will have analyzed the main loop before the *Sentinel Guard* goal is added to the agenda, it will have determined that the loop is buggy, because it does not input data on each pass through the loop. The bug demon deletes this bug from the current interpretation of the program.

BAD INPUT LOOP GUARD

Variables: ?Val, ?Pred
Template:

           (*in component* Process: *of goal Read & Process*)
               spanned by:

Guard: while ?Pred do
                  begin
                       subgoal Output Diagnostic()

Next: *subgoal Simple Input*(?Val)
                  end

Process: ?*
Posterior goals:

           Sentinel Guard((?New *from goal Read & Process*),
                       (?Stop *from goal Read & Process*))

Bug demons:

```
((λ (Inst)
    (and (eq? (HistInst-NodeType Inst) 'Plan)
         (eq? (Goal-Name (HistInst-PlanGoal Inst))
              'SentinelGuard)
         (LocalLabelBinding 'GuardedCode: Inst)
         (if (null? (LocalLabelBinding
                        'InternalGuard:
                        Inst))
             T
             (block
              (RemoveUnduplicatedPlan Inst)
              T)))))
```

BAD INPUT SKIP GUARD tests input for validity by placing an `if-then-else` statement inside the main loop.

BAD INPUT SKIP GUARD

Variables:	`?Val, ?Pred`
Template:	

(in component `Process:` *of goal Read & Process)*
      spanned by:

Guard:	`if ?Pred then`
	    subgoal Output Diagnostic `()`
	`else`

Process:	`?*`

BOGUS YES-NO PLAN reads a stream of data, and each time asks the user to type 'y' or 'n' to indicate whether or not to continue. The plan is not inherently "bogus", but it was so named because it sometimes is used in place of sentinel-controlled looping plans.

BOGUS YES-NO PLAN

Variables:	`?New, ?Yesno`
Template:	
Init:	*subgoal Input* `(?Yesno)`
Mainloop:	`while (?Yesno = 'y') do` `begin`
Next:	*subgoal Input* `(?New)`
Process:	`?*`
Next2:	*subgoal Input* `(?Yesno)` `end`

The following two plans are buggy attempts at implementing the goal *Compound Deduct*. They both use an incorrect variable in place of one of the values to be deducted.

BUGGY COMPOUND DEDUCT 1

Variables:	`?Total, ?New, ?Temp, ?Bogus var`
Template:	
Update:	`?Temp := (?Total - ?New)` `?Total := (?Temp - ?Bogusvar)`

BUGGY COMPOUND DEDUCT 2

Variables: ?Total, ?New, ?Temp, ?Bogus var
Template:

```
?Temp := (?New + ?Bogusvar)
```
Update: ?Total := (?Total - ?Temp)

The following plan implements one branch of a **case** statement.

CASE BRANCH

Variables: ?Var, ?Val
Template:

          (*in component* Process: *of goal Read & Process*)
```
case ?Var of
      Contains:
```
Guard: ?Val:
Guardedcode: ?*
```
end
```

CODE BLOCK is a simple **begin-end** pair, used to implement the goal *Goal Block*.

CODE BLOCK

Template:
```
begin
```
Process: ?*
```
end
```

COMBINE PARTIAL SUMS PLAN adds two variables together to yield a third.

COMBINE PARTIAL SUMS PLAN

Variables: ?Sum1, ?Sum2, ?Count
Template:
Update: ?Count := (?Sum1 + ?Sum2)

The following four plans are four different methods for deducting two values from a variable. They differ in the specific operations performed, and in the order in which they are performed.

COMPOUND DEDUCT PLAN 1

Variables:	?Total, ?New
Constants:	?Const
Template:	
Update:	?Total := (?Total - ?New)
	?Total := (?Total - ?Const)

COMPOUND DEDUCT PLAN 2

Variables:	?Total, ?New, ?Temp
Constants:	?Const
Template:	
Update:	?Temp := (?Total - ?New)
	?Total := (?Temp - ?Const)

COMPOUND DEDUCT PLAN 3

Variables:	?Total, ?New, ?Temp
Constants:	?Const
Template:	
	?Temp := (?New + ?Const)
Update:	?Total := (?Total - ?Temp)

COMPOUND DEDUCT PLAN 4

Variables:	?Total, ?New, ?Temp
Constants:	?Const
Template:	
	?Temp := (?Total - ?Const)
Update:	?Total := (?Temp - ?New)

CONDITION IF TEST surrounds a block of code with an `if` statement which checks whether or not a predicate ?Pred is true.

CONDITION IF TEST

Variables:	?Pred
Template:	
	(in component Process: *of goal Read & Process)*
Guard:	`if ?Pred then`
Guardedcode:	`?*`

CONDITIONED CONSTANT BACK-OUT, used to fix a variable ?Var to which a value ?Offset has erroneously been added, subtracts out the value when the predicate ?Pred turns true.

CONDITIONED CONSTANT BACK-OUT

Variables:	?Var, ?Pred
Constants:	?Offset
Template:	
	`if ?Pred then`
Update:	`->?Var := (?Var - ?Offset)`

The following plan is the same as the previous one, except that it subtracts out the value of a variable rather than subtracting out the value of a constant.

CONDITIONED VARIABLE BACK-OUT

Variables:	?Var, ?Pred, ?Offset
Template:	
	`if ?Pred then`
Update:	`->?Var := (?Var - ?Offset)`

COUNTER is an ordinary counter-variable plan.

COUNTER

Variables:	?Count
Template:	
Init:	`?Count := 0`
	(in component Process: *of goal Read & Process)*
Update:	`?Count := (?Count + 1)`

310

COUNTER-CONTROLLED FOR is a counter-controlled loop implemented using a for statement. This plan has a bug demon to check whether or not the plan appears in place of a sentinel-controlled looping plan, and if so, declares it to be buggy.

COUNTER-CONTROLLED FOR

```
Variables:              ?Max, ?Cnt, ?New
Template:
Initinput:    subgoal Input(?Max)
Mainloop:     for ?Cnt := 1 to ?Max do
                 begin
Next:                subgoal Input(?New)
Process:             ?*
              end
Bugdemons:
          ((λ (Inst)
            (if (PlanImplements? Inst
                               'SentinelControlledLoop)
               (let ((NewBug (New-Bug
                       'ImplementsWrongGoal)))
                 (set (Bug-HistInst NewBug) Inst)
                 (set (Bug-FoundStmt NewBug)
                     (car (LocalLabelBinding 'MainLoop:
                                              Inst)))
                 (set (Bug-GoalForms NewBug)
                     (list (DumbFindRightGoal
                            'SentinelControlledLoop
                            Inst)))
                 (set (HistInst-BugReport Inst)
                     (cons NewBug
                           (HistInst-BugReport Inst)))))
               T))
```

The following plan prints out an error message.

ERROR MESSAGE

```
Template:
Output:    writeln(?*)
```

EXCHANGE PLAN exchanges the values of two variables. It has a bug demon to check whether or not it is being used to implement a *Supercede Value* goal.

EXCHANGE PLAN

```
Variables:              ?Var, ?Val, ?Temp
Template:
Update:     begin
                ?Temp := ?Val
                ?Val := ?Var
                ?Var := ?Temp
            end
Bugdemons:
            ((λ (Inst)
              (if (eq? (Goal-Name (HistInst-PlanGoal Inst))
                       'SupercedeValue)
                  (let ((NewBug (New-Bug 'WrongPlanForGoal)))
                    (set (Bug-HistInst NewBug) Inst)
                    (set (Bug-FoundStmt NewBug)
                         (car (LocalLabelBinding 'Update:
                                                 Inst)))
                    (set (HistInst-BugReport Inst)
                         (cons NewBug
                               (HistInst-BugReport Inst)))))
              T))
```

FACTOR RUNNING TOTAL computes a running total of a series of fixed values, each equal to ?Factor.

FACTOR RUNNING TOTAL

```
Variables:           ?Total
Constants:           ?Factor
Template:
Init:       ?Total := 0
            (in component Process: of goal Read & Process)
Update:         ?Total := (?Total + ?Factor)
```

The following plan is a method for multiplying two numbers.

FINAL MULTIPLY PLAN

Variables: `?Factor 1, ?Product`
Constants: `?Factor 2`
Template:

        (*component* `Mainloop:` *of goal Read & Process*)
        followed by:
Update: `?Product := (?Factor1 * ?Factor2)`

GUARD EXCEPTION PLAN guards a block of code `?Code` against being executed when a predicate `?Pred` is true.

GUARD EXCEPTION PLAN

Variables: `?Pred`
Codevars: `?Code`
Template:

        if **NOT** `?Pred` then
          contains `?Code`

GUARDED BACK-OUT is a method of computing *Guarded Count*. It assumes that there is a count of the total number of values, and a count of the number of values for which `?Pred` is false. It subtracts one from the other, to yield a count of the number of values for which `?Pred` is true.

GUARDED BACK-OUT

Variables: `?Pred, ?Filtered, ?Count, ?Prefiltered`
Prior goals:

        Count((`?New` *from goal Read & Process*))
        Guarded Count((`?New` *from goal Read & Process*))
Added bindings:
        `?Count =>` (`?Count` *from goal Count*)
        `?Prefiltered =>` (`?Filtered` *from goal Guarded Count*)
Template:
        `?Plus := (?Count - ?Prefiltered)`

GUARDED COUNTER PLAN updates a counter `?Filtered` when a predicate, `?Pred`, is true.

GUARDED COUNTER PLAN

Variables:	`?Pred, ?Filtered, ?New`
Template:	
Init:	`?Filtered := 0`
	(*in component* `Process:` *of goal Read & Process*)
Guard:	`if ?Pred then`
Update:	`?Filtered := (?Filtered + 1)`

GUARDED REPETITIVE BACK-OUT is another method for implementing *Guarded Count*.

GUARDED REPETITIVE BACK-OUT

Variables:	`?Filtered, ?Pred, ?New`
Template:	
Init:	`?Plus := 0`
	(*in component* `Process:` *of goal Read & Process*)
	unordered set of:
Update:	`?Filtered := (?Filtered + 1)`
	`if *NOT* ?Pred then`
Backoutupdate:	`?Filtered := (?Filtered - 1)`

The following plan implements the goal *Guard Exception*. It wraps the guarded code in an `if-then-else` statement, and prints an error message when the exception condition occurs.

HACKED GUARD EXCEPTION PLAN

Variables:	`?Pred`
Codevars:	`?Code`
Template:	

```
if ?Pred then
    subgoal Output Diagnostic()
else
    contains ?Code
```

The following plan checks for the sentinel value `?Stop` being input.

HACKED SENTINEL SKIP GUARD

Variables:	`?New`
Constants:	`?Stop`
Template:	

```
Internalguard:
        if (?New = ?Stop) then
            subgoal Output Diagnostic ()
        else
Guardedcode:    ?*
```

INDIVIDUAL SENTINEL SKIP GUARD makes sure that a block of code `?GuardedCode:` is not executed when the sentinel value is processed.

INDIVIDUAL SENTINEL SKIP GUARD

Variables:	`?New`
Constants:	`?Stop`
Codevars:	`?GuardedCode:`
Template:	

```
        if (?New <> ?Stop) then
            contains ?GuardedCode:
```

LOOP GUARD EXCEPTION PLAN guards against an exception condition `?Pred` in the input by looping and re-inputing until the exception condition is not met.

LOOP GUARD EXCEPTION PLAN

Variables:	`?Pred, ?Val`
Codevars:	`?Code`
Template:	

```
Guard:    while ?Pred do
            begin
                subgoal Output Diagnostic ()
Next:            subgoal Simple Input (?Val)
            end
```

The following is the common plan for computing a maximum.

MAXIMUM PLAN

Variables: ?New, ?Max
Prior goals:
         Count ((?New *from goal Read & Process*))
Exception condition:
         ((?Count *from goal Count*) = 0)
Template:
Init: ?Max := 0
         (*in component* Process: *of goal Read & Process*)
Guard: if (?New > ?Max) then
Update: *subgoal Supercede Value* (?Max, ?New)

The following plan multiplies two numbers.

MULTIPLY PLAN

Variables: ?Factor 1, ?Product
Constants: ?Factor 2
Template:
Update: ?Product := (?Factor1 * ?Factor2)

The following plan inputs a value using a read statement.

READ PLAN

Variables: ?X
Template:
Input: read (?X)

The following plan inputs a value using a readln statement.

READLN PLAN

Variables: ?X
Template:
Input: readln (?X)

316

REPETITIVE AVERAGE is similar to AVERAGE PLAN, except that the average computation is performed repeatedly inside of the main loop. The effect of this is to prevent division by zero.

REPETITIVE AVERAGE

Variables: ?Avg, ?Sum, ?Count, ?New
Posterior goals:
          Count(?New, ?Count)
          Sum(?New, ?Sum)
Exception condition:
          (?Count = 0)
Template:
          (*in component* Process: *of goal Read & Process*)
Update: ?Avg := (?Sum / ?Count)

RUNNING ACCUMULATION adds successive values of ?New into a pre-defined variable ?Total.

RUNNING ACCUMULATION

Variables: ?Total, ?New
Template:
Update: ?Total := (?Total + ?New)

RUNNING AVERAGE computes an average by keeping a running average.

RUNNING AVERAGE

Variables: ?Avg, ?New, ?Count
Posterior goals:
          Count(?New, ?Count)
Exception condition:
          (?Count = 0)
Template:
Init: ?Avg := 0
          (*in component* Process: *of goal Read & Process*)
Update: ?Avg := (((?Avg * (?Count - 1)) + ?New) / ?Count)

RUNNING DEDUCTION deducts a series of values denoted by `?New` from a variable `?Total`.

RUNNING DEDUCTION

Variables:	`?Total, ?New`
Template:	
Update:	`?Total := (?Total - ?New)`

The following the classic running-total plan.

RUNNING TOTAL

Variables:	`?Total, ?New`
Template:	
Init:	`?Total := 0`
	(in component `Process:` *of goal Read & Process)*
Update:	`?Total := (?Total + ?New)`

The following four plans are implementations of the goal *Sentinel-Controlled Input Sequence.*

SENTINEL PROCESS READ REPEAT

Constants:	`?Stop`
Variables:	`?New`
Template:	
Initinput:	*subgoal* `Input(?New)`
Internalguard:	
	`if (?New <> ?Stop) then`
Mainloop:	`repeat`
Process:	`?*`
Next:	*subgoal* `Input(?New)`
	`until (?New = ?Stop)`

SENTINEL PROCESS READ WHILE

```
Constants:            ?Stop
Variables:            ?New
Template:
Initinput:    subgoal Input (?New)
Mainloop:     while (?New <> ?Stop) do
                    begin
Process:              ?*
Next:                 subgoal Input (?New)
              end
```

SENTINEL READ PROCESS REPEAT

```
Constants:            ?Stop
Variables:            ?New
Template:
Mainloop: ->repeat
Next:            subgoal Input (?New)
Internalguard:   subgoal Sentinel Guard (?New, ?Stop, Process: ?*)
              until (?New = ?Stop)
```

SENTINEL READ PROCESS WHILE

```
Constants:            ?Stop, ?Seedval
Variables:            ?New
Template:
Init:         ?New := ?Seedval
Mainloop:     while (?New <> ?Stop) do
                    begin
Next:                 subgoal Input (?New)
Internalguard:        subgoal Sentinel Guard (?New, ?Stop, Process: ?*)
              end
```

SENTINEL SKIP GUARD is a test for the sentinel value.

SENTINEL SKIP GUARD

```
Variables:           ?New
Constants:           ?Stop
Template:
Internalguard:
           if (?New <> ?Stop) then
Guardedcode:     ?*
```

SIMPLE VALIDATION LOOP is an implementation of the goal *Simple Input Validation*. It checks to make sure that an input datum ?Val is valid.

SIMPLE VALIDATION LOOP

```
Variables:               ?Val, ?Pred
Template:
Guard:       while ?Pred do
                begin
                    subgoal Output Diagnostic()
Next:               subgoal Simple Input (?Val)
                end
```

SUPERCEDE PLAN assigns the value of one variable to another variable.

SUPERCEDE PLAN

```
Variables:           ?Var, ?Val
Template:
Update:      ?Var := ?Val
```

TEST-EM-ALL IF is a buggy plan for checking input for validity. It uses an if statement rather than a loop, so it does not work correctly if two invalid data points are read in a row.

TEST-EM-ALL IF

Variables: ?Val, ?Pred
Template:
Guard: if ?Pred then
                    subgoal Output Diagnostic()
                else
                    ?*

The following three plans read a value, ?X, and check a validity predicate ?Pred.

VALIDATED INPUT PROCESS READ REPEAT

Variables: ?X, ?Pred
Template:
Input:
InitInput: *subgoal Simple Input(?X)*
                if ?Pred then
Mainloop: repeat
                        subgoal Output Diagnostic()
Next: *subgoal Simple Input(?X)*
                until *NOT* ?Pred

VALIDATED INPUT PROCESS READ WHILE

Variables: ?X, ?Pred
Template:
Input:
InitInput: *subgoal Simple Input(?X)*
Mainloop: while ?Pred do
                    begin
                        subgoal Output Diagnostic()
Next: *subgoal Simple Input(?X)*
                    end

VALIDATED INPUT READ PROCESS REPEAT

Variables:	?X, ?Pred
Template:	
Mainloop:	repeat
Input:	
Next:	*subgoal Simple Input* (?X)
	if ?Pred then
	subgoal Output Diagnostic ()
	until *NOT* ?Pred

The following plan subtracts a value ?Offset from a variable ?Var. This is to compensate for ?Offset having been erroneously added into ?Var by another plan.

VARIABLE BACK-OUT ADJUSTMENT

Variables:	?Var
Constants:	?Offset
Template:	
Update:	?Var := (?Var - ?Offset)

WRITELN PLAN and WRITE PLAN print out a value ?Val to the terminal.

WRITELN PLAN

Variables:	?Val
Template:	
Output:	writeln(?*, ?Val, ?*)

WRITE PLAN

Variables:	?Val
Template:	
Output:	write(?*, ?Val, ?*)

WRITE ERROR MESSAGE prints out an error message, using a write statement.

WRITE ERROR MESSAGE

Template:	
Output:	write(?*)

322

References

1. Adam, A. and Laurent, J. "LAURA, A System to Debug Student Programs". *Artificial Intelligence 15* (1980), 75-122.

2. Adelson, B. "Problem Solving and the Development of Abstract Categories in Programming Languages". *Memory and Cognition 9* (1981), 422-433.

3. Anderson, J., Boyle, F., and Yost, G. The Geometry Tutor. Proceedings of the Ninth IJCAI, IJCAI, August, 1985, pp. 1-7.

4. Balzer, R., Goldman, N., and Wile, D. "Informality in Program Specifications". *IEEE Transactions of Software Engineering SE-4*, 2 (March 1978), 94-103.

5. Balzer, R., N. Goldman. "Principles of Good Software Specification and Their Implications for Specification Languages". Proceedings of the Specfications for Reliable Software Conference , Boston, Massachusetts, April, 1979, pp. 58-67. (Also presented at the National Computer Conference, 1981).

6. Barnard, D.T. A Survey of Syntax Error Handling Techniques. Computer Science Research Group, Univ. of Toronto, 1976.

7. Barstow, D. R. The Roles of Knowledge and Deduction in Algorithm Creation. 178, Yale University Department of Computer Science, April, 1980.

8. Barstow, D.R. A Perspective on Automatic Programming. Proceedings of the Eighth IJCAI, IJCAI, August, 1983.

9. Bartlett, F.C.. *Remembering*. Cambridge University Press, Cambridge, 1932.

10. Bonar, J. and Soloway, E. Uncovering Principles of Novice Programming. SIGPLAN-SIGACT Tenth Symposium on the Principles of Programming Languages, 1983.

11. Bonar, J., Ehrlich, K., Soloway, E. "Collecting and Analyzing On-Line Protocols from Novice Programmers". *Behavioral Research Methods and Instrumentation 14* (1982), 203-209.

12. Bower, G.H., Black, J.B., Turner, T. "Scripts in Memory for Text". *Cognitive Psychology 11* (1979), 177-220.

13. Brooks, R. "Towards a Theory of the Comprehension of Computer Programs". *International Journal of Man-Machine Studies 18* (1983), 543-554.

14. Brown, J. S., Burton, R. R., and de Kleer, J. Pedagogical, Natural Language and Knowledge Engineering Techniques in SOPHIE I, II, and III. In *Intelligent Tutoring Systems*, Academic Press, New York, 1981.

15. Burton, R. Diagnosing Bugs in a Simple Procedural Skill. In *Intelligent Tutoring Systems*, Academic Press, 1982.

16. Chase, W.C. and Simon, H. "Perception in Chess". *Cognitive Psychology 4* (1973), 55-81.

17. Clancey, W.J. Classification Problem Solving. Proceedings of the Nat. Conf. on Art. Int., AAAI, August, 1984, pp. 49-55.

18. Clancey, W.J. Acquiring, Representing, and Evaluating a Competence Model of Diagnostic Strategy. In *The Nature of Expertise*, in press, 1985.

19. Conway, R.W., and Wilcox, T.R. "Design and Implementation of a diagnostic compiler for PL/I". *Communications of the ACM 16*, 3 (March 1973), 169-179.

20. Rich, C. Inspection Methods in Programming. MIT Artificial Intelligence Laboratory, June, 1981.

21. Davis, R. Diagnosis via Causal Reasoning: Paths of Interaction and the Locality Principle. Proc. of the Nat. Conf. on Artifical Intelligence, AAAI, August, 1983, pp. 88-94.

22. Davis, R., Shrobe, H., Hamscher, W., Wieckert, K., Shirley, M., and Polit, S. Diagnosis Based on Description of Structure and Function. Proceedings of the Second AAAI Conference, AAAI, August, 1982, pp. 137-142.

23. deGroot, A.D.. *Thought and Choice in Chess*. Mouton and Company, Paris, 1965.

24. Ehrlich, K., Soloway, E. An Empirical Investigation of the Tacit Plan Knowledge in Programming. In *Human Factors in Computer Systems*, Ablex, 1983.

25. Eisenstadt, M. Retrospective Zooming: A Knowledge Based Tracing and Debugging Methodology for Logic Programming. Proceedings of the Ninth International Joint Conference on Artificial Intelligence, IJCAI, 1985, pp. 717-719.

26. Fagan, M.E. "Design and Code Inspections to Reduce Errors in Program Development". *IBM Systems Journal 15*, 3 (July 1976), 182-211.

27. Farrell, R.G., Anderson, J.R., and Reiser, B.J. An Interactive Computer-Based Tutor for LISP. Proc. of the Nat. Conf. on Art. Int., August, 1984, pp. 106-109.

28. Forgy, C.L. OPS5 User's Manual. CMU-CS-81-135, Department of Computer Science, Carnegie-Mellon University, July, 1981.

29. Fosdick, L.D., and Osterweil, L.J. "Data Flow Analysis in Software Reliability". *Computing Surveys 8*, 3 (1976), 305-330.

30. Genesereth, M. R. *Automated Consultation for Complex Computer Systems.* Ph.D. Th., Harvard Univ., September 1978.

31. Genesereth, M. R. The Role of Plans in Intellegent Teaching Systems. Intellegent Tutoring Systems, Academic Press, New York, 1981.

32. Genesereth, M. Diagnosis Using Hierarchical Design Models. Proc. of the Nat. Conf. on Art. Intelligence, 1982, pp. 278-283.

33. Goguen, J.A., and Tardo, J.J. An Introduction to OBJ: A Language for Writing and Testing Formal Algebraic Program Specifications. Proc. Specification of Reliable Software Conf., Cambridge, Mass., 1979.

34. Graesser, A. C.. *Prose Comprehension Beyond the Word.* Springer-Verlag, New York, 1981.

35. Graham, S.L. and Rhodes, S.P. "Practical syntactic error recovery in compilers". *Communications of the ACM 18*, 11 (1975).

36. Harandi, M.T. Knowledge-Based Program Debugging: a Heuristic Model. Proceedings of the 1983 SOFTFAIR, SoftFair, 1983.

37. Heitmeyer, C.L. and McLean, J.D. "Abstract Requirements Specification: A New Approach and Its Application". *IEEE Transactions of Software Engineering SE-9*, 5 (Sept 1983).

38. Heninger, K.L. "Specifying Software Requirements for Complex Systems: New Techniques and Their Application". *IEEE Transactions of Software Engineering SE-6*, 1 (Jan. 1980).

39. James, E.B. and Partridge, D.P. "Adaptive correction of program statements". *Communications of the ACM 16*, 1 (January 1973).

40. Johnson, S.C. *YACC - Yet Another Compiler Compiler.* Bell Telephone Laboratories, Inc., Murray Hill, N.J., 1980.

41. Johnson, W.L. and Soloway, E. "PROUST: An Automatic Debugger for Pascal Programs". *Byte 10*, 4 (1985), 179-190.

42. Johnson, W.L., Soloway, E., Cutler, B., and Draper, S. Bug Collection: I. 296, Dept. of Computer Science, Yale University, October, 1983.

43. Kant, E., and Newell, A. Problem Solving Techniques for the Design of Algorithms. CMU-CS-82-145, Department of Computer Science, Carnegie-Mellon University, November, 1982.

44. Kernighan, B.W., and Lesk, M.E. *LEARN -- Computer-Aided Instruction on UNIX*. Bell Telephone Laboratories, Inc., Murray Hill, N.J., 1979.

45. King, J.C. "A New Approach to Program Testing". *Programming Methodology Lecture Notes in Computer Science 23* (1970), 278-290.

46. Lukey, F.J. "Understanding and Debugging Programs". *International Journal of Man-Machine Studies 12* (1980), 189-202.

47. McDermott, D.V. "Contexts and Data Dependencies: A Synthesis". *IEEE Transactions on Pattern Analysis and Machine Intelligence PAMI-5*, 3 (1983), 237-246.

48. McKeithen, K.B., Reitman, J.S., Rueter, H.H., Hirtle, S.C. "Knowledge Organization and Skill Differences in Computer Programmers". *Cognitive Psychology 13* (1981), 307-325.

49. Myers, G.J. "A Controlled Experiment in Program Testing and Code Walkthroughs/Inspections". *Communications of the ACM 21*, 21 (1978).

50. Rich, C. A Formal Representation for Plans in the Programmer's Apprentice. Proc. of the Seventh Int. Joint Conf. on Artificial Intelligence, ICJAI, August, 1981, pp. 1044-1052.

51. Sacerdoti, E.D. *A Structure for Plans and Behavior*. Elsevier North-Holland, Inc., 1977.

52. Schank, R.C. and Abelson, R.. *Scripts, Plans, Goals and Understanding*. Lawrence Erlbaum Associates, Hillsdale New Jersey, 1977.

53. Sedlmeyer, R. L. and Johnson, P. E. Diagnostic Reasoning in Software Fault Localization. Proceedings of the SIGSOFT Workshop on High-Level Debugging, SIGSOFT, Asilomar, Calif., 1983.

54. Shapiro, D. G. Sniffer: a System that Understands Bugs. AI Memo 638, MIT Artificial Intelligence Laboratory, June, 1981.

55. Shapiro, E.. *Algorithmic Program Debugging*. MIT Press, Cambridge, Mass., 1982.

56. Shneiderman, B. "Exploratory Experiments in Programmer Behavior". *International Journal of Computer and Information Sciences 5,2* (1976), 123-143.

57. Shortliffe, E.H.. *Computer-Based Medical Consultations: MYCIN*. American Elsevier Publishing Co., New York, 1976.

58. Sleeman, D. A rule directed modelling system. In Michalski, R., Carbonell, J., and Mitchell, T.M., Ed., *Machine Learning*, Tioga Press, Palo Alto, CA, 1983.

59. Soloway, E., Rubin, E., Woolf, B., Bonar, J., and Johnson, W. L. "MENO-II: An AI-Based Programming Tutor". *Journal of Computer-Based Instruction 10*, 1 (1983).

60. Soloway, E. and Ehrlich, K. "Empirical Investigations of Programming Knowledge". *IEEE Transactions of Software Engineering SE-10*, 5 (1984).

61. Soloway, E., Ehrlich, K., Bonar, J., and Greenspan, J. What do Novices Know about Programming. In A. Badre and B. Shneiderman, Ed., *Directions in Human-Computer Interactions*, Ablex Inc., Norwood, New Jersey, 1982.

62. Soloway, E., Bonar, J., and Ehrlich, K. "Cognitive Strategies and Looping Constructs: An Empirical Study". *Communications of the ACM 26* (November 1983).

63. Spohrer, J.C., Pope, E., Lipman, M., Sack, W., Freiman, S., Littman, D., Johnson, L., Soloway, E. Bugs in Novice Programs, and Misconceptions in Novice Programmers. Proceedings of the World Conference of Computers in Education, World Conference of Computers in Education, 1985.

64. Spohrer, J., Soloway, E., and Pope. E. "A Goal/Plan Analysis of Buggy Novice Programs". *Human-Computer Interaction 1*, 2 (1985, 163-207.

65. Swartout, W. The Gist Behavior Explainer. Proceedings of the National Conference on Artificial Intelligence, AAAI, Washington, D.C., 1983. (Also available as ISI/RR-83-3).

66. Teichroew, D., and Hershey, E.A. III. "PSL/PSA: A Computer-Aided Technique for Structured Documentation and Analysis of Information Processing Systems". *IEEE Transactions of Software Engineering SE-3*, 1 (January 1977).

67. Warren Teitelman. *INTERLISP Reference Manual.* Xerox Palo Alto Research Center, 1978.

68. Wertz, H. "Stereotyped Program Debugging: an Aid for Novice Programmers". *International Journal of Man-Machine Studies 16* (1982), 379-392.

69. Wescourt, K. T., Beard, M., Gould, L., and Barr, A. Knowledge-based CAI: CINS for Individualized Curriculum Sequencing. 290, Stanford Institute for Mathematical Studies in the Social Sciences, Psychology and Education Series, October, 1977.

70. Woods, W.A. "Optimal Search Strategies for Speech Understanding Control". *Artificial Intelligence 18*, 3 (1981), 295-326.

71. Zave, P. "An Operational Approach to Requirements Specification for Embedded Systems". *IEEE Transactions of Software Engineering SE-8*, 3 (May 1982), 250-269.

Index

329